The High
KINGDOM
THE LIVING COUNTRYSIDE

A Reader's Digest selection

THE HIGH KINGDOM

First Edition Copyright © 1985
The Reader's Digest Association Limited, Berkeley Square House
Berkeley Square, London W1X 6AB
Reprinted with amendments 1989

Copyright © 1985
Reader's Digest Association Far East Limited
Philippines Copyright 1984
Reader's Digest Association Far East Ltd

Originally published as a partwork,
The Living Countryside
Copyright © 1981, 1982, 1983, 1984, 1985
Eaglemoss Publications Ltd and Orbis Publishing Ltd

® READER'S DIGEST, THE DIGEST and the Pegasus logo
are registered trademarks of
The Reader's Digest Association, Inc, of Pleasantville, New York, USA

PRINTED IN SPAIN

ISBN 0 276 39655 3

The High KINGDOM

THE LIVING COUNTRYSIDE

PUBLISHED BY THE READER'S DIGEST ASSOCIATION LIMITED
LONDON   NEW YORK   MONTREAL   SYDNEY   CAPE TOWN

Originally published in partwork form
by Eaglemoss Publications Limited and Orbis Publishing Limited

Consultant

Robert Gibbons

Contributors

Contents

Introduction

Life on windswept mountain tops 8
Exploring rock pavements 12
The underground world of caves 15
Life on perilous scree slopes 19
Heather moorlands 24
Blanket bogs: a cloak of peat 28
Ireland's peat moorlands 34

Trees and shrubs

Birchwoods of Britain 40
The smallest trees in Britain 44
Rowan: hardy magical tree 47
Fragrant bog myrtle 50
Berry-bearing moorland plants 53
Heather mixture 56

Flowers, ferns and mosses

The arctic-alpines of Ben Lawers 62
Alpine flowers 67
Mountain snow-patch plants 70
Hardy mountain saxifrages 72
Plants that eat animals 75
Bracken: beautiful but fatal 78
Rare ferns of our uplands 80
Ancient and modern clubmosses 82
Peat-forming sphagnum mosses 84
Mosses and liverworts of bogs 88

Cold-blood creatures

Silver-blue salmon 93
The trout: a fish for all waters 95
The charr: stranded lake fish 98
Three mountain butterflies 100
Mayflies & stoneflies 102

Birds

The eagle: king of the birds 107
Peregrine: prince of birds 111
Ospreys: Highland rarities 115
Buzzards: rugged birds of prey 119
Moorland merlins 122
The snowy owl: a rare visitor 126
Snow buntings: Arctic visitors 128
Game birds of our moorlands 130
Black grouse 133
Upland plovers 136
Raven and chough: two cliff birds 139
Ring ouzel: a mountain blackbird 142
The wheatear: bird of the open spaces 145
Pipits of meadows and rocky coasts 148

Mammals

Mountain and moorland mammals 154
The frenzied rut of the red deer 158
Return of the reindeer 162
The wildcat: a fierce predator 166
Gregarious goats of remote hills 169
Hares of heather moorland 173
Otters in a Scottish winter 176
Lakeland Fell ponies 179
The Welsh mountain pony 182
Adaptable Highland ponies 186

Index 190

The High
KINGDOM

Introduction

The upland habitat is a simple one, rarely being three-dimensional or layered like a lowland woodland, yet it is complex and continuously variable, its plant and animal life being dominated by the need to survive constantly harsh winters and frequently poor summers. The resulting communities and species are among the most exciting and the least known features in Britain for the naturalist.

Many parts of our mountains and uplands are bleak, cold and windswept, but they are surprisingly rich in plants and animals, many of them occurring in no other habitat. The uplands are among the most obviously artificial of all habitats since, although almost all land up to the natural tree-line (which may be as high as 600m/2000ft) *should* be wooded, hardly any now *is* – this bareness being due entirely to the activities of man. At the same time, hardly any of the uplands have been ploughed or drained and there is more semi-natural vegetation, relating closely to the local conditions and occurring in larger blocks, than in any other habitat.

Our uplands have changed dramatically from totally bare after the last Ice Age (about 10,000 years ago), through a long period of domination by woodland, to the present time when 'open' peaty and grassy habitats abound. Much of our native wildlife has failed to adapt to these changes, with the result that our mountains and moors are poor in species.

In a few places, such as Ben Lawers, there are relics of the rich flora that developed after the Ice Age, but they are greatly prized as rarities. And many animals that flourished in the one-time forest have now gone – yet golden eagles, ravens, harriers, red grouse and many other open country birds – and mammals – of special interest remain.

Left: Borrowdale in Cumbria – autumn has tinted the boggy moorland grasses and the fringing birch trees with rich gold.

LIFE ON WINDSWEPT MOUNTAIN TOPS

Up on the snow-covered mountain tops a small community of animals and plants has adapted to raging winds, searing cold and long, dark nights. In winter ptarmigan and mountain hares turn white and their furry feet act as snow-shoes; mice and shrews dig snow tunnels, while hardy plants cling to rocks.

In the Cairngorms you might come across a herd of reindeer, plentiful in Britain during the Great Ice Age. In 1952 they were reintroduced and now roam freely over nearly 6000 acres in Glenmore Forest Park. Unlike many creatures that seek shelter on the lower slopes, the hardy reindeer stay up on drier ground.

In the north and west of the British Isles is an expanse of semi-wilderness, quite unlike the rest of our landscape; here lofty peaks, snow-covered for much of the year, rise to a height of over 1220m (4000ft). The severe climate and steepness of the slopes mean that they are still very remote: only determined climbers and skiers brave the heights. But the mountainsides are not quite as desolate as they look: a small but sturdy community of plants and animals has adapted to these harsh conditions and, hidden from sight for months by a protective mantle of snow, ekes out a precarious existence.

Altitude has profound effects on climate and wildlife. For a start there are no trees, not simply because there is too little soil on bare mountainsides, but because it is too cold and windy for them. Even the hardiest trees need an average temperature of above 10°C (50°F) for at least two months of the year. At 700m (2300ft) it might just be warm enough in some places; but for every extra 150m (500ft) above sea level, the average temperature falls by about one degree. 1000m (3300ft) is well beyond the tree limit and parts of the mountain ranges in North Wales and Scotland are even higher than this.

Hardy plants Only plants adapted to alpine conditions grow above the tree line. Some grow in permanently wet places where water collects, but others face the problem of water shortage. Rain runs off rocky mountainsides and on the steepest ground there is little soil to trap the water. In winter, water is frozen as ice or snow and so cannot be used by plants. Searing wind presents a further difficulty, buffeting the plants and drying out the soil. For example, on the summit of Ben Nevis which dominates the landscape near Fort William, gales of 50mph or more blow on at least 250 days of the year.

Many of these plants are succulents which cope with the dry conditions by storing water in fleshy leaves and stems. Rarely more than a few centimetres tall, the plants cling firmly to the rock and pockets of warmer soil. The soil is scant and poor because the hard rocks weather very slowly and release few nutrients into the soil. Lichens and mosses form thick carpets, able to withstand weeks of drying out, swiftly absorbing water from rain or snow showers. Larger plants, such as tough grasses and the low shrubby bilberry, grow in sheltered nooks, their roots anchored in cracks between the rocks. Others, such as saxifrage (which means rock breaker), form low cushions, the temperature inside the clump being higher and more stable than that outside. There are also a number of evergreens such as crowberry which can use the sun's energy for growth all the year round, even in the dim light filtering through the snow.

Snow to the rescue Snow is very cold stuff, though not nearly as cold as the mountain air which often reaches −10°C (14°F) or lower in winter. A covering of snow actually protects the plants and soil creatures from the cold: if it is −5°C (23°F) on the surface, it may only be 0°C (32°F) underneath the snow. Frost, too, is kept at bay. When there is no snow frost freezes the soil solid and kills plants, while dry air steals away any remaining moisture. Although the growing and feeding processes of all plants are slowed down under this mantle of snow, the plants survive.

Without this plant life most of the creatures that live on the mountain tops could not survive. Tiny soil animals, such as mites, weevils, springtails and small beetles, live among the plant roots. Several of them are flightless; feeding underground they do not need to come above the surface and risk being blown away. Many, including springtails and mites, produce a glycerol antifreeze which prevents them from freezing solid. They in turn become an important source of food for larger animals, and particularly birds, which move up the mountainsides during the more hospitable summer months.

Burrowing mammals In patches of grass these animal communities are numerous enough to support pygmy and common shrews, which can be found on our highest peaks in winter. In Wales, the wood mouse ekes out a meagre living on rocky screes near the summit of Snowdon. Once the problem of food is solved, these small mammals have one big advantage over the larger animals: they can escape the bitter conditions by burrowing under the snow and hiding beneath the rocks.

Above the snow the creatures dependent on the vegetation must literally scratch for a living. Principal among them is the ptarmigan, a kind of mountain grouse which is rarely seen below 650m (2100ft) and is most at home on steep, stony ground. There the wind scours snow off the shrubs, exposing the shoots, berries and leaves which form the mainstay of the ptarmigan's diet. Ptarmigan have been remarkably tolerant of intrusion by skiers and mountaineers. They can be seen strutting through the snow below the chair lifts at places like Glenshee. A small black and white bird, the snow bunting, which arrives for the winter from the Arctic, has also come

The structure of mountains
A cross-section of the land reveals layers of different rocks, deposited at various periods over millions of years. There are three main groups.
Igneous, such as black basalt and granite, formed from molten larva forced out from the earth's core. Much of the Cairngorms and the Wicklow Mountains are topped with granite. You can recognise it by the glinting crystals of mica, quartz and feldspar embedded in it.
Sedimentary, such as limestone and shale, formed from layers of mineral sediments or the remains of plants and creatures compressed at the bottom of the sea. The Cambrians are a mixture of shales and sandstones; the core of the craggy Pennines is limestone.
Metamorphic, such as slate and gneiss, formed when igneous or sedimentary rock was changed by heat and chemical action. It is often dark, banded and wavy as a result of folding, breaking easily into flakes and sheets, as in the slate of the Welsh mountains. Most of the Scottish Highlands rocks are metamorphic.

The oldest mountains, based on gneiss, are in the Outer Hebrides and the north-west Highlands. The youngest, the Pennines and mountains of south Wales, were thrown up some 270 million years ago. Once as high as the Himalayas, the peaks have been much eroded by persistent weathering.

The ptarmigan is well adapted to the snowy mountain tops: stiff, comb-like feathers on its feet serve as snow-shoes, preventing it from sinking into the soft snow while its strong claws can dig out plant shoots or even a hollow for overnight roosting.

to terms with humans and now commonly feeds around car parks and from litter bins. A small number of snow buntings usually remain in the Scottish mountains to breed, building their moss-lined nests on small ledges or in rock crevices.

Winter whiteness The brown mountain hare shares a strange characteristic with the ptarmigan and stoat: its coat turns white in winter. At first sight the reason for this seems to be the effective camouflage in a white, snowy terrain. Certainly if they remained brown, as in summer, they would be highly conspicuous. However, predators are relatively scarce at high altitudes during the winter. So it may well be that a white coat primarily gives protection against cold rather than predators. White bodies radiate heat less rapidly than dark ones, so winter whiteness may be a way of conserving body heat. Temperature seems to trigger off this colour change. The colder it is in November, the quicker the change occurs. Lowland stoats, which normally stay reddish brown through winter, have been exposed to low temperatures and their coats rapidly change to white.

If you climb up a mountainside in the winter months the only evidence of living creatures you may see is an occasional track—perhaps that of a hare or a ptarmigan. Most of the resident wildlife will be sheltering under the snow or in rock crevices, protecting themselves from the cold and wind.

The mountain hare, smaller than its lowland relative the brown hare, moults from brown to white as winter approaches and retains its white coat until spring. The Irish mountain hare, however, only develops a piebald coat or does not change colour at all. In winter the mountain hare feeds almost entirely on heather but will eat the twigs of willow or birch if the heather is covered in very deep snow.

How plant types change with increasing altitude

The higher up a mountain you go the colder and more windswept it becomes. Plants are correspondingly smaller and hug the ground more closely nearer the summit, where only small patches of lichens cling to the bare rocks. A few hardy cushion plants, such as mossy saxifrage and cushion pink, can survive at almost any level; but most have a maximum altitude at which they normally grow. Change between vegetation zones is gradual, but the majority of species mainly grow within the zones shown on the right. Each mountain is different, and the plant species vary according to soil types, rainfall, snow cover, the steepness of the slope and its drainage.

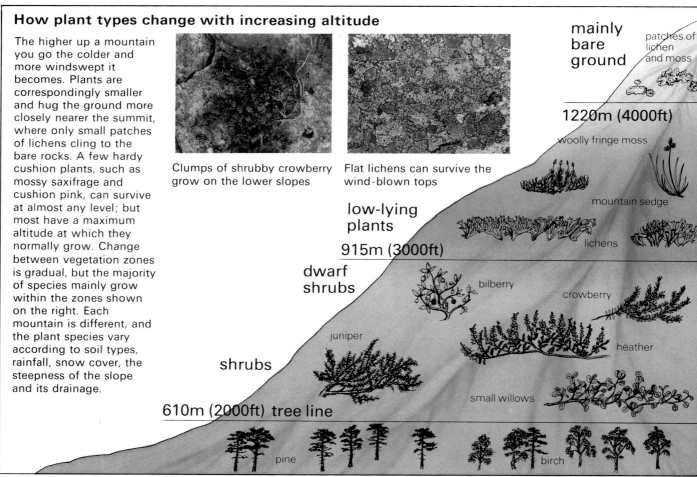

Clumps of shrubby crowberry grow on the lower slopes

Flat lichens can survive the wind-blown tops

mainly bare ground — patches of lichen and moss

1220m (4000ft)

woolly fringe moss

mountain sedge

low-lying plants

915m (3000ft)

lichens

dwarf shrubs

bilberry

crowberry

heather

juniper

shrubs

small willows

610m (2000ft) tree line

pine

birch

Britain's mountains

Typical mountain residents over 760m (2500ft)

mountain hare (not Wales or Lake District)
field vole
mole (up to 915m (3000ft) on good soils)
pygmy shrew
buzzard
raven
wren (up to 915m (3000ft), descends in hard weather)

mountain ringlet butterfly (Highlands and Lake District only)
large black slug
craneflies
spiders
beetles
weevils
mites
springtails

Some Scottish residents. . .

reindeer (Cairngorms only)
ptarmigan
golden eagle
black mountain moth
mountain burnet moth (very rare)
northern dart moth

. .and visitors

snow bunting
Lapland bunting (rare)
shorelark

Visitors in spring and summer

fox
stoat
ring ouzel
golden plover
wheatear
meadow pipit
dotterel (rare)

North Harris

NORTH-WEST HIGHLANDS

Some snow usually lasts all the year round on the highest Scottish mountains

Ben Nevis 1343m (4406ft)
Snow usually falls in September, and begins to melt in May

Bla Bheinn
Cuillin Hills
Rhum
Mull

Cairngorms
Cairn Gorm 1246m (4088ft)

Monadhliath Mts

GRAMPIANS

The rare alpine milkvetch and small alpine gentian only grow on a few mountains in Scotland

Arran
Tweedsmuir Hills
Cheviot Hills

Shalloch on Minnoch
Merrick

Snow fell on the Pennines as late as June in 1975

CUMBRIAN MTS
Sca Fell 977m (3205ft)

Colour change of mountain hare often incomplete

PENNINES

Nephin
Croagh Patrick
Mweelrea Mts

Mourne Mts

Wicklow Mts
Blackstairs Mts

Snowdon 1086m (3563ft)

Berwyn Mts
Cader Idris

Spiderwort only grows on a few mountains in Snowdonia

Slieve Mish Mts
Carrauntoohil 1041m (3415ft)
Macgillycuddy's Reeks

Galty Mts
Comeragh Mts
Knockmealdown Mts

Black Mts

CAMBRIAN MTS

Mynydd Du
Brecon Beacons

No colour change of mountain hare in Ireland

Places where mountain-top plants and animals can be viewed from the road

A9 between Inverness and Aviemore (Grampians)
Coire Cas ski centre on Cairn Gorm (Cairngorms)
Lecht road between Cock Bridge and Tomintoul (Grampians)
From Loch Kishorn to Applecross (Wester Ross)
Snowdon railway (Snowdon)

Key

☐ land exceeding 300m (1000ft)

■ parts of mountain ranges exceeding 760m (2500ft)

▲ individual mountains exceeding 760m (2500ft)

EXPLORING ROCK PAVEMENTS

High above fields and villages a hilltop limestone pavement, like that over Malham Cove in Yorkshire (below), attracts a host of walkers and naturalists. The pavement crevices form a habitat where plant and animal communities live sheltered and secure.

An expanse of bare white rock stands at the head of a high escarpment. Nearby, a little group of sheep rests silently, sheltered from the heat of summer by a lonely clump of trees. The scene has a biblical air, and if asked to guess its whereabouts, you might first be tempted to say the Middle East. Few would be quick to tell its true location–the hill country of northern England. And few would guess that this barren scene with its shimmering surface of rock was shaped by ice. Long ago the original limestone was worn down to its flat table shape under the immense weight and grinding power of millions of tons of ice.

During the later ice ages, up to a million

years ago, glaciers and ice sheets worked their way down across England as far south as where the Midlands are today. The wide, graceful U-shaped valleys of the Scottish Highlands, the Lake District and Snowdonia, often holding a blue lake in their deepest part, mark the paths glaciers once took.

Many of us can recognise the sweeping shape of these beautiful valleys as the result of glacial movement; but the rock pavements appear different; it seems hard to connect them with the glacial valleys – and yet they were created by the same process.

The rock is limestone. During the ice ages, the piled-high ice sheets carried a mighty mass of boulders and small stones, which worked as a vast abrasive, scraping and wearing down the limestone to produce a smooth sheet.

When warmer weather returned and the ice melted away, the boulders and stones were left behind on the pavement top, where many of them still stand today as evidence of the glacial age.

Since the last ice age the rock has been subject to open-air weathering. For more than ten thousand years rain has dissolved and washed away the surface of the limestone, and in places this enlarged the hairline cracks that are found in the limestone. These were originally caused by changes in the pressure on the earth's crust, for example when the ice sheet melted away relieving the rock of its burden. The cracks often form rectangular patterns, from which these limestone expanses gained the name of pavements.

There are a few specialised words used for the unique features of the rock pavement. The pieces that look like paving slabs are known as clints, and the cracks between are called grikes.

Etched into the surface of the clints there are shallow grooves called runnels, which drain into the grikes. When the pavement is sloping, the runnels follow the direction of the slope; but where the pavements are more or less level they form patterns which sometimes resemble the spokes of a wheel.

The usual width of a grike is a few inches; grikes vary in size from thin crevices to occasional huge troughs which could quite easily accommodate a sheep.

Plant colonizers Little light penetrates the deepest grikes, and their lower levels hold scarcely any plant life. If any plant can make use of this chimney-like habitat it is likely to be a moss or a liverwort. Water can cut underground channels and hollows in the most unexpected routes through limestone, and in some places you can lie with your ear to the surface of the rock and hear the water running a few feet below the pavement surface. In places like this, where water is not far away, the opposite-leaved golden saxifrage may grow.

Even the shallower grikes can be damp and

humid and, with the shade provided by the close rock walls, the conditions resemble those of a woodland floor. Wild flowers and ferns do well in these crevices. When you approach the pavement from a distance you would imagine it to be a dry lifeless habitat, but step up on to the top and you'll be lured onwards, to look for plants concealed down every grike.

Typical finds in these crevices are herb robert, hart's tongue fern, dog's mercury, sanicle, hedge woundwort, lady fern, hard-shield fern, herb paris, lily of the valley and plenty of others besides.

Plants of rocky habitats also come into their own on the limestone pavement, and you are quite likely to see wall spleenwort, maidenhair spleenwort, brittle bladder fern, wall lettuce and limestone polypody fern. The rigid buckler fern is a rare plant elsewhere in the British Isles, but is well established on some pavements to the east of Morecambe Bay.

Where sheep graze the pavements in hill country, the leading shoots of young trees

Above: Not all rock pavements are on the hilltops: this one, showing a grike brimming over with silverweed, is on the shore of Lough Coole in Ireland.

Below: Boulders resting on the top of the pavement shelter the underlying rock from erosion by rain. Over the centuries the surrounding surface is worn down, leaving the boulder perched upon a pedestal. Boulders that have been moved a long way are called glacial erratics. This is one of the Norber Boulders on the Ingleborough pavement in Yorkshire, a glacial erratic that was transported there by the ice.

that start to grow in the grikes are normally bitten off as soon as they protrude above the surface. But where woods surround the pavement–allowing it to become a secluded clearing–shrubs such as juniper and yew grow and form a layer like a green mat over the clint surface.

Ash saplings often take root in the grikes in these clearings, but all too often the narrow confines of the rocky habitat constrict the roots, arresting growth and condemning the trees to remain forever stunted.

Other occupants Spiders seem to have a great liking for the grikes, and often spread their webs across crevices that look like miniature canyons. Only one bird species appears to be interested in this easy source of food and that is the wren, whose fondness for caves is well known.

Other visitors may be less fortunate. It has been known for a lapwing to be found trapped at the bottom of a grike; and sometimes the skeleton of a sheep shows just how treacherous these places can be.

Where to find limestone pavements In England large outcrops are found in the Yorkshire Dales, where hill walkers on Ingleborough and Whernside get a bird's eye view of the white expanses, and where, above Malham Cove (as you can see in the photograph on page 12) the passage of many feet has actually polished the surface of the limestone. These are mountain pavements,

Above: Bloody cranesbill *(Geranium sanguineum)* growing in one of the series of limestone pavements on the Burren, County Clare in Ireland.

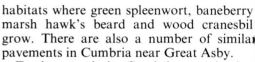

Below: This grike is very deep but near enough to the edge of the cliff to be open to light and air, and so provide a home for ferns and small plants.

habitats where green spleenwort, baneberry marsh hawk's beard and wood cranesbill grow. There are also a number of similar pavements in Cumbria near Great Asby.

Further south in Cumbria, on the low wooded hills surrounding Morecambe Bay, the pavements, which lie hidden under hazel and yew, support other species of plants such as the dark-red helleborine, the angular Solomon's seal and the rusty back fern.

The pavements of western Ireland also support the rusty back fern. The Irish outcrops are found mostly in the north of County Clare and South Galway. One splendid example is the Burren, a sweeping range of pavements that rise up from sea level to 300m (1000ft), making a scene of unique beauty.

Plundering man Limestone pavements are not widespread: it has been estimated in a recent survey that all the outcrops in the United Kingdom put together only amount to about 5300 acres of pavement. And, sad to relate, they certainly belong in the category of natural habitats that are being damaged and destroyed by the work of man.

The clints are attractive with their intricate runnels and waterworn surface, and they have for long been highly valued as rockery stone. People used to lever off the smaller individual clints, prising them off with crowbars. Some of their crowbars evidently became too deeply embedded in the rock to be freed, and can still be seen today, standing like bizarre rusted gate posts. But with the advent of powerful tractors, even the most massive pavements are at risk, and very large clints can be torn from the underlying rock, with far more damaging effect.

So, if you are planning a rockery and have thought of using waterworn limestone, think again. For every stone that is taken away, a rare natural habitat is reduced. A few areas of limestone pavement have been safeguarded in nature reserves, but the sad fact is that where pavements have been destroyed, they are not renewed: for new ones to be formed, we would indeed have to wait for another ice age to start the process all over again.

THE UNDERGROUND WORLD OF CAVES

Beneath our limestone hills lie series after series of deep cave systems, carved out of the stone by the action of countless years of corroding water. They form our last truly wild places, being remote and difficult of access, yet even in their darkness there is active, scurrying life.

Above: These extraordinary stalactite and stalagmite formations are to be found inside the Otter Hole Cave in the Forest of Dean. Over the course of many years minerals from the constantly dripping water build up into fantastic architectural shapes and patterns.

What could be more mysterious than an ancient, rock-bound chasm opening into the earth's surface, gulping a fast flowing stream into the darkness below? Its dank interior seems an unlikely home for any living creature. The rough rock walls glisten with beads of water, and the floor is of sticky, orange-brown clay. The only other colours are the varied hues of brown, interrupted by the glistening white of what look like slender hanging straws. These are stalactites in their first stage of growth. But life is persistent and astonishingly adaptable: take a close look at a mud bank or wall-pocket, and there you will see living things – small creatures that hop and scurry about. The cave fauna is an

unsuspected, improbable community, linked to the outside world only by trickling water and the coming and going of swirling bats.

Food from outside Life revolves around the sun. Green plants trap solar energy and manufacture food on which animals depend. But light penetrates only a few metres into the underground world so that no green plants can live in a deep cave. However, fragments of twig and leaf may be carried from the surface into the depths by a stream, and may be stranded on its banks where small scavengers of plant remains can reach them. The droppings of visiting bats still hold a little food energy from the bats' rich diet of insects caught in the air above fields and

Cave formation
Rainwater, weakly acidic after its passage through the soil, corrodes its way into limestone along lines of weakness. At first the channels are tiny, but some enlarge and capture the main flow. As water is conducted away, passages are drained and cavers can enter. Our major caving areas are in the Yorkshire Dales, the Peak District, the Brecon Beacons and the Mendips.

woods. This energy is passed on to the cave flies, beetles and millipedes which feed on the droppings.

A niche for winter The huge rock mass in which the cave lies is little influenced by short-term changes in temperature so that the interior remains at about the mean annual temperature, summer and winter alike. This makes caves ideal hibernation sites for bats and insects. Bats are frequently found in Devon, Somerset and in the Welsh caves, but further north they are scarce below ground. The insects that hibernate in caves–the herald moth (*Scoliopteryx libatrix*), the tissue moth (*Triphosa dubitata*) and various flies and mosquitoes–are widespread in all British cave areas.

Cave dwelling has its own problems, even for the temporary winter visitors. Most obvious is the lack of light. Bats have excellent hearing and can rely on ultrasonic squeaks to pinpoint even the smallest obstacles as they fly through the cave. The slow-moving invertebrates on the cave floor are able to use their antennae to feel their way, while an acute sense of smell will guide them to their food.

Hazards of hibernating There are, however, more subtle problems, one such being the draught. Many caves have two or more entrances, and if these are at different heights an air current is generated. In winter the cave is warmer than the outside world, so the relatively warm air rises out through the upper entrance, to be replaced by cold, denser air that streams in at the lower entrance. The cave walls impart their warmth to the new air, which then rises and continues the flow within the cave.

This chimney effect can cause serious problems for hibernating animals. As cold air warms, it exerts a drying effect on cave walls and their inhabitants. The small insects have extremely limited water reserves, and would not take long to dehydrate. Even bats are threatened. They may cluster closely to trap moist air between their bodies, or may snuggle deep into narrow roof crevices, away from the drying air current. Usually, however, they try to find a blocked cave, free from

Above: A herald moth hibernating on the cave roof. In the course of time water droplets have condensed on its wings from the saturated air. Herald moths are commonly found hibernating in the transition zone of many British caves from late autumn till spring. They may otherwise hibernate in barns, belfries, roofs and under the arches of stone bridges.

any draughts, in which to roost, precisely to avoid this problem.

While dry air may cause problems for the species that visit the cave, saturated air may be more difficult to cope with and has led to even more radical adaptations. An insect's equivalent of blood (the haemolymph) has a high content of water but in a cave the air can become extremely moist, and in such conditions–which are normal in the deep cave–some of the water may be absorbed into the body fluids of the insect. This leads to water poisoning unless the insect has a way of getting rid of the excess water. Freshwater animals possess a kind of water pump which keeps their body fluids up to the right concentration, and many of the deep cave creatures have developed one too.

Land or water animals? With the problem of water balance solved, there is little or no distinction between the land and water dwelling creatures of the deep cave. Aquatic animals such as the shrimp-like amphipod *Niphargus fontanus* and the isopod *Proasellus cavaticus* (a small white water louse) move from pool to pool across the damp cave floor. They may be joined in the water by 'terrestrial' millipedes, beetles and the small, knobbly woodlouse *Androniscus dentiger*. Having once adopted an aquatic type of water balance system, the deep cave specialists cannot cope with dry atmospheres, and this is one factor that restricts them to caves.

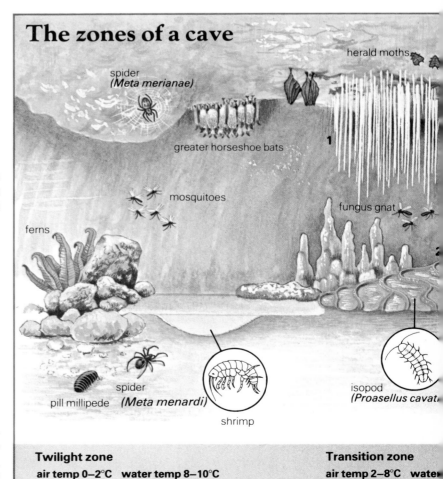

The zones of a cave

herald moths

spider
(Meta merianae)

greater horseshoe bats

mosquitoes

ferns

fungus gnat

spider
(Meta menardi)

pill millipede

shrimp

isopod
(Proasellus cavat...)

Twilight zone
air temp 0–2°C   water temp 8–10°C

Transition zone
air temp 2–8°C   water

Permanent cave dwellers So many creatures are dependent on caves and unable to live elsewhere that biologists have given them a collective name – troglobites. Many of them are blind, white invertebrates – dwelling in total darkness they have no need for vision or body pigment, and in the course of evolution they have lost both. In Britain most aquatic troglobites are confined to the south west, south Wales and East Anglia. These are areas south of, or only just north of, the southern limits reached by the great ice sheets during the most recent ice age.

The ice sheets probably wiped out all cave specialists in the area beneath them, but the creatures are slowly inching back northwards year by year, using flooded crevices in the rocks and deep gravel beds of rivers as migration routes from one cave region to another. They cannot follow surface migration routes because, lacking any form of skin pigment, they are completely unprotected from the damaging effect of ultraviolet light in the sun's rays. For them, daylight is therefore lethal and they are trapped underground for ever.

Saving precious energy Food is in short supply in the deep cave, and some troglobite specialisations are effective in saving energy and therefore food. These include slow rates of growth and great efficiency in movement and the actions needed to capture prey or take plant food. Another adaptation is the

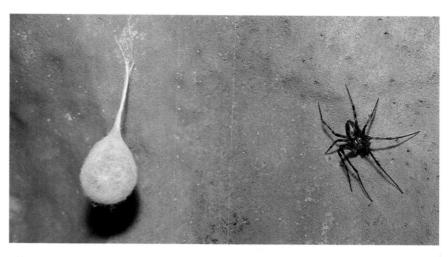

Above: A cave spider, *Meta menardi*, keeping guard over its egg sac.

Right: *Proasellus cavaticus* is an isopod, related to the woodlouse, that can be seen in caves of the Mendip Hills and South Wales. This one has made its home in a film of water on a flowstone bank, where it grazes on patches of bacteria. These are visible in its gut as a dark central line running along the body.

ability to breed successfully by means of a single egg, or only a few eggs. This compares with the myriads of eggs laid by many other creatures, for example insects.

Many of the deep cave insects have lost some or all of their larval stages of growth, and it is thought that this may also act as an adaptation that saves energy. The process of metamorphosis often involves peak periods of feeding which, in the inhospitable cave environment, may simply not be possible.

Troglobite eggs are unusually well stocked with food so that the young are big and strong when they emerge, and thus are well equipped for survival. A troglobite species can therefore avoid the high wastage – in loss to predators or in mortality of other kinds – that is often a feature of life for wild populations.

Plant life in the dark While green plants are absent from caves, many lower plants manage to eke out a living. Fungi feed on washed-in vegetation and may take a heavy toll of hibernating insects whose resistance to fungal infection may have been lowered by water poisoning. Even further down the evolutionary scale are the organisms that form powdery patches on cave walls. Looking like lichens and often called wall fungi, these are members of a group called the actinomycetes. Their colonies are often beaded with small water droplets, giving them a jewel-like appearance in the caver's headlamp.

spider
(*Porrhoma*)

tterer's bat

3

◀ water flow

ground beetle
(*Trechus micros*)

amphipod
(*Niphargus fontanus*)

Deep cave

air temp 10°C   water temp 10°C

Conditions for life
In a cave, as in many other habitats, variations in living conditions produce a series of life zones, each with a distinctive community. The twilight zone reaches the limit of light penetration, the dark transition zone beyond has a variable climate, while the deep cave has a steady temperature and saturated humidity.

Water-formed stone
Stalagmites stand and stalactites hang. They are the accumulated mineral deposits from dripping water. Straw stalactites are in the process of being formed (**1**). Rimstone is formed at the rim of a pool as water slowly overflows (**2**). Flowstone (**3**) is made when a film of water flows down a sloping surface, depositing a smooth sheet of calcite.

Bacteria are everywhere in the cave and, together with fungi, form the main food of the animal community.

The food chain Tiny springtails are voracious feeders on the spreading branches (hyphae) and spores of fungi. They often cluster on pool surfaces where most predators cannot venture and where the humidity is always high. Those braving the cave walls face the danger of blundering into a spider's web, where certain death awaits them. Most cave spiders belong to the genus *Porrhomma*, which is one of the genera of money-spiders. Our only cave-limited spider is the rare *Porrhomma rosenhaueri*. Occupying another lowly position in the cave food chain are the tiny pink worms that live in mud banks. These, the enchytraeids, are easy prey for the small ground beetle *Trechus micros* which, in Britain, is thought to breed only underground.

Upsetting the balance The cave community is perfectly adapted to function on a tight energy budget. Many troglobites survive with population densities at such a low level that even a slight drop in numbers can consign them to local extinction, and recolonization can be slow. Fortunately the deep cave is a stable habitat.

Even so, man's influence can reach into the depths of a cave. Tipping nutrient-rich sewage or refuse into a convenient sinkhole may solve a problem for the farmer, but it can have serious effects on the ecosystem in a cave below. While the slow-breeding troglobites are for once comfortably provided with food, the less cave-adapted species undergo a population explosion amid such plenty.

Numbers—first of the primitive plants, then the herbivores which eat them, and finally their predators—build up rapidly. The predators wreak indiscriminate havoc among

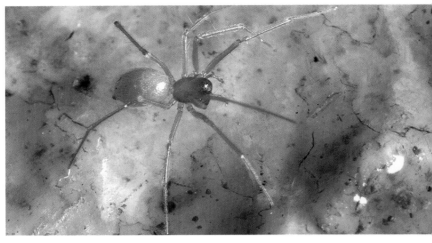

Above: Blind and spindly legged, the tiny spider *Porrhomma rosenhaueri* is known in Britain in just two small caves in Wales. It spins a gossamer sheet-web in remote crevices, to catch the pinhead-sized springtails on which it feeds.

Right: Most cave fungi do not produce fruiting bodies and when they do they are unlike the familiar mushrooms above ground. They can only develop if a large enough supply of food is provided—for example, a dead insect.

Below: The entrance is the only part of the cave where light is sufficient for plants to occur naturally—here are ferns, mosses and grass.

their prey, troglobites and non-specialised species alike. Eventually a steady state is regained, but in the upheaval the troglobites may well have been wiped out: it will be many years before the community recovers its original variety and balance.

Limestone quarries However, such inadvertent tampering with the balance of cave life is of less importance when compared with the wholesale destruction of the cave habitat by quarrying. Extensive caves in Britain are developed only in limestone. Fortunately we have plenty of cavernous limestone, but the perpetual need for cement, road aggregate and building stone can only be met by blasting away limestone hillsides with their unique fauna and flora. Conservation bodies are taking a new interest in caves and the Nature Conservancy Council has denoted a number of caves throughout Britain as Sites of Special Scientific Interest, a first step towards ensuring their future conservation. This signals an increase in public awareness of the special role of caves as yet another fascinating habitat.

LIFE ON PERILOUS SCREE SLOPES

Scree slopes – banks of loose, bare stones where living things could at any moment be buried by rock falls – may seem barren. Yet, although they are not rich in species, they do in fact support their own range of animals and plants.

Many mountainsides exposed to weathering have broken into vertical cliffs whose loosened fragments are scattered down the slopes below by the force of gravity. Such spreads of disintegrated rock are known as scree or, less commonly, talus. They are common in upland districts and contribute greatly to the wildness of the landscape.

Types of scree Typically, the stones of a scree are sharp and angular, not rounded like those worn by water. Many screes begin at the top of a gully in the cliffs and broaden gradually as they stretch down the slope. Often there are many screes side by side and, although they start as separate streams of stones, they merge into each other lower down to form one large spread of scree.

Most cliffs and screes are found on the north and east sides of our mountains because there they are most exposed to frost. There are several types of screes. They can be of small stones, huge blocks or any size in between. Some screes are steeper than others, but usually they are not extremely steep since, over the years, the stones work their way down to accumulate at lower levels, thus making the slope less severe and more stable. The stones are then said to be lying at an angle of repose. Such screes can usually be walked across, but seldom with any comfort because the stones either move under your feet or are so big that they have to be scrambled over. Screes composed of thin, flat slates are very loose and almost impossible to walk across.

Primary plant colonization Vegetation colonizes screes only very slowly. First come those strange plants, the lichens, each a union of an alga with a fungus. Extremely hardy, they can grow on bare, exposed surfaces at high altitudes; as they cling to the rock they help to wear it away by producing acids which slowly eat into it, gradually crumbling it to form the soil needed by the next colonizers – the mosses. Meanwhile, the frost and other agents of erosion (sun, wind and rain) are also attacking the scree, slowly breaking it down to form soil between the stones. If the parent rock in the cliffs is soft and rotten, then soil forms comparatively quickly, but in screes of hard rock this process is very slow.

Above and left: Steep scree slopes in the Lake District. Although screes like these are too unstable a habitat for most plants and animals, they are successfully colonized by a small number of particularly adaptable species. From a conservation point of view, scree is of special value because it is one of the few surviving types of habitat to have been left relatively undisturbed by man. It can therefore be classed along with mountain cliffs and corrie lakes as an almost natural — and therefore precious — element in the mountain scene.

Previous page, left: This scree slope (on Ben Lomond in Scotland) is fairly stable, as can be seen from the grasses and other vegetation growing among the stones.

Previous page, right: Since most of the rocks in Britain are lacking in calcium, the plants found on scree formed from these rocks are calcifuges — lime-haters. One such plant is this bell heather, a typical scree colonizer.

Right: Few birds frequent screes, but the wheatear is one that may site its nest under the stones.

One of the commonest and most conspicuous mosses of some screes is the woolly hair-moss, which forms large grey-green cushions or even spreads as a continuous carpet visible from far away. As soil and humus begin to gather in screes, then the first flowering plants and ferns become established. These pioneers in their turn add to the soil by the annual dying down and decaying of their leaves and stems. So, in the course of time, if conditions are right, these larger plants may succeed in covering a whole scree so completely that from a distance it ceases to look like a scree at all.

Advantages of scree life What is it that enables some plants to colonize a scree slope despite the obvious disadvantages? First, the very fact that it is too harsh a place for most species means that there is less competition to grow in a scree than in most other habitats; therefore it is open to colonization by adaptable, aggressive plants.

Another virtue of screes is their usually excellent drainage, which ensures that con-

stantly renewed supplies of perhaps mineral-rich water are reaching the roots of the plants. Yet another advantage of good drainage is that there is little danger of the root-rot that afflicts many plants in stagnant water. With their rapid run-off of water it might be thought that screes must suffer from drought, and indeed this may be true of those with southern aspects. But the rainfall in our mountains is so great (usually between 2540-5080mm/100-200in a year) that most screes remain perennially watered, especially those on the shadowy sides of the uplands.

Calcifuges and calcicoles What plants you find on a scree is largely dictated by the chemical content of the rock. Because most of the rocks of British mountains lack calcium (lime) it follows that most of our screes are colonized by plants which can manage with very little or no lime at their roots.

Typical of these calcifuges (lime-haters) are bilberry, common heather, bell heather, crowberry, cowberry, wood-sorrel and heath bedstraw. On some mountainsides the screes are patched bright green with parsley fern, but this elegant plant is strangely absent from other screes that seem to be perfectly suitable for it. Several kinds of upland grasses, such as sheep's fescue, wavy hair-grass and sweet vernal-grass, are common invaders of acid screes. More local are the beech fern, oak fern, bladder fern, sea campion and many others.

Screes which form from the decay of lime-rich cliffs are naturally lime-rich themselves and become a habitat for some lime-loving plants (calcicoles). So, instead of the bilberry, heather and parsley fern of acid ground, these calcareous screes are occupied by mossy saxifrage, yellow saxifrage, alpine willow-herb, alpine scurvygrass, mountain sorrel, spring sandwort, butterwort and others. Some of these fall on to the scree from the cliffs when the rocks give way. Others may simply slide off a sloping ledge when the soil in which they are growing becomes sodden with heavy rain.

Strip vegetation Where scree covers a whole mountainside, it is unlikely to be uniformly stable. More often it exists as alternating vertical bands of firm and loose material. The loose strips are usually those below gullies in the cliffs because that is where erosion is proceeding briskly and sending down a constantly renewed stream of rock fragments and other debris.

The stable screes, on the other hand, normally lie below cliffs which are more resistant to the weather and therefore produce less scree debris. Or, in some places, a stable strip may lie not below a cliff but under some great detached boulder that has slipped half-way down the slope but then become stuck. There it acts as a brake on the downsliding of the scree, so creating a stable strip immediately below. Because vegetation can form only on stable scree, what we often see on a scree slope are plants growing in vertical lines separated by strips of loose scree with no vegetation at all.

Block scree The coarsest type of scree consists of huge boulders that may be several metres across. They are often the result of rocks splitting off cliffs weakened by cracks. Because these huge masses of detached rock usually slide or roll all the way down the slope, block scree is typically found towards the bottom of a mountainside, and there it may cover a large area. Some block scree at high altitudes is poor in plant life, except for lichens, because its hard surfaces are so exposed to the drying effects of wind and sun. But in shaded corries where there is perennial moisture, the block scree can become overgrown by some of the plants that flourish in the cliffs above.

Deep among the boulders of a block scree you may discover quite a different sort of habitat from that of the open mountainside—a sheltered, shadowy world where mosses and liverworts thrive in abundance and where the

Right: In the relatively few areas in Britain where the rocks are lime-rich, a variety of calcicole plants—lime-lovers—can be found. They include this attractive alpine willowherb with its reddish-purple flowers, red sepals and pinkish seeds pods. It is usually to be found in wet places on mountains and flowers in July and August. Other calcicoles on screes are mountain sorrel, alpine scurvygrass and spring sandwort.

Above: Yellow mountain saxifrage flourishing amid large scree boulders on the side of a mountain. It flowers from June to September in wet areas.

Below: Strange though it may seem, a few mammals frequent areas of scree. Block scree, in particular, provides excellent hiding places for foxes during the day. They emerge at nightfall to hunt across the high grasslands and bogs.

accumulation of humus is deep enough fo some of the larger ferns more typical of damp shady woods—lady fern, male fern and broad buckler for example. Some block scree i draped with thick mats of juniper.

Woodland on scree On screes, as on al slopes, such nutrients as the soil contains ar always being carried downhill by water. Th result is that there is usually more fertility an vegetation on the lower parts of a scree tha higher up. Below about 400-430m (1300 1400ft) which, in many districts, is the natura tree line, scree may be covered by woodlan which is suppressed on neighbouring grass land by the nibbling of sheep. Although mos scree is accessible to sheep, it is far less attract ive to them than grassland, and under suc light grazing pressure it is frequently pos sible for woodland to develop.

High-level woodland colonizing limeles block scree usually consists of oak with scattering of birch, rowan and holly. The tree are mostly wind-stunted and their trunks an branches are adorned with mosses and poly pody ferns. The boulders under the trees ar green with mosses, leaving little room fo flowering plants. Animal life is scanty com pared with that of lowland woods. Wel known upland oakwoods on block scree ar the Keskadale and Birkrigg Oaks in the Lak District and Wistman's Wood on Dartmoo

Woodland has also developed locally o upland scree whose rocks are lime-rich. Th

dominant tree here is usually ash, with perhaps a mixture of whitebeams and yews.
There may be a rich ground flora of calcicole
plants, such as lily-of-the-valley, green helle-
bore, herb paris and spurge laurel. Such ash-
woods are well known in parts of the Lake
District, the Peak District and Wales on the
carboniferous limestone, but they are also
found on other lime-rich screes—on igneous
rocks, for instance.

Animals of scree slopes A stable scree well
clothed with plants provides food and shelter
for invertebrates such as centipedes, wood-
lice, spiders and beetles—all animals which
can avoid the worst of the winter weather by
withdrawing deep among the stones.

Block scree is also an excellent retreat for
such mammals as the stoat, weasel, polecat,
pine marten and fox. They lie up by day in
the caverns under the rocks and come out at
nightfall to forage across the high grasslands
and bogs. They prey on rabbits, hares, mice,
voles and a variety of small birds and their
eggs. Being highly mobile animals, they are
not, of course, restricted to the scree habitat
alone, and range far and wide.

The birds of screes are few and far between,
most typical being the wheatear. This bird
uses the tops of rocks as look-out posts from
where it can spot its invertebrate prey. It also
hides its nest safely out of harm's way under
the scree stones. Ring ouzels, too, often
forage on screes that lie below the heathery
gullies where they breed.

Highly characteristic of block scree is the
wren, which spends much of its day down
among the great boulders, living on insects,
spiders and other small creatures. Its loud,
shrill song (unusual for such a small bird) can
be quite startling when it suddenly breaks the
silence of a mountain scree.

The only other widespread frequenter of
screes is the meadow pipit. It often feeds and
nests on screes, especially those with plenty of
vegetation. High-level screes on some Scottish
mountains are an important part of the
tundra-like world of the hardy ptarmigan, one
of the few birds in Britain that changes in
colour from brown in summer to white in
winter.

Above: Parsley fern on steep, slaty scree. On some scree slopes this plant forms bright green patches, but on others it is strangely absent.

Right: A view of Llanberis Pass in Snowdonia, with highly mobile, unstable scree on the right. This type of scree is very dangerous to walk on— once the small, loose stones start sliding, they may well precipitate a tumbling avalanche.
Often many screes exist side by side and, although they start as separate streams of stones, they merge into each other lower down the slope to form one large spread of loose stones and debris. Some cliffs shatter to form screes composed entirely of thin, flat slates; these make the loosest of all screes and can be almost impossible to walk across (like the spoil heaps of slate quarries).

The action of frost on rock

Mountain summits are under constant attack by the process of weathering, one of whose most penetrating weapons is frost. Most of the rock of our mountains has been deeply fissured by pressures in the earth's crust. Rainwater trickles down into these cracks (**a**) and, in winter, freezes hard. Then, because ice expands as it forms (**b**), the cracks open slightly. Next winter they open a little more and this frost action, repeated year after year, eventually causes the rock to split (**c**). Cliffs subjected to this type of weathering break into loosened fragments that are scattered down the slopes in the form of scree.

vertical section through rock

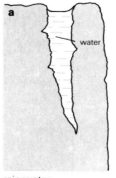

rain water fills crack

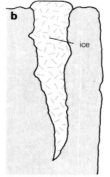

ice forms, enlarging crack slightly

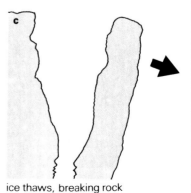

ice thaws, breaking rock into fragments

HEATHER MOORLAND

Go for a walk on the moors and you will soon be knee-deep in purple swaying heather, where the whirr of a flock of grouse flying low and fast over the brow of the hill is a lonely drama in a vast scene.

Widely distributed in northern Britain, the main heather moorland areas are found in the Peak District, North York Moors, Northumberland and the Southern Uplands and Eastern Highlands of Scotland. Other areas in the country may still retain remnants of a heather moorland vegetation but are now largely dominated by hill grasses. These are the home of grazing animals such as sheep and possibly deer, rather than grouse which is always associated with heather moorland.

All these moorlands have been formed since the last great Ice Age came to an end about 10,000 BC; the chief factor in their formation was a wet climatic period about 5000 to 6000 BC during which sphagnum mosses flour-

Above: In fine weather, moors are places of unending peace and solitude. On this heather moor in Perthshire the pine tree acts as a landmark that can be seen for miles around.

shed, covering large expanses of upland Britain in blanket bogs. Over a great many hundreds of years layers of sphagnum have built up, and these became peat.

Peat underlies most of our moorlands, sometimes to a depth of several feet. The vegetation which grew on the peat in ancient times was scrub willow, birch and pine, with cotton sedge in the wetter areas and heathers and grasses in the drier parts. When man started to settle the rocky uplands, perhaps five thousand years ago, trees were cleared to provide grazing; at a later stage the moors came to be managed for grouse and this caused vast areas to be covered with heather.

Eliminating the competition The maintenance of heather moorlands for grouse shooting (and in some cases for sheep grazing) has not been achieved without cost to other animals and plants. The main work of gamekeepers has been to persecute, by gun and trap, the other wildlife which either compete with the grouse for food or may kill the grouse themselves. Foxes, stoats and weasels are the grouse's main mammal enemies, and amongst birds both the predators and the ravens and crows have been killed to save the grouse.

You may nevertheless be lucky enough to see birds of prey – kestrels and the merlin, perhaps, but you have less chance of seeing peregrine falcon, buzzard or hen harrier. The eagle, which bred as far south as the Peak District until the early 18th century is now

Heather's central role

Heather plays a central role in the life of a moorland community, first as a food plant for herbivores, and then for the predators which feed on them. The diagram below is simplified:

for example, kestrels will also eat voles; and not shown are the small insects in the leaf and twig litter below the heather, and the seasonal visits of bees gathering nectar.

golden eagle
carrion crow (eats eggs)
fox
hen harrier
golden eagle
red grouse
hare
kestrel
fox
emperor moth larva
heather
dead sheep
fox
carrion crow
fox
meadow pipit
vole
short-eared owl

■ carnivores

■ herbivores

Left: Devon's Dartmoor has miles of grass-covered scenery, dotted with scrub and rocky outcrops of granite. In the distance is Wistman's Wood, famous for its stunted oaks and moss-covered boulders.

Below: Moors are a feature of the upland areas. Scotland has the largest moorland area, followed by Ireland, Northern England and Wales.

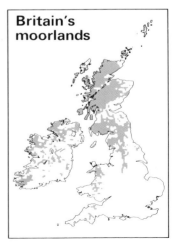

Britain's moorlands

confined mainly to the Scottish highlands.

During the summer the moors are visited by several birds that breed there. Notable among these are the golden plover, with its mournful 'peeping' call and the dunlin, a rather less timid bird. Both tend to prefer slightly wetter areas for nesting. The curlew, like the plover and dunlin, winters by the coast and migrates up to the moors in spring to breed, preferring tall heather in which to nest. Its gliding flight and bubbling call are a feature of the moors in spring. Three song-birds are particularly associated with the moors in summer: skylark, twite and, in greater numbers, the meadow pipit, with its twittering song and parachuting downward flight.

Insects of the moors Apart from the grouse, all these birds feed mainly on the numerous insects which the heather supports. Each species of insect specialises in its way of deriving a living from the heather: feeding from the sap of the plant are frog hoppers (whose larvae make cuckoo spit), and leaf hoppers. Eating the leafy shoots are the larvae of several moths, notably the fox moth, northern eggar and, most spectacular of all, the emperor moth.

Another insect closely associated with heather is the heather beetle. This can occasionally reach plague proportions and seriously damage the heather, sometimes with an effect on grouse numbers locally.

The litter which accumulates beneath the heather is food for springtails, whilst preda-tory spiders, harvestmen and beetle larvae feed on the plant-eating species.

Cotton grass and bilberry On wetter moor-land, cotton grass is often the commonest plant. Cotton grass supports fewer insects than does heather, although in the wet peat on which it grows several insect larvae may be found – particularly cranefly larvae, which play an important part in the moorland food-chain, especially as food for the breeding dunlin and golden plover. Also growing in wet peaty areas, the attractive pink-flowered cross-leaved heath adds a dash of colour.

In dry areas, the redder and larger-flowered bell heather is often found alongside the common heather or ling. The flowering of bell heather begins earlier and lasts much longer than that of the common heather. Other dry places may contain bilberry and its close relative, the red-berried cowberry.

Where sheep graze heavily on a moor that is not regularly burnt, grass often tends to take over from the heathers. Sometimes the grass is succeeded by bracken, which can spread quickly and exclude other plants by its dense shade.

Social change and the moors The country-side is always changing and the moorlands are no exception. Changes in the activity of man can greatly alter the natural environ-ment. An increasing demand for wood creates new plantations of conifers; demand

for water, too, continues to rise and bring new reservoirs into being. Another growing requirement of modern society is open areas for leisure activities, and so more walkers and holidaymakers appear than before – increasing the risk of fires in dry seasons. It may be, too, that smoke and gases from industry harm the moorland communities.

It is not surprising, then, that the total area of our moorlands has suffered a mea-surable reduction in the past forty years. It is hard to imagine that the conifer plantations and uniform grasslands which are replacing them will be as rich in natural interest or as full of that peculiarly lonely, weatherbeaten charm of Britain's upland heather moors.

Above: The red grouse of British moorlands is a native sub-species that is not found in other countries and is therefore the subject of attentive care by gamekeepers. It has four main requirements: old heather for cover, young heather, which is the staple diet, grit to swallow and water to drink. Grit and water are available naturally, but the mixture of young and old heather is enhanced by burning. When a patch has been burnt, young shoots spring up which provide more nutritious food for the grouse and its chicks.

Above left: Bilberry, which on dry moors can grow in extensive patches, is essentially a woodland rather than a moorland plant. This provides a clue to the history of the moors — long ago they used to be woodlands and scrub. Several of the moths and beetles of the moors are considered to be moorland forms of woodland species.

Heathlands and moorlands of Britain

Heathland and moorland are in many ways similar habitats, characterised by nutrient-poor soils and a distinct flora and fauna. But there are some differences. Moorland, which occurs mainly in upland Britain, has a wet, sometimes boggy soil with plants typical of bogs such as bog asphodel possibly present, though ling may be absent. Heathland, on the other hand, is found predominantly in lowland Britain and has a dry soil and ling or heath is always present.

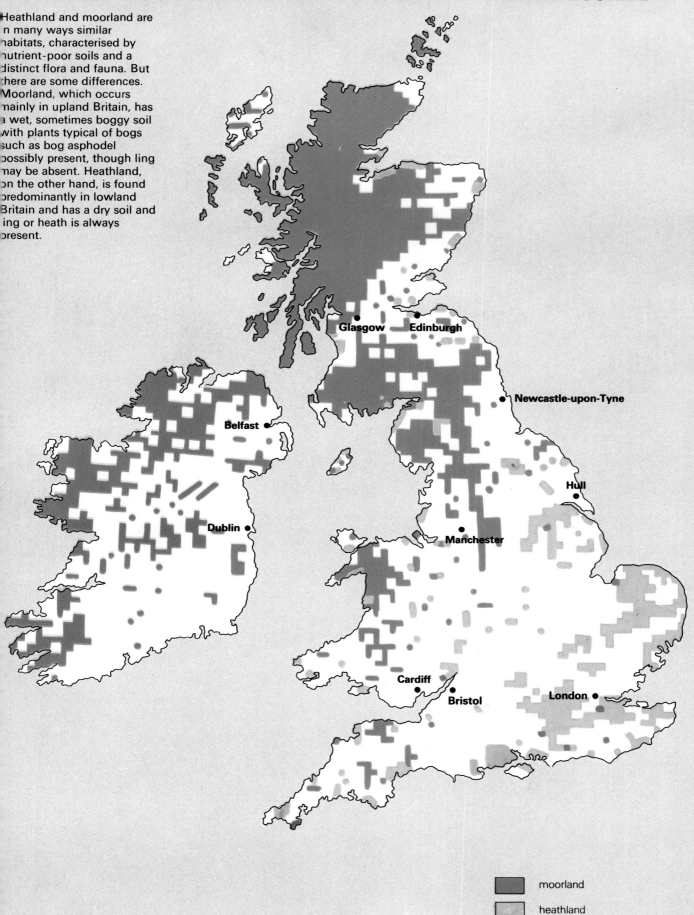

Glasgow

Edinburgh

Newcastle-upon-Tyne

Belfast

Hull

Dublin

Manchester

Cardiff

Bristol

London

moorland

heathland

27

BLANKET BOGS: A CLOAK OF PEAT

Most of our 'moorland' is more accurately described as blanket bog. The Pennines, Dartmoor, upland Wales and many of Scotland's heather-covered moors consist largely of blanket bog – wild, untamed land still awaiting the first cut of the plough.

Left: One plant that is often found in shallow water in bogs, fens and the edges of lakes is the bogbean – it grows 15-30cm (6-12in) in height and bears racemes of white or reddish flowers.

To some extent the general concept of bogs as dismal places is well-founded because blanket bogs depend for their formation first and foremost on the climate – the wetter the better. Britain lies directly in the path of moisture-laden westerly air-streams that sweep in from the Atlantic, bringing the rain which is literally the life-blood of our moorland areas

Above: Sphagnum moss—a riot of colour. That tiny bog mosses like this could have such profound effects over a wide area of Britain seems incredible, but the whole development of blanket bogs is closely bound up with this small but extremely important group of bryophytes.

Left: Pool and hummock bog —although such areas appear to be bleak, barren wastelands, they actually harbour many of our most fascinating and unusual plant species—most notable among them being the carnivorous butterworts, bladderworts and sundews.

Below: You can sometimes find an adder basking on a hummock in a blanket bog on a warm day.

The sphagnum blanket The process of blanket bog formation begins with the damp climate maintaining a waterlogged soil. This, together with the hard, acid rocks which dominate most of our northern and upland areas, combine to produce particularly difficult conditions for plant growth. However, species of the genus *Sphagnum* (bog moss) are superbly adapted to such conditions. Where waterlogging is particularly acute, such as in shallow basins, broad plateaux and gentle slopes, the small but brightly coloured bog mosses gradually form extensive carpets that cloak the thin, sodden soil.

Looked at under the microscope, the leaf of a sphagnum moss is seen to consist of extremely narrow, living green cells (containing chlorophyll) that are squeezed between, and dwarfed by, enormous empty cells (hyaline cells) which make up the bulk of the leaf. These hyaline cells are used for water storage—with cells this size the sphagnum plant is able to hold many times its own weight of water. Consequently, as sphagnum forms its 'carpets', the ground, already wet from the rainfall, becomes increasingly sodden because the sphagnum carpets are able to absorb and bind the majority of the rain where it falls.

Such conditions disrupt the usual course of biological growth, death and decomposition– the most efficient bacteria involved in decomposition require oxygen, which is not available because of the high water table. Anaerobic bacteria (those requiring no oxygen) are able to begin the process, but are much less efficient and therefore unable to achieve complete decomposition. Consequently the dead remains of the previous year's growth slowly accumulate beneath the living sphagnum layer. (We are generally more familiar with this accumulation of dead but undecomposed bog moss as 'peat'.)

Formation and development It appears that extensive blanket bog formation began about 5000BC when Britain's climate was extremely wet and fairly warm. Growth of the moss carpets is not rapid–about 2mm a year is the average–but over a period of six to seven thousand years this has been quite sufficient

to produce peat depths of up to 5m (16ft). Whole landscapes have vanished under layers of peat several feet thick because the original nuclei of peat developing in the hollows, on level ground and on gentle slopes began to coalesce to form a complete blanket, leaving exposed only the steepest slopes (30 degrees or more) where water is still able to drain freely.

Surprisingly, the bog surface remains water-logged, even though it may be perched 5m (16ft) above the mineral soil, because the power of sphagnum to bind water is stronger than the pull of gravity. Walk across the surface of a deep blanket bog–even when it covers a gentle slope–and it will be soft and spongy, sometimes quaking, and often (at least in the far north and west) riddled with a maze of peaty bog pools or *dubh lochans* (*dubh* meaning black and *lochan* being a small lake).

The actual nature of the surface patterns is largely controlled by the climate. The relatively dry conditions of the Pennines (about 1500mm/59in of rain a year) allow ample time for the majority of surface water to run off the downslope or evaporate. Pools of open water

Above: Red grouse (female) sitting on her nest. This species is attracted to blanket bogs to feed on such plant species as heath.

Opposite page: Strangely enough, heather, although always associated with moorlands, plays only a small part in most blanket bog vegetation. It is a species intolerant of extremely wet conditions and is therefore generally restricted to the higher hummocks. Only on the thinner, much steeper soils does it form its broad purple sheets. Its place on the true blanket bog is taken by cross-leaved heath (shown here) which is often mistaken for bell-heather. However, bell-heather is a plant of thin peat in the far west of Britain, while cross-leaved heath occurs mainly on deeper peats.

are therefore comparatively rare on the Pennine peats, the surface instead consisting of hummocks of bog mosses separated by shallow damp hollows. The far north-west of Scotland, on the other hand, has almost 2300mm (90½in) of rain each year. Such a volume of water cannot possibly be lost entirely through run-off and evaporation, and the excess collects as pools. In time these pools become established in complex but stable patterns, the nature of these patterns being determined by the type of blanket bog formation.

Types of blanket bog Watershed bogs are those occupying the broad, level ridges of ground that form watersheds between river systems. Here the pools tend to be broadly circular, often several feet deep, and separated by wide ridges of drier bog vegetation.

Valley-side flows, as their name suggests, occupy the gently sloping ground of river valleys. At times this can mean a surface slope of up to 20 degrees, but the pools formed on these slopes are quite stable. Each pool is very narrow (up to 1m/3ft across) but extremely long (sometimes as much as 50m/164ft), and lies along the slope, parallel to the contours. Between this pool and the next is a ridge of peat, equally long and narrow, dominated by drier bog vegetation; downslope from this is the next pool. Remarkably, although these two pools may be separated by only a narrow ridge of peat, the difference in water level between the two pools may be as much as 50cm (20in). That such a pattern can remain stable is due entirely to the water-retaining properties of sphagnum peat. From the air these surface patterns resemble strange, alien landscapes, but for the species which inhabit them they are the major source of habitat diversity in an otherwise unbroken landscape. Even so the highest hummocks barely reach 1m (3ft high.

Carnivores of the plant world Most plant

Blanket bog plants

The insectivorous plants of Britain's blanket bogs are distributed in a variety of quite specific areas. The round-leaved sundew, for instance, is found on the hummocks, the great sundew on and around the pool margins and the long-leaved sundew in shallow hollows. Bladderwort flourishes in the bog pools. Each species of sphagnum (nos 1-6) also has its own distinctive place in the surface patterns of the blanket bog. They carpet the ground in brilliant colours.

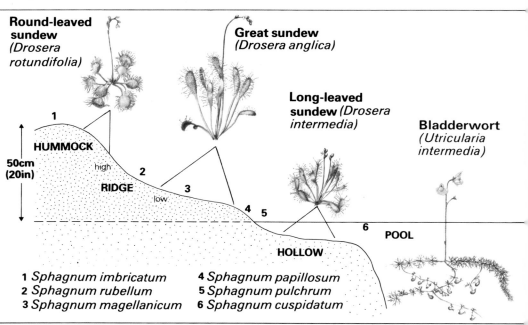

Round-leaved sundew (*Drosera rotundifolia*)

Great sundew (*Drosera anglica*)

Long-leaved sundew (*Drosera intermedia*)

Bladderwort (*Utricularia intermedia*)

50cm (20in)

HUMMOCK
high
RIDGE
low
HOLLOW
POOL

1
2
3
4 5
6

1 *Sphagnum imbricatum*
2 *Sphagnum rubellum*
3 *Sphagnum magellanicum*
4 *Sphagnum papillosum*
5 *Sphagnum pulchrum*
6 *Sphagnum cuspidatum*

find the constantly high water table of a bog intolerable, and the thickness of peat prevents even the deepest-rooting species from reaching the subsoil. The peat itself offers little in the way of nutrients; indeed, the major source of minerals available to the growing surface once the peat layer is more than 60-90cm (2-3ft) thick is the very rain that started the whole process off. Clearly this is a miserably poor input, but species must either find this sufficient or else make use of alternative sources.

Perhaps the most famous of these alternatives is that utilised by the carnivorous plants – the sundews, bladderworts and butterworts. Anyone who has been on a walking holiday in Scotland in mid-summer will be aware that the moors are inhabited by swarms of blood-thirsty midges and horse-flies or clegs. Here is ample food for the sticky leaf-glands of the sundews to trap and digest slowly, releasing vital nutrients to the plant. All three species of British sundew – the round-leaved, great and long-leaved – are found on our blanket bogs, each inhabiting a slightly different part of the surface pattern. The round-leaved sundew occurs on hummocks, the great sundew along the pool margins and the long-leaved sundew in shallow hollows. Butterwort, another carnivorous species, traps insects like the sundews but makes its leaves rather more slippery than sticky. Insects are therefore unable to crawl round the upcurled leaf edges and become trapped, to be slowly digested by the glands on the leaf surface. Bladderwort, found in the bog pools, uses a more violent method of ambush: trailing from the leaves are a number of small bladders, each of which has a hair trigger. When this is brushed by a passing water flea, the lid of the bladder flips open, water and the unfortunate flea are sucked in, and the lid snaps shut.

Another well-known species of blanket bogs is common cottongrass. The russet glow its leaves give to the vegetation cover in the autumn is often a clear and simple guide to the wettest areas of ground; in Orkney its white cotton seed heads were traditionally gathered, spun and woven into bridal stockings. In the early spring by far the most vivid splashes of colour are provided by a small lily, the bog asphodel.

To all these other colours, the moss carpet itself adds its own vivid swathes of greens, yellows, oranges, reds and browns. Each species of sphagnum has its own place in the surface patterns, and each is characterised by its own distinctive colouring.

Blanket bog animals Compared to the bustling life of a woodland, a blanket bog can, at first sight, appear to be a bleak and lifeless place – but appearances can be deceptive. This is red deer and grouse country, and golden eagles soar on thermals above the bogs, while merlins flash by, hugging the ground to pick off startled meadow pipits. Short-eared owls quarter the ground on stiff,

Above: A bird to watch for in the sky over northern blanket bogs – the magnificent golden eagle.

Below: Blanket bogs like this are under threat. Huge areas of blanket bogs are being ploughed for forestry, as here, other areas have been earmarked for possible use in peat-fuelled power stations, a number of farmers are attempting to transform peat into rye-grass pasture and, most insidious of all, the practice of hill-burning or 'muirburn' (carried out to encourage the growth of heather) is destroying thousands of acres of the very ground it claims to improve. Burning destroys the living layer of sphagnum and without its living layer a blanket bog cannot grow; instead it slowly decomposes.

bowed wings, while hen harriers drift low over the ground on V-shaped wings, waiting t snatch up small birds and nestlings.

Adders, too, can be seen on blanket bog basking on warm moss hummocks in the su before slithering off to hunt for frogs, toac or newts in the small pools, and dragonflie such as the black darter or the metallic re damselfly patrol these same pools in rhythmic dance, swooping to grab smalle flying insects. In the pools larval forms c insects chase and are chased by other larva while adult water beetles prey on all th largest of these.

Above all, capturing the very essence of ou moorlands with their haunting and evocativ cries, are two birds – waders that spend th winter feeding on our estuaries but return t the hills in the spring to breed. The dunlin ar the golden plover are almost invariably foun together, so much so that in the Pennines the association has earned the diminutive dunli the name 'plover's page'. Both run from hum mock to hummock on clockwork-like leg their plaintive calls travelling vast distance

Blanket bogs of Britain

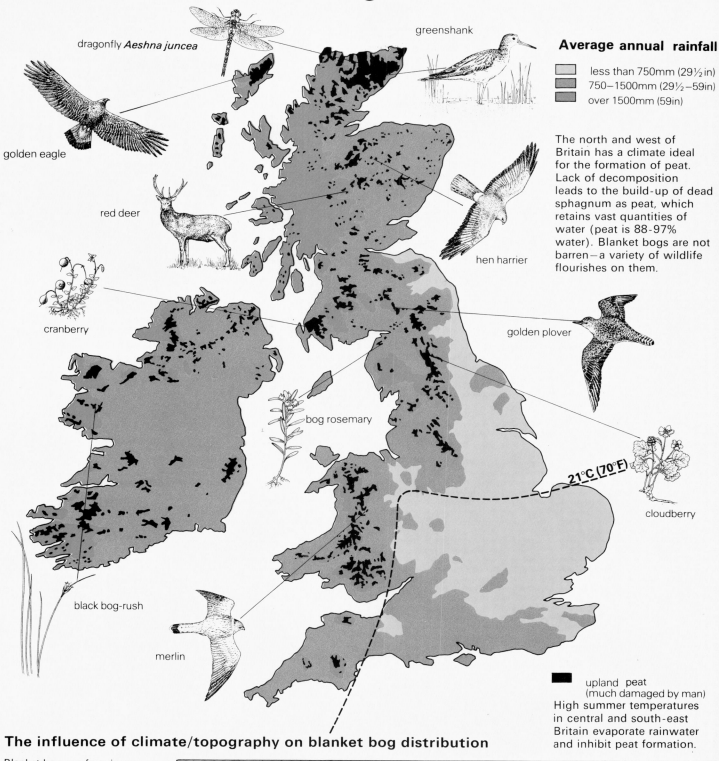

dragonfly *Aeshna juncea*

greenshank

golden eagle

red deer

cranberry

hen harrier

golden plover

bog rosemary

21°C (70°F)

cloudberry

black bog-rush

merlin

Average annual rainfall

less than 750mm (29½ in)
750–1500mm (29½–59in)
over 1500mm (59in)

The north and west of Britain has a climate ideal for the formation of peat. Lack of decomposition leads to the build-up of dead sphagnum as peat, which retains vast quantities of water (peat is 88-97% water). Blanket bogs are not barren—a variety of wildlife flourishes on them.

upland peat (much damaged by man)
High summer temperatures in central and south-east Britain evaporate rainwater and inhibit peat formation.

The influence of climate/topography on blanket bog distribution

Blanket bog can form in any area where the annual rainfall is more than 750mm (29½in) — except where high summer temperatures evaporate the water quickly. Excess surface water collects as pools with ridges of peat between, the surface patterns varying according to climate and slope. Shown here are three types.

peat
peat with dubh lochans

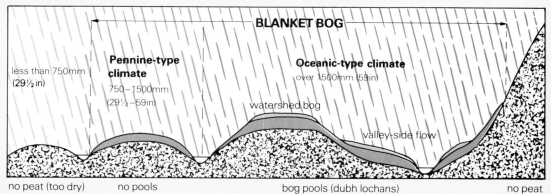

less than 750mm (29½ in)

Pennine-type climate
750–1500mm (29½–59in)

BLANKET BOG

Oceanic-type climate
over 1500mm (59in)

watershed bog

valley-side flow

no peat (too dry)

no pools (not wet enough)

bog pools (dubh lochans)

no peat (too steep)

IRELAND'S PEAT MOORLANDS

One seventh of Ireland is covered with peat. For centuries people have been cutting it for fuel, but modern harvesting methods mean that most of Ireland's peat—and with it its bogs and fens— could disappear over the next 30 years.

Above: In areas such as the west of Ireland, where the landscape is predominantly sloping rather than hilly, blanket bog forms in preference to raised bog. This picture, taken in Connemara, shows a typical stretch of blanket bog. In the foreground are the white seeding heads of cotton-grass, a common plant of bogs and acid fens. In the background are the famous Twelve Bens of Connemara, the tallest of which is 730m (2395ft) above sea level.

Peat is composed entirely of the partly decomposed bodies of dead plants. The moist, cool climate of Ireland, poor drainage and gentle slopes have all contributed to the development of peat, and man has also played a part. In well-drained (and therefore drier) habitats the remains of dead plants decompose due to the action of bacteria and fungi. But, where there is too much water that will not drain away, anaerobic conditions develop –no oxygen is available to the decomposing agents, the bacteria and the fungi. They cannot do their work, and so dead plants do not decay but remain more or less intact. Over the years layer upon layer of undecomposed material builds up to form peat. The process is

slow, but during the 10,000 years since the last Ice Age more than 10m (33ft) of peat have accumulated in some Irish bogs.

There are two basic types of peat, one formed from fen, the other from raised bog or blanket bog. Since fen and bog support quite different types of vegetation, fen peat and bog peat differ in their compositions.

Fen peat Sometimes called sedge peat, fen peat forms where there is plenty of water– usually in the form of a small lake–and a plentiful supply of plant nutrients. During the early post-glacial period such conditions abounded in Ireland in the numerous small lakes that occupied the hollows between the low rounded hills known as drumlins. Aquatic plants and species typical of lake margins, such as sedges and rushes, grew lushly. When they died, the remains sank to the lake bottoms and accumulated as rotting vegetable matter. Because there was little through-flow of water anaerobic conditions developed and peat began to form on the lake-bed. Slowly the lakes filled with peat, until there was no visible water, just a sodden fen.

Raised and blanket bogs When the lake became completely filled with fen peat the accumulating surface mat of vegetation began to rise above the water table, and conditions changed. The plants on the mat were now unable to take up nutrients in the water of the lake and therefore nutrient-poor, acidic conditions developed –acidic because the

cids released by the partially decayed vegetation were no longer neutralised by the
nutrients in the water. The result was that
plants requiring richer, less acidic habitats died
out. The fen had turned into a bog, and a new
plant community developed dominated by
various species of *Sphagnum*–mosses typical
of bogs.

In this type of bog, known as a raised bog,
the only way that nutrients can reach the
surface vegetation is in the rain water which,
of course, contains almost no dissolved salts.
Thus the surface becomes more acidic and
only plants capable of tolerating these special
conditions survive.

Among the plants found on raised bogs are
the insectivorous sundews, which gain their
essential minerals and nitrogen from the
insects that they trap. In bog pools, bladderwort, another insectivore, is sometimes
found. As well as *Sphagnum* moss, the raised
bogs are inhabited by cotton-grass (actually a
sedge), bog asphodel, bog myrtle and various
grasses including purple moor-grass. Many
members of the heath family tolerate wet, acid
bogs, including cross-leaved heath, bog rosemary and ling. The peat formed from these
plants is composed mainly of *Sphagnum* moss
with smaller quantities of heathers, grasses
and sedges.

Raised bogs develop in hollows, where
lakes or fens formed, and occasionally on
other flat areas of land. But on the gentle slopes
of western Ireland, a different type of bog–
blanket bog– has formed. In these areas the
rainfall is high and evaporation low. The
constant drenching of the land means that
plant nutrients are rapidly leached away. The
acid from decaying plants is not neutralised by
dissolved mineral salts, so that conditions
similar to those on raised bogs arise. The
remains of plants do not decompose, and a
blanket of peat (rarely deeper than 2m/6ft)
envelopes the slopes, except the steepest ones.
The plants inhabiting blanket bogs are the
same as those on raised bogs–heathers, purple
moor-grass, sedges, *Sphagnum* moss and
others.

Records of the past Man has assisted the
spread of blanket peat in western Ireland. The

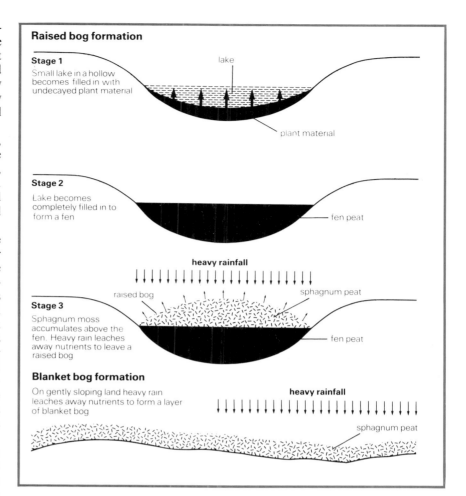

Above: The formation of
raised and blanket bogs.
Note how fen is a stage
towards the creation of a
raised bog.

Right: An old abandoned
peat face where cutting once
took place. Such faces are
slowly recolonized by bog
plants. Here, heather and
various species of lichen
have moved in.

Below: Bog rosemary, a plant
closely related to heather,
can survive in the acid
conditions of a bog.

Bogs and peat workings

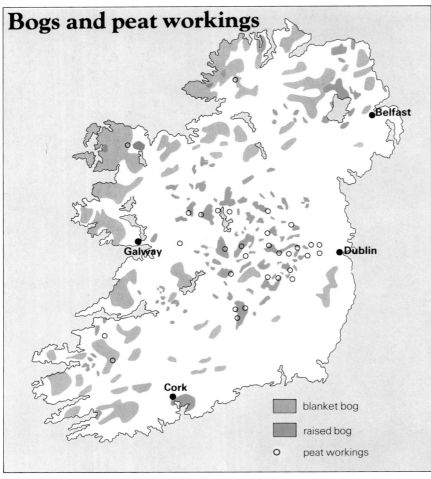

blanket bog

raised bog

○ peat workings

Stone Age and Bronze Age people cut dow the woodlands that developed after the Ic Age, and in the clearings practised primitiv agriculture. After they moved on, or died ou the woodlands did not always regenerat because the soil was too impoverished. Th blanket of peat slowly covered the remains of the dwelling houses, tombs and even th ancient fields of these people. It is fortunat for us that the peat has preserved these trace of our ancestors, for archaeologists can lear much from the peat-engulfed remains.

Peat is a marvellous preservative and th bogs of Ireland sometimes yield surprisin evidence of past epochs—the preserved bodie of people have been unearthed as well a hoards of butter. The stumps of trees are ofte revealed when peat is removed. Some of thes are the remains of Scots pines which grew i abundance about 7000 years ago. Othe stumps are of oak. The wood is well preserve and has been used for a variety of purposes building, fuel, and carving into ornaments o food vessels.

The peat also serves as a record of th environment throughout the 10,000 yea since the last Ice Age. Each layer contain information about the plants growing in th fen or bog, and nearby, at that time. B studying the preserved remains—pollen grain fruits and seeds, flowers, wood and leaves botanists can build up a picture of th succession of vegetation.

Above: The distribution of blanket bogs and raised bogs in Ireland. The former tend to occur in the west of Ireland, and also the north, while the latter are confined mostly to central Ireland. Also marked are the sites where the peat is being extracted.

Left: Bog asphodel is a perennial member of the lily family that spreads through bogs and fens by means of underground runners. It grows to a height of 40cm (16in) and flowers in July and August.

Right: Some plants of bogs supplement their meagre nutrient intake by trapping and digesting insects. Sundews, such as this great sundew, achieve this by having sticky leaves.

Peat as fuel The great peatlands of Ireland are not just a habitat for plants and animals, or a living archive preserving details of past epochs. They provide a valuable resource – peat – in a country which, until recently had no other reserves of fuel.

From the time immemorial, people have been cutting peat by hand for fuel. This was done by digging into the bog to form a vertical face, from which the sods of turf were scooped using an implement like a garden spade. The sods, each about 30cm (1ft) long and 10cm (4in) square, were gathered into small stacks to dry during the summer. Then they were formed into larger stacks and finally carted, usually in baskets on the backs of donkeys, to the farmhouse. Turf fires provided warmth and were used for cooking; they were never allowed to go out.

Modern methods Nowadays, this source of energy is harnessed in specially designed power stations. The Republic of Ireland is the only country, apart from the Soviet Union and Finland, in which electricity is generated in peat-fired power stations. The six major peat stations consumed 3 million tonnes of peat in 1988 and there are several smaller stations supplied with peat by local peat-cutters.

The Irish Peat Board, Bord na Móna, now has 80,000ha (200,000 acres) of bog under active use. As well as the peat for the electricity stations, Bord na Móna also extracts peat for the production of briquettes – highly compressed peat for use as a domestic fuel instead of coal – and for use in horticulture. Irish moss peat is exported throughout the world for use in nurseries and gardens, and over 1.3 million cubic metres of moss peat was extracted in 1983. Plans are already in hand to open a further 30,000ha (70,000 acres) for peat extractions.

The peat is 'mined' on a vast scale using specially designed machines, like giant combine harvesters. They operate in various ways. Some scoop the top 1cm (½in) off the bog, and leave a loose layer of powdered peat to dry. This is later gathered by other machines and used in the briquette and moss peat factories, and in power stations as milled peat. Other machines cut the raw peat into sods like those produced by the traditional hand-cutting. Each machine can harvest 5000 tonnes of peat a month.

Concern for the future While this commercial exploitation provides a valuable resource, it causes as much damage to the landscape as open-cast mining. For all practical purposes peat is not a renewable resource, and at the present rate of exploitation there will be no large bogs left in 30 years. There is now a considerable anxiety that these ancient habitats will be eliminated, and there is special concern for the few remaining intact fens and large raised bogs. In Northern Ireland, a number of valuable bogs have been acquired as nature reserves, and in the Republic they have now fully accepted the need to preserve

Above: Traditional peat-cutting in operation in County Kerry. The sods of peat have been stacked into groups and will later be taken away to dry out for the winter.

Below: Few plants are capable of surviving in such acidic conditions as those tolerated by *Sphagnum* moss. The species shown here is *S. capillifolium*, one of the more common species of bogs, where it is usually found on the top of hummocks.

and to conserve bog and peatland habitats.

Given 10,000 years, and no disturbance, the peatlands would regenerate naturally, but that does not mean Ireland should destroy all its bogs. Small-scale cutting by local people does some harm, but it also does good, for the old, abandoned, peat-faces provide habitats for interesting plants. But the large-scale 'mining' is different – it can be completely destructive. A better balance is therefore needed between the need for fuels and the need to retain some of these habitats as living bogs. This is gradually occurring, due to a better understanding between the Irish Peatland Conservation Council and the Irish Peat Board.

Trees and shrubs of mountain and moorland

Mountains do not conjure up instant ideas of trees and shrubs, yet there are woody plants right up to the high tops, and once all our lower mountain slopes up to 600m (2000ft) or so were covered by forests, this natural tree-line being the point above which sizeable trees cannot grow.

Woody plants are probably the most flexible and adaptable of all our plants in their growth form. Junipers, for example, can vary from being small trees in sheltered lower valleys to tight prostrate cushions a few inches high on mountain tops and exposed coastal sites; and the rowan tree grows from sea level up to nearly 1000m (3300ft), varying from a graceful tree up to 20m (66ft) tall to a stunted shrub just a metre (3ft) or so high. Other trees have a closely related alpine 'cousin' which has evolved an identity of its own. For example, the familiar silver birch has a tiny relative – the dwarf birch – which grows to just a few centimetres tall, way up in the mountains, but is just as woody. The willows, too, are familiar in the form of pussy willow shrubs in the lowlands, but there are several specialised dwarf species such as the tiny least willow or the net-veined willow which only grow high on mountains.

Here and there in the mountains you can see glimpses of what the original woodland cover must have been like – the old Caledonian forest remnants in the Highlands, the birchwoods of places like Craigellachie, or a rocky gorge-side oakwood in the Welsh Hills – and such places are alive with mountain wildlife. The additional shelter, humidity and complexity allow very many more species to survive, particularly invertebrates, mammals and birds.

The edges of woodlands, too, are vital places where the wood gradually gives way to open moorland or grassland. These areas of interface give the best of both worlds, with most of the advantages of woodland plus sunshine too, but they are all too rare now as the native woodlands have gone. The straight ranks of planted conifers are not an adequate substitute.

Left: The bearberry, one of the rarer members of the heather family to be found on moors and heaths, is a protected species. It has evergreen leaves and bears small shiny red berries in the autumn.

CHECKLIST

This checklist is a guide to some of the trees and shrubs you will find on mountains and moorlands. Although you will not see them all in the same place, you should be able to spot many of them throughout the changing seasons. The species listed in **bold type** *are described in detail.*

Bayberry
Bearberry
Bell heather
Bilberry
Blue heath
Bog bilberry
Bog myrtle
Bog rosemary
Cowberry
Cranberry
Creeping willow
Cross-leaved heath
Dwarf birch
Dwarf juniper
Dorset heath
Irish heath
Juniper
Least willow
Ling
Net-leaved willow
Rowan
Scots pine
Silver birch
Strawberry tree
Woolly willow

Left: The rowan or mountain ash is perhaps the most beautiful of all our native trees — and it truly deserves its reputation for it has something to offer in almost every season: large heads of scented white flowers in spring, clusters of deep red or orange berries in late summer, and a magnificent display of yellow and orange leaves in autumn.

BIRCHWOODS OF BRITAIN

The steep hillsides of the Scottish Highlands are colonized in many areas by downy birch. On the lighter, drier soils of south-east England silver birchwoods are more common. Both habitats support a variety of animal and plant life.

moorlands occurring only locally; and two tree species, downy and silver birch, both of which are widespread and common. Of these the downy is slightly hardier than the silver birch and is the dominant birch in the cold wet areas of upland Britain, especially in the Highlands.

At the end of the Ice Age birch and pine were the first trees to advance north into Britain and form forests. Then, as the climate continued to improve, these two species were largely replaced by forests, mainly of oak, until eventually birch and pine were dominant only in the cooler climate of the Highlands. Remnants of these forests show that while pine defeated birch on the richer Highland soils, birch survives where pine fails on poorer soils. Where, as often occurs, the soils are mixed, pine and birch grow side by side.

Woods almost purely of birch flourish on many Highland glensides up to about 600m (2000ft). Few other trees grow among them, but by far the commonest is rowan. Of vast extent in early prehistoric times, these woods have been declining ever since Neolithic man began to destroy them and prevent their regeneration by the introduction of grazing animals. The surviving birchwoods of Scotland vary greatly. A few consist of fine, well-grown trees–though never as magnificent as those of Scandinavia. Where conditions are harsh the woods are made up of contorted, diseased and insect-ridden trees not reaching 6m (20ft) in height. The usual end of such degenerate woods is to be gradually destroyed by gales.

How the birch spreads Birch is an eager colonizer. Its multitudinous seeds are small and light and may be carried far by the wind. So in the absence of grazing animals, birchwoods can develop on wet or dry grasslands, peaty or sandy heaths and commons, sites of

Birches are among the world's hardiest trees, growing in forests all round the Northern Hemisphere right up to the edge of the tundra. They are abundant in temperate regions also. Out of a world total of about 40 species, three birches are native in the British Isles: dwarf birch–a very small shrub of high Scottish

Above: Silver birches, with a ground-layer of bracken. Petty whin (right), lesser twayblade and chickweed wintergreen are some of the choicer species of wild flowers to be found growing in birchwoods.

elled woodland, screes and even the infertile waste-tips of collieries and slate quarries. At first the seedlings may be crowded together but they soon eliminate their weaker numbers by competition until, by the time the survivors develop into mature trees, they are usually well spaced. There are two reasons why they do not grow close to each other: during gales their tough whippy branches lash at neighbouring trees; and below ground there is similar intense rivalry as each tree's hungry roots spread widely near the surface and challenge those of other trees.

While downy birch is commoner in upland Britain, silver birch is characteristic of the lighter, drier soils of south-east England, except those on chalk which contain too much lime for either species. These ecological differences are, however, only slight. Very often the two grow in the same wood. And even in the Scottish Highlands, especially in the east, there are woods of silver birch; while there are occasional woods dominated by downy birch in the south of England, particularly on wetter soils.

In the colder parts of the Northern Hemisphere birch makes climax forest. In the mild climate of much of the British Isles birch competes with temperate-zone trees and a birchwood here is usually a transitional stage in the formation of a different kind of wood. While still in its early stages it may be invaded by oaks as jays bring acorns, bury them among the birches and then forget them. Eventually the birches are smothered by the growing oaks (or by beeches, pines, sycamores and other large trees). Conditions are more favourable for the birchwoods high in the Scottish Highlands, because at many sites the conditions are too harsh and infertile for rival types of woodland to challenge birch.

At first sight the larger Scottish birchwoods

Above: A family of birch shieldbugs—a female and nymphs. The other shieldbug found in birchwoods is the parent bug, famous to entomologists because the female has a habit rare among insects: she stands on guard to protect her progeny.

Below left: Boletus fungi, such as this brown birch bolete, are common in birchwoods and are usually found close to the base of the trees.

Below: The stoat lives in a wide range of habitats including birchwoods. Another carnivore, the wild cat, roams over Highland birchwoods, and where pines grow among the birches the pine marten may also be present.

may seem like relics of climax forest. Yet if we could observe them over a long enough period we would probably find that they are far less permanent. A birch lives only 70-80 years and birchwoods seldom show signs of active regeneration within the wood. Often there are no young trees at all and the old trees all look about the same age, suggesting that they colonized the site when the area was not being grazed for a few years. So it may be that even in the Highlands the birchwoods are always on the move, here this century but gone the next.

Woodland layers Because the trees are usually well spaced, light reaches the floor easily, so provided grazing is not too severe (few birchwoods are fenced) there may be well developed field and ground layers. On the impoverished acid soils of Scottish hillsides the vegetation under the trees is usually poor in species, frequently consisting of spreads of bilberry, crowberry, heather, wavy hair-grass or bracken, and occasionally a dense shrub layer of juniper.

Squeezing in here and there amongst these

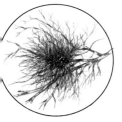

1 witch's broom

2 long-tailed tit

3 large emerald moth

4 willow warbler

5 birch sawfly

6 redpoll

7 moss
Hylocomium splendens

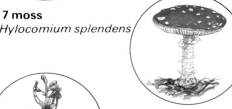

8 fly agaric

9 lesser twayblade

10 wood sorrel

Left: Some of the plants and animals you can find in a birchwood. Right at the top of the **tree layer** are dense clusters of twigs known as witch's broom. When there are many in one tree they look like a number of untidy rooks' nests. They can be caused by a fungus or a mite and are thought to be connected with an upsetting of the tree's hormone balance. In summer you might see the beautiful large emerald moth, though its delicate green colour makes it difficult to spot among the leaves. Its twig-like caterpillar feeds on birch leaves. Another insect found high up among the trees is the birch sawfly, whose white caterpillars are easily seen feeding on the leaves. The adult flies slowly around the trees rather than settling on the leaves. Among the birds of the tree layer are the insect-eating willow warbler and the seed-eating redpoll, as well as the more omnivorous long-tailed tit. Down in the **field layer** wild flowers such as lesser twayblade and wood sorrel grow with mosses such as *Hylocomium splendens*, while several fungi are particularly associated with birchwoods, the most striking being the fly agaric.

Below: Surprisingly, no butterfly larva eats the leaves of birch; but very locally Scottish birchwoods are the habitat of the rare chequered skipper whose foodplants are woodland grasses. It flies in late May and June.

dominant species are such wild flowers as yellow tormentil, white heath bedstraw and heath milkwort, which has flowers that may be pink, blue or white. There are many mosses, the great carpeters being those which also spread widely over the ground in the nearby woods of pine and sessile oak: *Rhytidiadelphus loreus*, *Pleurozium schreberi* and *Plagiothecium undulatum*, for example.

Though our birchwoods are rich in edible fungi, few people eat them. Yet every autumn in the Continental birch forests they are gathered to be dried and kept for winter eating. One that is definitely not to be eaten is the spectacular scarlet-capped, white spotted fly agaric. This is one of several fungi whose mycelia live in intimate association with the root tips of birches. Among others are ugly milk-cap, coconut-scented milk-cap and brown birch bolete.

Animal life Since birch has been so abundant over a vast reach of time it is inevitable that many insects have become adapted to a birchwood existence. Thus there are more than 120 kinds of larger moths which live on birch, a figure exceeded only by those on oak. Most of these birch feeders live on other species as well, oak especially, as is natural since birch and oak so often grow together. And some moths such as the mottled umber defoliate birches just as efficiently as they strip the oaks.

While no mammals or birds are peculiar to British birchwoods many species found in other woodlands also live there. The most distinctive mammals are red and roe deer in their seasonal wanderings, and wild cats whose numbers are gradually increasing. In woods of birch mixed with pine, another rare mammal, the pine marten, finds shelter. Typical summer birds of these Highland woods are chaffinch, willow warbler, tree pipit, robin, redstart and various tits, and occasionally redwings. All over the British Isles birch seed is a major food of finches, especially flocks of redpolls and siskins which take the seeds off the trees in autumn and from the ground in winter. Woodpeckers, jays and squirrels, both red and grey, also take the seeds.

THE SMALLEST TREES IN BRITAIN

Willows and birches are generally thought of as tall graceful trees; likewise juniper is to most people a large bush. But there are some willows, birches and junipers growing in Britain that are hardly taller than a daisy. These are our dwarf 'trees'.

Most of our dwarf trees belong to one genus, the willows. The smallest of them could easily be missed from a distance of a few yards and, far from providing a perch for birds, would be hard pressed to support a modest-sized insect. This minute tree is least willow. It has a long, much-branched underground rhizome which creeps over a large area. From this arise short aerial branches rarely more than 3cm (1in) long, which vary from being upright to lying flat along the ground. Each branch normally bears between two and five thin, toothed, rounded leaves with prominent veins.

In common with other willows, least willow bears catkins. These are borne on short stalks after the leaves appear–usually in June. All

willow catkins are aggregations of male or female flowers. In this species the male flowers are much reduced, usually consisting of just two stamens. The female catkins are made up of several oval capsules which turn reddish when ripe.

Least willow is an alpine species, rarely being found below 600m (2000ft), though it does descend to as low as 100m (300ft) in Sutherland because of the climate of that area. It can be found in Wales, Yorkshire, the Lake District and on all suitable Scottish mountains. It occurs on mountain tops and rock ledges where almost nothing else can grow.

Big brother Net-leaved or reticulate willow can be regarded as least willow's big brother though it is not a great deal bigger. This plant is even more attractive than its smaller relative, with leaves that are covered early in the season with long silky hairs. These disappear later on, revealing the prominent net-veining on the undersides of the leaves that give this plant its name. The catkins appear on terminal stalks after the leaves have unfurled.

Reticulate willow has a very local distribution in Britain. It is more demanding than least willow since it requires a base-rich soil to grow in. It is typically found at heights of between 600m (2000ft) and 1100m (3600ft) or the ledges of just such a base-rich rock.

Not so small willows As well as these two tiny willows there are at least two others that though not quite so small, are still a long way from most people's idea of a willow.

Creeping willow is a small prostrate shrub found on dune slacks, wet heaths and moors. It hardly ever grows taller than 10cm (4in) and its catkins appear before the leaves.

Woolly willow is a giant compared with the species so far mentioned. It can reach a height

Above: The grey-green foliage of creeping willow (*Salix repens*), interspersed with strands of marsh horsetail.

Opposite page: The best place to look for the dwarf birch is on boggy moorland.

Right: As with other willow species, the male and female catkins of creeping willow are borne on separate plants. The female catkins mature to form the fluffy white seed heads shown here.

of 1m (3ft) and is a rare plant of damp, base-rich ledges on Scottish mountains. The leaves are twice as long as they are broad and at first they are covered with silky hairs on both surfaces. Later on the upper surface loses these hairs and becomes dark green, but the lower surface retains them. The catkins are golden yellow and oval if they are male or cylindrical if female.

Dwarf juniper Juniper brings to mind a large bush, typically up to 3m (10ft) tall, but it is a very variable plant and specimens from one locality can look quite different from those growing somewhere else. There is, however, a mountain form which looks distinct enough to be called a subspecies; it is known as subspecies *nana*. Unlike ordinary juniper, the mountain form is hardly prickly to the touch, its leaves are not borne at such a wide angle to the stem, nor do they come to a point so suddenly.

Subspecies *nana* is found on mountains in north Wales, northern England, Scotland and Ireland. It has a trailing habit of growth (unlike the upright habit of ordinary juniper) and in extreme conditions it forms a hummock, usually up to 30cm (1ft) long and rising to no more than about 8cm (3in) high in the middle.

Dwarf birch Birches are familiar to everybody as large silver-barked trees. The silver birch normally grows to a height of about 25m (80ft) but, like the willows, it has a much

Above: The mountain form of juniper, known as *Juniperus communis* subspecies *nana*, has a trailing habit of growth. In extremely adverse conditions it forms a small hummock no more than 30cm (1ft) across and about 8cm (3in) high at the centre.

Below: The tiniest of all our small willows is least willow (*Salix herbacea*) whose leaves are less than 2cm ($\frac{3}{4}$in) long. Shown here are the capsule-like fruits; the reddish tinges show that they are ripe.

smaller relative that forms a distinct species. This is dwarf birch, a rare plant and always an exciting find for the botanist working in the field.

Dwarf birch is a low-growing shrub with stems that may grow to a height of 1m (3ft) though it is much more often encountered as a shrub about 30cm (1ft) tall. It is a spreading plant with stiff downy twigs that are dark brown in colour. The leaves are borne alternately along the shoots and are up to 2cm ($\frac{3}{4}$in) long, more or less rounded and with a deeply toothed margin. When mature the leaves are a bright glossy green, and it has been reported that they develop a golden tint before they fall in the autumn.

Like willows, the flowers of dwarf birch are borne in catkins, which are either male or female, but, unlike willows, catkins of different sexes are found on the same plant. The catkins are oval and borne in the axils of the leaves, the males are about 8mm long and the females 5-10mm.

Dwarf birch has a very local distribution, being found on moorland—especially boggy moorland—at altitudes between 250m (800ft) and 900m (3000ft). In Britain it is found no further south than the Yorkshire–Durham border and is most common in Scotland. Elsewhere in the world it has an Arctic distribution, occurring in northern Europe, Siberia, the Alaskan tundra and around the North Pole.

Dwarf trees

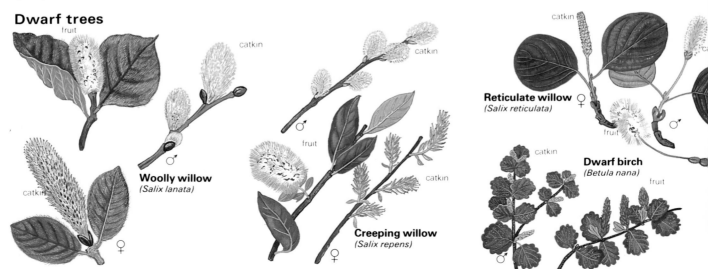

fruit
catkin

Woolly willow
(*Salix lanata*)

catkin
♂
♀

catkin

catkin

fruit

Creeping willow
(*Salix repens*)
♀

catkin

catkin

Reticulate willow ♀
(*Salix reticulata*)

fruit
♂

catkin

Dwarf birch
(*Betula nana*)
fruit
♂

ROWAN: HARDY MAGICAL TREE

The rowan has something to offer for most of the year. Its graceful foliage emerges in spring, splashes of white blossom appear in summer, and in autumn and early winter the tree is decorated with dense hanging bunches of bright red berries.

The rowan (below) is a native tree most usually associated with high country. Indeed, it is also known as mountain ash, but it is totally unrelated to the common ash, and differs in all respects apart from its compound leaves.

In the British Isles rowan grows at altitudes up to 950m (3115ft) which is higher than any other native broadleaved tree. It also occurs throughout the lowlands, favouring sandy or gravelly soils which tend to be rather acid. On bleak mountainsides it forms a stunted, windswept tree only a few metres tall, but on the more sheltered lowlands it can reach 20m (65ft) in height. Because its berries are devoured by birds and the seeds widely

dispersed in their droppings, the rowan appears in a variety of habitats including woodland, scrubby hillsides, heaths and hedgerows.

Multi-purpose species The rowan's versatile form has, not surprisingly, made it a firm favourite with landscape gardeners. It is widely planted in parks and gardens, on motorway embankments and golf courses, for it stands up well to the stresses of urban life. Foresters have also used it as a nurse tree in plantations of hard woods when the light shade of its foliage promotes the growth of the hard wood saplings—until they eventually outgrow it and form a close canopy which is often too dark underneath for the rowan to survive for long.

Handsome appearance The slim trunk is covered with smooth slate-grey bark which is marked with shallow horizontal scars. The limbs tend to grow upwards to form a rather loosely branched crown which allows plenty of light through and so does not appreciably suppress plant growth beneath. The twigs are pale brown, sometimes tinged with violet. The alternate buds, 10-15cm (4-6in) long, and the brownish-purple bud scales are fringed with fine silky white hairs.

The foliage unfurls towards the end of April. The leaf stalks, 10-25cm (4-10in) long, bear from five to eight opposite pairs of leaflets and are tipped with a single terminal leaflet. Each leaflet has serrated edges and is

Above: Rowan berries are rich in Vitamin C and can be made into delicious jelly that goes well with game.

Below: Rowan flowers have a sweet, musty smell, rather like hawthorn blossom.

bright green on its upper surface, but pal underneath.

Rowan leaves fall relatively early in t autumn, but not before they have acquir colourful autumn tones of yellow and orang

The rowan blossoms in May or Jur producing dense, flat-topped inflorescenc made up of many tiny flowers, each with fi creamy white petals. Although the individu flowers are very small, because they a tightly packed together they are conspicuo and attract a variety of prospective polli ators, including flies, beetles and bees.

After fertilisation the flowers are succeed by green berries. They ripen by Septemb and provide a glorious display of bright, shii fruits varying in colour from orange scarlet. Generally this attractive sight short-lived, because birds find the fru irresistible and soon strip the trees bare.

Blackbirds, thrushes, fieldfares and re wings all take their share. The handson waxwing, a winter visitor from northe Europe, which in some years migrates he in large numbers, is particularly fond rowan berries. It has been reported that bir sown rowan seeds germinate the followi spring, whereas normally they remain dor ant in the soil for 18 months. This may be d to the abrasive action of the bird's gut whi acts upon the seed-coat, allowing moisture enter, so germination occurs sooner tha usual when the berries fall to the ground.

The rowan's Latin name, *Sorbus aucupar* means 'fowler's service tree', which refers the past use of the berries as bait by bi trappers. In some districts the berries a known as 'hen-drunks', because chicke apparently became intoxicated after gorgi themselves on the fallen fruits. In Wales t berries were fermented in ale to produce alcoholic drink with similar effects.

To the human palate the fruits have a rather harsh, sour taste, but they are still used to make jelly that goes well with game dishes such as hare and venison.

Magical tree The rowan has a special place in our folklore, especially in northern regions. Many of the superstitions connected with it originated from ancient Nordic visitors from Scandinavia. The word rowan is probably derived from the Norse *runa*, which means a charm, and relates to the tree's reputation for warding off evil.

In Scotland and Ireland the rowan's magical powers were greatly revered. A branch was always nailed to cattle sheds to protect the animals from witchcraft and sorcery. Similarly Highland crofters planted a rowan tree outside their homes to keep witches at bay. Indeed, another local name for the tree is witch-wood, and an old rhyme sings its praises:

Rowan tree and red thread,
Hold the witches all in dread.

In Wales, Ireland and some northern counties of England, the rowan was often planted in churchyards. This was to keep the dead in their graves and prevent any ghosts appearing in the neighbourhood.

The wood is dense and strong and was valued by crofters living in the sparsely wooded glens of Scotland and Ireland.

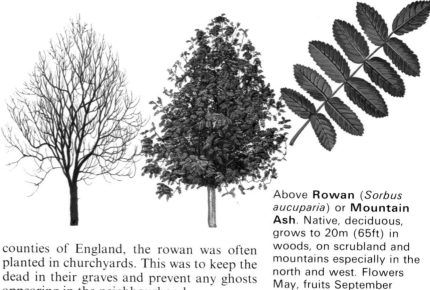

Above **Rowan** (*Sorbus aucuparia*) or **Mountain Ash**. Native, deciduous, grows to 20m (65ft) in woods, on scrubland and mountains especially in the north and west. Flowers May, fruits September onwards.

Below: The rowan in full fruit growing on Dartmoor.

Above: A stand of bog myrtle flowering in early May before the leaves have unfurled. Irish legend has it that bog myrtle was once a tall tree until its wood was used to build the Cross. But then, out of shame and remorse, it shrank to its present lowly stature.

Bog myrtle (*Myrica gale*). Native deciduous shrub found in damp habitats in most parts of Britain; particularly common in the north and west.

Bayberry (*Myrica carolinensis*). Deciduous shrub native to the eastern United States. Established in the New Forest, Hampshire.

FRAGRANT BOG MYRTLE

Bog myrtle, one of our most powerfully aromatic shrubs, grows in bogs and fens and has the remarkable property of being able to change sex from one year to the next.

Bog myrtle, or sweet gale as it is often called, is the only British representative of the family Myricaceae. All members of this family of small trees and shrubs have leaves covered with small resinous glands that give off an aromatic scent. The flowers are normally borne in the form of catkins, a feature that causes many botanists to place this family near to the birch family, Betulaceae, though its exact position in the classification system is still not settled.

Bog myrtle is a plant of moist places, such as bogs, fens and the margins of streams. It occurs in most parts of the British Isles and in some areas, especially parts of Scotland, Ireland, Wales and western England, it can be the dominant vegetation. Conversely, however, it is unaccountably absent from some areas where it might be expected to grow, notably in parts of the Midlands and in the eastern half of the border between England and Scotland. Bog myrtle can be found at considerable altitudes; in the eastern Highlands of Scotland, for example, it grows up to about 550m (1800ft) above sea level.

Suckering shrub Bog myrtle is a small deciduous shrub usually growing to a height of 1.2m (4ft), though occasionally becoming taller. It often spreads by sending out suckering shoots, by this means sometimes forming large stands of pure bog myrtle.

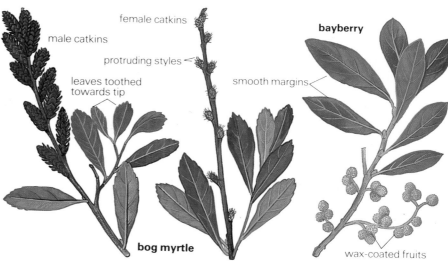

male catkins

female catkins

protruding styles

leaves toothed towards tip

bayberry

smooth margins

bog myrtle

wax-coated fruits

The leaves are lance-shaped and are at their widest near the tip rather than in the middle or near the stalk end. (This shape is known as oblanceolate.) The margins have a few forward-pointing teeth at intervals. The upper surfaces are greyish-green and hairless, while the lower surfaces are a fresher-looking green and pubescent (hairy). The leaves, stems (which are usually purplish-brown) and all other parts of the plant are scattered with aromatic glands, which are yellow when young but become darker with age. These glands exude a sweet fragrance somewhat reminiscent of eucalyptus, but without the overtone of menthol.

Sex change The most remarkable feature of bog myrtle is the way in which some plants change sex from one year to the next. All bog myrtle plants bear either male or female flowers, as do many other plant species. But, among the British flora bog myrtle is one of just a very few plants that exhibit this curious phenomenon of changing sex (the common ash is another one that does). As well as male plants becoming female and *vice versa*, single-sex plants may suddenly bear flowers of both sexes one year, or they may even bear inflorescences containing both male and female flowers.

Almost invariably, however, individual male and female flowers are borne on separate inflorescences usually known as catkins, though the term is not strictly accurate. The male catkins are borne on last year's shoots, usually before the new season's leaves appear in April and May. Each catkin is 7-15cm (3-6in) long and consists of a number of reddish-brown scales bearing several yellow anthers tinged with red. The female catkins have a similar structure, the same reddish-brown scales containing a pair of long crimson

Left: The fruits of bog myrtle are borne in catkin-like structures. Each fruit is a nutlet 2-3mm long and bearing two wings. Like the rest of the plant it is covered with tiny yellow glands. The leaves are 2-6cm (1-2½in) long with a few scattered teeth towards the tip.

Below: Male flowers of bog myrtle. Despite the sweetish fragrance of this plant, which accounts for one of its many common names – sweet gale – all parts have a bitter taste, none more so than the male catkins.

styles that protrude well beyond the scale and are noticeable at a distance.

Pollination is by the wind. The fruits mature through the summer, forming a flattened hard berry or nutlet with two wings. Like the rest of the plant, the fruits are covered with glands, and they also have a greyish-white waxy coating. Despite the presence of the wings, the fruits are far too heavy to be carried on the wind any distance. Instead, they simply fall to the ground beneath the plant. There is no evidence that animals or birds feed on them and thereby distribute the seeds.

American relative A species closely related to bog myrtle has become established in at least one place in the New Forest, despite being native to the eastern United States. This plant is bayberry. It grows in slightly drier soils than bog myrtle and appears to spread only by suckers, for its seeds are not viable here. Bayberry is similar in appearance to bog myrtle, the only differences being that it is somewhat taller, the catkins appear at the same time as the leaves and the fruits are covered in a thicker layer of wax.

BERRY-BEARING MOORLAND PLANTS

Most of the berry-bearing plants found on our upland moorlands belong to just one family – the heather family. They include the bilberry and the cranberry and also such rare natives as the blue heath and the alpine bearberry.

There are 15 genera in the heather family growing in the British Isles today. Many of these contain plants that are not native but were introduced for their ornamental qualities–indeed, the family includes some of our most popular and attractive garden plants. Some, such as rhododendrons, subsequently escaped into the wild and became naturalised.

As well as the familiar heaths and heathers the family contains a considerable diversity of species: some form large trees, others small shrubs; some have bell-shaped flowers similar to those of heaths, while the flowers of other species look quite different. Nevertheless there are certain unifying characters. All the species, whether large or small, are basically woody. All the British species, with the exception of the strawberry tree, need an acid soil. The leaves are usually narrow, leathery and evergreen, and the flowers have four or five petals normally joined to form a tube, the corolla.

Bilberry relatives One of the largest genera in Britain is *Vaccinium*, which has four native members. The best known is *Vaccinium myrtillus*, commonly called bilberry, whortleberry, blaeberry, whinberry and hurt in different parts of the country. It grows from sea level up to a height of more than 1200m (4000ft), though it is more frequent in hilly areas. It more often grows in open woods than

Above: Bearberry (*Arctostaphylos uva-ursi*) bears pale pink flowers.

Opposite page: Bearberry's fruits are bright red; note how its stems trail.

Above: At high altitudes bilberry is sometimes so abundant that it supplants other species and forms what are known as 'bilberry summits'. The dark blue berries, whether eaten raw or made into jams or jellies, have long been valued by man.

53

Above: Cowberry is a common shrub on the hillsides of Scotland, Wales and northern England, where it creeps along the ground sometimes forming large patches. Its red fruits are, like bilberry fruits, edible, and the two species often hybridise, the product being known as *Vaccinium × intermedium*. This hybrid was first recorded in 1870 and occurs in various places in northern England and, rarely, in Scotland.

Above left: Cowberry flowers. Whereas bilberry bears its flowers singly or in pairs, cowberry flowers are borne in clusters at the ends of its stems. The corolla, formed by the petals fusing together, is more deeply lobed in cowberry than it is in bilberry.

Left: Flowers of *Kalmia angustifolia*, a North American species naturalised in just a few sites in Britain, though it is known to have been present at some of these sites since early this century.

do other members of the family. It ha vigorous rhizomes which can soon form wic open patches. Its fruits–dark bluish berries are very popular with birds (and man) ye seedlings of this plant are rarely seen eve though the seeds must be dispersed by th birds.

Bilberry is a deciduous plant, unlike i close relative, *V. vitis-idaea*, known common as cowberry, which is evergreen. This specie is a dwarf shrub common in many uplan parts of Britain and is often confused wit bearberry (*Arctostaphylos uva-ursi*), anothe member of the heather family though of different genus. Cowberry, however, can b distinguished by its narrower, paler gree leaves. Both plants have red berries, but thos of cowberry lose their calyx early on in th season.

Bog bilberry (*V. uliginosum*) is anothe moorland plant, despite its common name. occurs only in northern Britain, and eve there rarely outside the north-west.

Bilberry, cowberry and bog bilberry a have bell-shaped flowers similar to heaths an heathers, but cranberry (*V. oxycoccos*), ou final native member of the genus *Vacciniun* has quite different flowers. Instead of its peta being united to form a tube they are ber backwards to leave the stamens exposec Cranberry is a species of mossy bogs and ha declined drastically as its habitat has bee drained for agricultural purposes.

Rare natives Three members of the heat family are very rare, though native, and a found on just a few mountains in Scotlanc One of the most interesting of these is th misleadingly named blue heath (*Phyllodo caerulea*). Very rare indeed, this specie grows in just two places in the Scottis Highlands and produces pink–not blue!–bel shaped flowers in early summer. Its commo name comes from the fact that its flowers a supposed to dry blue, though it takes believing eye to accept that.

Another rare native is trailing azale (*Loiseleuria procumbens*), which bears only passing resemblance to the plants mor familiarly known as azaleas. It spreads alon the ground forming a carpet, and produce tiny, pink (occasionally white) funnel-shape flowers. It grows on just a few mountains i central and northern Scotland, always hig up.

The third member of this group is alpir bearberry (*Arctostaphylos alpinus*). Foun only on mountain moorlands in northern an north-western Scotland, its leaves have distinctive and attractive pattern of n veining and turn a rich red in autumn befo they fall off. Its bell-shaped flowers are whi and its berries black.

Doubtful natives Two of our largest an most attractive species, the strawberry tr and the rhododendron, may possibly k native to the British Isles, though no one ca be sure. The strawberry tree (*Arbutus uned*

s been recorded in south-west Ireland from
far back as Tudor times, some 400 years
o or more, when it was already famous. One
the attractions of this tree is that it can bear
white, heather-like flowers at the same time
its red 'strawberry' fruits appear.

Rhododendrons were native in Ireland, and
ssibly also in Britain, until a few thousand
rs ago when they died out. They were
troduced about two hundred years ago,
tably *Rhododendron ponticum*, *R. maximum*
d *R. catawbiense*. These species were
ssed by several nurserymen, and the
ulting hybrids spread to many parts of the
untryside by both sucker and seed.

Garden escapes The final group of plants in
e heather family are the garden escapes. An
ample is *Pernettya mucronata* from the
uthernmost part of Chile, which occurs very
ally in the wild in Britain.

Closely related is *Gaultheria* from North
merica, a shrub sometimes planted to
ovide food for pheasants. Also from North
merica is *Kalmia* which has particularly
eresting flowers, for the stamens are bent

back into pouches in the corolla–when the
pollen is ripe the slightest touch causes them
to spring up and jerk the pollen on to a visiting
insect or the flower's own stigma. *Ledum
palustre*, again a North American species,
occurs in scattered bogs from Surrey to
Perthshire and looks similar to a small
rhododendron.

Above: Flowers and fruits of
Gaultheria shallon, a native
of North America,
occasionally becoming
naturalised in Britain. Note
the similarity between its
flowers and those of heaths,
with the petals fused into a
bell shape.

elatives of heather

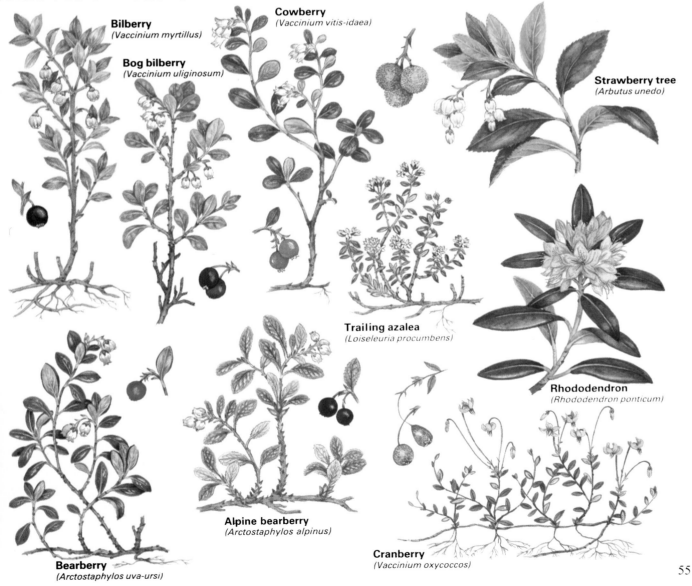

Bilberry
(Vaccinium myrtillus)

Bog bilberry
(Vaccinium uliginosum)

Cowberry
(Vaccinium vitis-idaea)

Strawberry tree
(Arbutus unedo)

Trailing azalea
(Loiseleuria procumbens)

Rhododendron
(Rhododendron ponticum)

Bearberry
(Arctostaphylos uva-ursi)

Alpine bearberry
(Arctostaphylos alpinus)

Cranberry
(Vaccinium oxycoccos)

HEATHER MIXTURE

By late summer and early autumn many moorland areas in the British Isles are aglow with a patchwork of flowering heather and heaths in glorious shades of deep pink and purple.

The best known species of the heather family is the true heather (*Calluna vulgaris*), or ling as it is often known. Along with several other British species of heaths, it belongs to the Ericaceae family which has more than 1350 species scattered throughout the world. Ling and heaths are similar in size and colour, they thrive in the same conditions and often bloom at the same time of year. Many people refer to ling and heaths as heather.

Ling is common throughout the British Isles. It is a robust evergreen species of bogs, moors, open woods, sandy heathland and highlands up to 700m (2300ft), and it thrives especially on well-drained soils. It does not grow much taller than a metre (3ft), its pliable

Above: Bell-heather, flowering with ling. The two species are commonly found growing together on heaths and moors with acid soils.

Right: Bell-heather flowers have small sepals and brightly coloured bell-shape flowers clustered towards the tips of the stems. Bell-heather blooms from July to September.
Ht 60cm (24in).

ugh woody stems becoming twisted and
ngled around one another as it sprawls
cross the ground.

The pairs of short, stalkless green leaves,
rising directly from the stem, have two pro-
ctions at their base. Those that grow from
e short side stems are close together and
ften overlapping, while those on the main
em are more spaced out.

Heather comes into flower in mid July and
ay continue until the end of September.
he pale purple flowers are solitary, either on
e main stem or on lateral branches. They
re rounded in appearance and have four
ny sepal-like structures at their bases. The
ale purple stigma and style of the female

Above: Bog rosemary – a
close relative of heather –
grows on bogs and high
moorlands and wet heaths.

Left: The flowers of cross-
leaved heath are clustered
together in bunches at the tip
of the stems.

parts protrude from the centre of each flower.
After fertilisation the flowers lose their colour
and form dark brown capsules which are
easily detached in the wind. White forms of
heather occur sporadically in the wild and are
much favoured by collectors and gypsies as
they are supposed to bring good luck.

Nectar pots Heather flowers are prolific
producers of nectar and are much sought
after by bees. Each flower has eight nectaries
which are arranged alternately with the
stamens. As the plant matures the nectar
flow diminishes, but other factors such as the
nature of the soil and the subsoil, the age of
the plant, the amount of rainfall and the
altitude, all influence the nectar flow.

Dark heather honey is highly regarded. It is
expensive because it is thick and has to be
pressed from the comb, thus destroying it so
that it cannot be used again.

Heather provides cover and food for a
number of birds and insects. The Scottish
heather moors give ideal cover for the
famous red grouse which feed on the tender
young heather shoots; small heather beetles
are found deep in the foliage; and the green
larvae of a particularly spectacular moth, the
emperor, feeds on heather in June, July and
August – you can recognise them by the distinctive black markings on their bright green
bodies, with blackish bristles arising from
warts along their length.

Heaths Six native heaths are found in the
British Isles. Two of the most common species
grow throughout the country, in similar
conditions to ling, to an altitude of 700m
(2300ft): the bell-heather (*Erica cinerea*),
sometimes known as purple bell-
heather or Scottish heather, also occurs on
heaths and moors with true heather; it tends
to grow in drier areas than its close relative
the cross-leaved heath (*E. tetralix*).

Both species grow as shrubs up to 60cm (24in) high. Bell-heather is a straggling species that is characteristically found on dryish areas that are often surrounded by bogs. It flowers earlier than true heather, with deeper purple, much larger, distinct bell-shaped flowers. The flowers are borne in groups towards the tip of the stem at the base of clusters of thin leaves. The leaves tend to grow in whorls of three up the stem. The deep rich colours of bell-heather are often responsible for the glowing autumnal purple hues that are so typical of the Scottish Highlands.

Bell-heather is attractive to honey bees, which make deep port-coloured honey from the nectar. Bumble bees sometimes make holes at the base of the petals in order to get at the nectar, and honey bees exploit this short cut.

Cross-leaved heath looks rather like bell-heather but it tends to grow in wetter areas. It gets its name from the whorls of four leaves along the stem. You can also distinguish it from bell-heather by its drooping flowers, which are arranged in clusters at the tip of the stem. Each bloom is pendulous and moves in the wind, but after pollination, usually by small insects, the fruits become upright. Cross-leaved heath is also self-pollinated.

Heather and heaths have been extensively hybridised by horticulturists, and very many different varieties exist. There are a number of

Left: Heather, or ling as it is often known, is our only native species of true heather. It flowers from August to September on moors, bogs and in woodland on acid soils throughout the British Isles. Ht 100cm (40in).

gardens open to the public where visitors can see different heaths in flower during each month of the year. Two of the best places to see a really choice variety of species are the Botanic Gardens in Edinburgh, and the Ness Botanic Gardens on the Wirral in Cheshire. Here you can find a marvellous array of richly coloured species.

Below: Heather has long been used for numerous purposes: you can tie several of its twiggy branches together to make a good broom; a patch of heather, so long as it is nowhere near gorse, makes a comfortable outdoor bed on a long moorland walk, and in the past it was often used to stuff mattresses. The stems were woven for thatching, and it also made good fuel.

Heaths and heathers

1 Cross-leaved heath
(*Erica tetralix*).
2 Bell-heather (*Erica cinerea*).
3 Ling (*Calluna vulgaris*).
4 Irish heath (*Erica erigena*).
5 *Erica terminalis*.
6 *Erica lusitanica*.
7 Dorset heath (*Erica ciliaris*).
8 Cornish heath (*Erica vagans*).
9 St Dabeoc's heath
(*Daboecia cantabrica*).
10 Mackay's heath (*Erica mackaiana*).
11 Bog rosemary
(*Andromeda polifolia*).

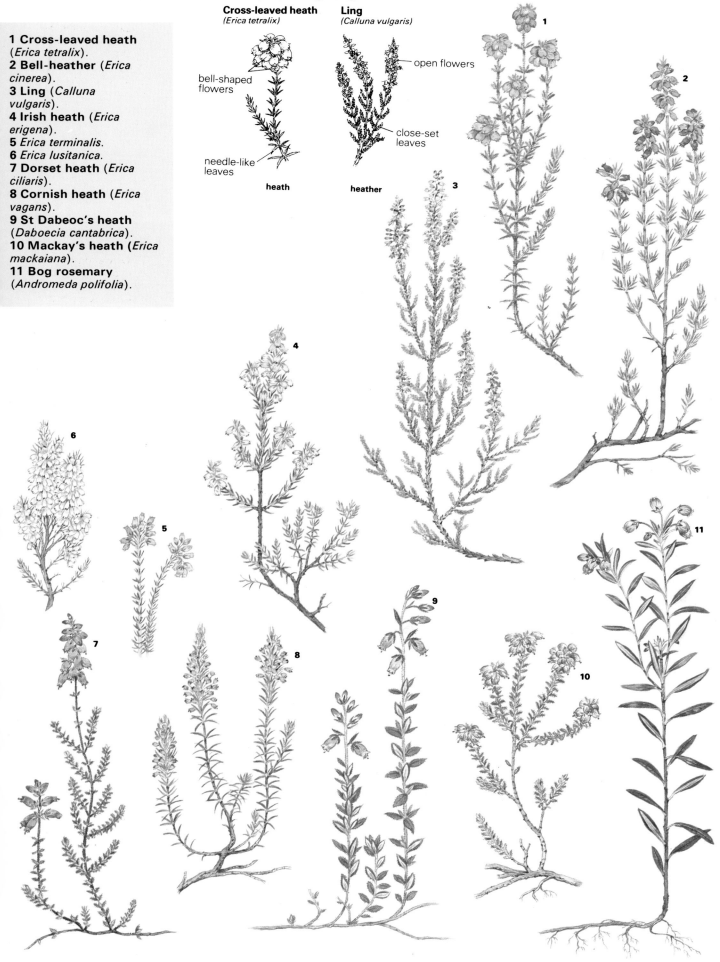

Cross-leaved heath
(*Erica tetralix*)

Ling
(*Calluna vulgaris*)

bell-shaped flowers

needle-like leaves

heath

open flowers

close-set leaves

heather

Flowers, ferns and mosses of mountain and moorland

For a variety of reasons – some historical, some ecological – by far the richest concentrations of alpine flowers occur in mountain areas where lime-rich rocks predominate. The lime in the soil has tended to inhibit peat formation, and most such rocks weather easily, giving a continuous supply of the open, nutrient-rich habitats in which most species occur. Ben Lawers, with its lime-rich schists, is a mecca for botanists, having almost two-thirds of the British mountain flora on its slopes and cliffs, while other lime-rich areas such as Upper Teesdale, Glen Cova and Caenlochan are almost equally favoured.

Although mountain habitats might superficially appear uniform in contrast to the patchwork mosaic of the lowlands, a close look will reveal that each species occupies its own particular niche on the mountain. Some, especially the saxifrages, depend on rills and springheads, while others need a slow gradual 'flushing' of water moving through the soil. Some species favour the protection of hollows where snow lies late in the year, while others require high ridges where the snow clears early and exposure is extreme, but where there is little competition. Other species, especially taller ones such as the elegant globeflower or the alpine sow-thistle, prefer cliff ledges where they can avoid grazing animals and where nutrient levels tend to be higher. Similarly, screes, gullies, grasslands, lake-shores and all the other microhabitats have their own particular species.

At higher altitudes insects are less abundant than in the lowlands, so it is more difficult for plants to be pollinated. This is one of the reasons why so many alpine flowers are brightly coloured and often nectar-rich – the few insects that are about have to be strongly attracted. Other species, such as the alpine meadow-rue, have come to rely more on wind pollination – there being no shortage of gusty days to blow the pollen around.

Left: The lovely, low-growing purple saxifrage is one of the earliest of our arctic-alpine flowers to appear, often before all the snow of winter has melted. It is most at home on damp rocks and mountain cliffs.

CHECKLIST

This checklist is a guide to some of the flowers, ferns and mosses you will find on mountains and moorlands. Although you will not see them all in the same place, you should be able to spot many of them throughout the changing seasons. The species listed in **bold type** *are described in detail.*

Alpine cinquefoil
Alpine fleabane
Alpine forget-me-not
Alpine lady's mantle
Alpine meadow rue
Alpine mouse ear
Alpine speedwell
Alpine woodsia
Bracken
Common bladderwort
Common butterwort
Cotton grass
Clubmosses
Globeflower
Great sundew
Intermediate sundew
Killarney fern
Least cudweed
Liverworts
Moss campion
Mossy cyphel
Mountain avens
Mountain sorrel
Oblong woodsia
Pale butterwort
Parsley fern
Pyramidal bugle
Purple moor grass
Roseroot
Round-leaved sundew
Saxifrages
Sea campion
Snow gentian
Sphagnum mosses
Spring sandwort
Stiff sedge
Tormentil
Tunbridge filmy fern
Wavy hair grass
Wilson's filmy fern

Left: The sundew is a tiny but beautiful plant that grows in bogs and on moors — but it has a deadly secret. It is one of just a handful of plants in this country that are insectivorous, trapping small insects with the sticky 'glue' at the end of the hairs on each paddle-shaped leaf.

THE ARCTIC-ALPINES OF BEN LAWERS

Most of the Scottish Highlands are covered by poor acid soils which support very few plant species. But the mountain of Ben Lawers, by the side of Loch Tay in Perthshire, is different, for its soils are less acidic, making it one of the best sites for alpine and arctic plants in Britain.

The unique soil conditions on Ben Lawers and its abundant mountain flora–in contrast to the rest of the Scottish Highlands–are explained by the nature of the underlying rock. This is composed of sediments laid down many millions of years ago when sea covered the area. These sedimentary rocks then sank down towards the hotter centre of the earth, below the surface crust. When they were forced up again by a series of folding movements they formed a mountain range. Such great heat and pressure changed the nature of the rocks, however, and they no longer resembled sedimentary rocks–they were schists, and some contained semi-precious garnet stones.

These schists form one or two of the main soil types on Ben Lawers, and occur mostly on the upper slopes. The other main soil type is glacial drift–clays, sand and gravels deposited by glaciers when the ice retreated at the end of the Ice Age. Even within these two main soil types variations exist, for the effect of drainage and weathering in different parts of the mountain can be dramatic.

Leached glacial drift The sands, gravels and clays deposited by glaciers cover most of the lower slopes of Ben Lawers. These soils are usually impoverished, a state caused by rain water passing through a layer of humus on the soil surface and washing out (leaching) organic acids from the decomposing material.

Above: The summit of Ben Lawers, taken from neighbouring Beinn Ghlas. Ben Lawers is part of the Breadalbane mountain range and lies near Aberfeldy in Perthshire. Rising 909m (3984ft), it has been require visiting for generations of botanists, ever since its flora was first documented by James Dickson in 1789. In contrast to most mountains in the Scottish Highlands, Ben Lawers is built of rocks which were originally composed of sediments and then subjected to intense heat and pressure. The resulting schists are finely fragmented rocks which hav a tendency to split in one plane.

Above: Mossy cyphel, with its small green flowers, is a cushion-forming plant found on the rocky ledges of Ben Lawers.

Left: The rocky ledges, of which there are many, support some of the mountain's most interesting plants for the soils are rich in minerals. Here, nutrients in the soil are constantly added as a result of soil movement and rock falls, so leaching does not have the same impact as it does on other parts of Ben Lawers.

Below: Moss campion is an attractive alpine species with pink star-like flowers; it also thrives on the rocky ledges.

s this acidic water penetrates the depths of e soil it removes various soluble salts vital to e growth of a diverse plant community. The il which is left is essentially a mixture of or peat and sand and gives rise to an interesting vegetational cover dominated mat-grass, a supremely acid-tolerant plant. Sometimes these impoverished soils are nstantly water-logged, making it possible r the acid-tolerant *Sphagnum* moss to grow. ese water-logged areas gradually develop to full-scale bogs supporting cotton-grass d bog asphodel.

Flushed soils In some parts of the lower pes the leaching out of minerals is comnsated by the constant addition of minerals ched out of soils higher up, or by water rrying small pieces of rock that have been ently weathered away. This process is own as flushing. It may be seasonal, with eltwater from winter snows providing the tra nutrients; it may be permanent, as in eas where water comes to the surface and ws down; or it may be a dry process where e soil at the base of a scree is kept topped up the simple process of gaining material from ove.

Wet flushes—a result of the first two ocesses—contain the largest number of plant cies, especially sedges and rushes. These the most interesting glacial drift soils on

the lower slopes of Ben Lawers.

Schist soils It is the soils composed of broken down schist, however, which provide a home for the particularly special plants of the mountain. As you climb Ben Lawers you will notice that the appearance of this more crumbly schist is marked also by the appearance of more varied plant communities. Alpine lady's mantle is one of the first plants to be seen, and on the less easily grazed areas it will often be joined by patches of moss campion with its attractive pink flowers.

Gradually ascending the slope you will also begin to notice the effect which the wind has on the vegetation. The wind is a great dehydrator, and the plants that survive it are some of the most highly adapted on the mountain. The moss *Rhacomitrium* is a characteristic plant of these conditions, and growing with it you may find the sedge *Carex bigelowii*, a stiff-leaved plant. A few lichens

Above: In good seasons large numbers of alpine forget-me-not grow on Ben Lawers on the cliff ledges and also on the turf below.

Left: Alpine fleabane is an extremely rare plant, found only in certain parts of Scotland, growing at high altitudes on rocky ledges. In this country it was first discovered on Ben Lawers in 1789 by James Dickson.

Opposite page: Drooping saxifrage, though long ago discovered on Ben Lawers, has hardly ever been recorded in flower, but 1983 was an exceptional year.

Below: The rocks beside Lochan nan Cat, below Ben Lawers, support a variety of mosses and lichens.

may also be found as can the rush *Juncus trifidus* which occurs in the more sheltered spots.

Nutrient-poor communities on the schist, where much leaching is evident, are dominated by the ubiquitous mat-grass, present in patches that exactly mark the winter snow drifts which gave the plants protection. These poor soils are also characterised by an abundance of alpine lady's mantle, bilberry and various grasses and lichens.

Rocky ledges As on the glacial soils, the most interesting habitats on the schist soils occur where flushing, or other pressures that delay complete leaching out of nutrients, happen regularly. One such habitat is rocky ledges, of which there are many on the upp slopes of Ben Lawers. A ledge may form any time, simply by soil movement, or fro the contents of another fall, as a ledge washed away.

Some of the plants that grow here a natural cliff-dwellers, such as rose-root ar alpine saxifrage, nearly always found presse close against the rock. Other well-know plants include sea campion, mountain sorr and the early flowering purple saxifrage. C certain ledges you may find alpine fleabane beautiful little plant–alpine speedwell, ar one of the classic arctic-alpine plants, alpir mouse-ear chickweed.

The rocky ledges are also known to suppo two species of willows. These 'trees' neve exceed 15cm (6in) in height, and are hard recognisable as willows. The least willow fairly common over the higher areas, but i relative, the net-leaved willow, is mo particular in its distribution. This is also th larger of the two and, with its beautiful veined leaves, the more attractive.

above: Spring sandwort grows in compact tufts close to the ground and so is protected from fierce biting winds.

favours acid soils on mountains and also on lower slopes, particularly among heather moorland. It has strong woody roots which were once used by fishermen in the Western Isles in tanning their nets when tree bark was not available.

Damp gully species The natural process of rainwater erosion tends to wash soil down the mountain side and this can collect to quite a depth on ledges and in gully-bottoms. Here, if the area is fairly sheltered and remains moist, quite a lush vegetation has a chance to develop.

The globe flower, an obvious member of the buttercup family, has large round yellow blooms up to 5cm (2in) across, and deeply cut leaves. It is not confined to mountains, growing just as well in wet ground in lower hilly districts.

Alpine meadow rue, however, is a true mountain species, rarely found below 455m (1500ft). The unusual flowers are known as pollen-flowers, because insects are attracted solely to the mass of yellow anthers – there are no petals, nectar or scent. Visiting insects, usually flies, cling to the bunches of anthers, although wind pollination may also take place.

flowers is pollinated by flies. But some other mountain plants are self-pollinated – at such high altitudes they cannot depend on insect visitors. The alpine cinquefoil, on the other hand, can produce seeds without any fertilisation of its bright yellow flowers – a process called apomixis.

Another relatively tall plant – tormentil –

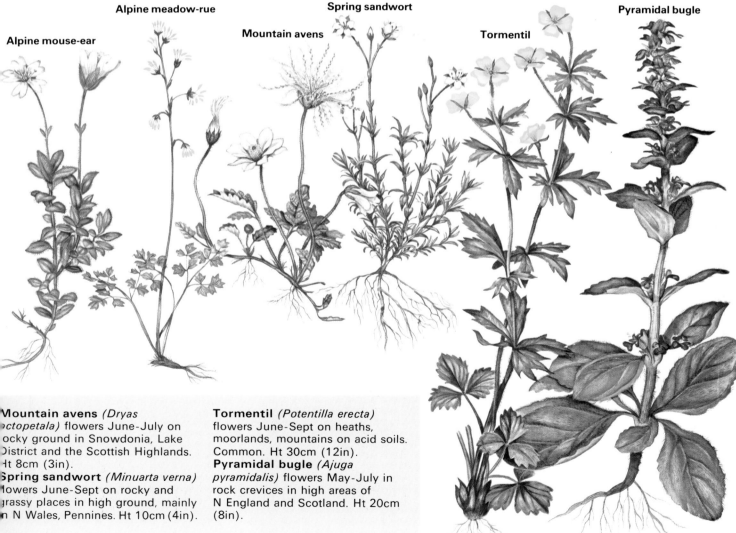

Alpine mouse-ear

Alpine meadow-rue

Mountain avens

Spring sandwort

Tormentil

Pyramidal bugle

Mountain avens *(Dryas octopetala)* flowers June-July on rocky ground in Snowdonia, Lake District and the Scottish Highlands. Ht 8cm (3in).
Spring sandwort *(Minuarta verna)* flowers June-Sept on rocky and grassy places in high ground, mainly in N Wales, Pennines. Ht 10cm (4in).

Tormentil *(Potentilla erecta)* flowers June-Sept on heaths, moorlands, mountains on acid soils. Common. Ht 30cm (12in).
Pyramidal bugle *(Ajuga pyramidalis)* flowers May-July in rock crevices in high areas of N England and Scotland. Ht 20cm (8in).

MOUNTAIN SNOW-PATCH PLANTS

Despite being so exposed, mountain plants form thriving communities, even where the ground is covered by snow for much of the year.

One factor that makes mountain plants so interesting is the number of different habitats to be found within a relatively small area. Cliff ledges, screes and damp gullies all have very different communities of plants and these in turn may vary according to altitude or aspect.

Snow patch plants A quite distinctive association of species is one that surrounds late-lying snow patches that often persist into late summer, especially in a summer following a very cold winter. The centre of such a patch might remain snow-covered throughout the year, or be uncovered for a few weeks only. Surrounding it are a series of definite zones, each with a characteristic flora. The species growing in the innermost zone may be uncovered – and so free to grow and photosynthesise – for only two or three months each year; only a few species of liverworts can grow in these conditions. In the next zone, where plants may be uncovered for three to four months per year, mosses such as *Polytrichum norvegicum* may be found, together with the fir clubmoss and a few cushion-forming alpines, such as the starry saxifrage.

Acid and alkaline soil dwellers The outermost zones surrounding the snow patch provide a home for several interesting species of flowering plants. One of these is the least cudweed. This tiny, tufted species is a member of the daisy family, somewhat resembling edelweiss, to which it is distantly related. Its

Above: *Diapensia lapponica* is something of a mountain rarity. Properly an Arctic species, its tiny white flowers are found on only one mountain in western Scotland.

Below: Alpine lady's mantle (*Alchemilla alpina*) has a covering of silky hairs on the underside of its leaves which helps to protect them from the water of melting snows. In flower from June to August, it is seen here on Ben Lawers in the Grampians.

woolly leaves are densely covered with tin hairs, which help to keep it dry when th snow melts, and it produces small, compa spikes of whitish flowers with papery brow bracts in July. The least cudweed is especial characteristic of late-lying snow patches b requires acid conditions and is found only c the acid granites of the Cairngorms and Sky

On the Cairngorms it may be found grov ing alongside alpine lady's mantle. Th pretty, fairly low-growing plant is mo common in snow hollows which, being she tered, have better-quality and more abundar soil than in the surrounding areas.

Many of the species that grow around sno patches flourish regardless of the soil typ Sibbaldia is one such species. It belongs to th rose family, like the alpine lady's mantle, an is a small, compactly tufted plant with blu green leaves and tiny yellow-petalled or peta less flowers.

A very different species of the outermo snow patch zone is one of the mounta sedges – stiff sedge. It has narrow recurve leaves which grow from a creeping rhizon and flowers that are typical of the sedge They are purple-black in colour and upwar pointing with brown bracts; the fema flower spike is below the male. Stiff sed often grows alongside such grasses as th wavy hair grass (in acid conditions) and alpi meadow grass, and a shrub, the least willo This is the smallest of Britain's w

ows, forming prostrate mats of woody, creeping stems with bright green leaves.

Colonizers and pioneers Snow patches are only one of many micro-habitats on our mountains. Screes and patches of bare, stony soil, freshly formed from the mountain rocks, provide a home for many plants that demand an open situation where they are not shaded out by other species. The pioneers, or colonizing species, of the mountains are particularly demanding in this respect; one such species is *Koenigia islandica*.

A tiny plant, with small yellowish-green flowers that appear in summer, it often grows alone, covering large areas of the bare, stony soil. It is an unusual species in several ways. Firstly, it is an annual, whereas most mountain plants are perennials. Secondly, it is very limited in its British distribution, growing only on certain mountains on the islands of Skye and Mull, although other habitats suitable for its growth are found on other mountains. Thirdly, it was not discovered in Britain until 1934 and even then it was wrongly classified, being classified properly only as recently as 1950.

Diapensia lapponica is another relatively recent discovery, being found on a mountain ridge near Fort William in western Scotland in 1951. Here it grows on a patch of quartzite rock which is very different from the surrounding schist forming the rest of the ridge. It forms perennial compact cushions with leathery, evergreen leaves and white flowers which appear in May and June.

Species of the lower slopes Large areas of Britain's mountains – such as the acid granite of the Cairngorms and the sandstone of the Pennines – are sometimes considered rather dull from a botanical viewpoint. However, they are often covered by wide expanses of heather, bilberry, cowberry, crowberry and other dwarf shrubs that are adapted to living in acid conditions. Where the rainfall is very high or drainage is poor, layers of peat may accumulate over a long period of time. If these layers are very thick, the composition of the underlying rock ceases to influence the vegetation. Also, on heather moors there may be outcrops of less acid rock above ground, like the thin bands of limestone which occur in the sandstones of Ingleborough and Penyghent.

These limestone bands provide a home for many interesting montane species, including several saxifrages, of which the most attractive is probably the purple saxifrage. This is a mat-forming perennial with solitary, rosy-purple flowers borne at the ends of the lower stems in March and April. By way of contrast the yellow mountain saxifrage produces red-spotted yellow flowers at the ends of erect rosettes in the spring, while Dovedale moss, a mossy saxifrage with larger rosettes, resembles some garden saxifrages. Its flowering shoots, which are about 15cm (6in) high, bear pure white flowers from April to June.

Species found around snow patches

Below: **Least willow** (*Salix herbacea*). On mountain tops. Catkins appear in spring. Ht to 2cm (¾in).

Right: **Wavy hair grass** (*Deschampsia flexuosa*). On moors, sandy or peaty soil. Flowers June-July. Ht to 2m (78in).

Below: **Least cudweed** (*Gnaphalium supinum*). On mountains in Scotland. Flowers July-Aug. Ht to 7.5cm (3in).

Above: **Stiff sedge** (*Carex bigelowii*). On stony soil, mountains. Flowers June-July. Ht to 15cm (6in).

Right: Sibbaldia (*Sibbaldia procumbens*) is a member of the rose family. A small, creeping plant, it produces tiny yellow-petalled or petal-less flowers in its leaf axils from July to August.

Below: *Koenigia islandica* is rather an unusual species to find on mountain tops for it belongs to the Polygonaceae, a family of plants more often associated with wet lowlands than inhospitable mountain ridges.

Strange find

surface

HARDY MOUNTAIN SAXIFRAGES

Delicate though they may look, saxifrages are hardy plants well adapted to the rigours of their native habitats on exposed mountains.

In Britain the saxifrage family (Saxifragaceae) is represented by two groups of plants. The largest is the genus *Saxifraga*, after which the family is named, but there are also two species in another genus, *Chrysoplenium*.

Saxifrages are predominantly mountain plants, the Highlands of Scotland being the best place in Britain to see them. Many have very restricted distributions; the drooping saxifrage, for example, is now nearly extinct in this country and survives only on the summit of Ben Lawers in Scotland. Others, such as the Dovedale moss (which, despite its name, is a saxifrage), are more common and not confined just to the highest altitudes but may be found lower down – to the delight of both naturalist and walker alike.

Rosettes and cushions Britain's saxifrages can be divided into two types according to their manner of growth: those that form rosettes and those that form cushions. The rosette types have a compact rosette of leaves spreading from the top of a very short stem, or stock as it is more usually known. The leaves are commonly pressed close to the ground.

The cushion saxifrages, on the other hand, consist of a great many short stems arising from the main root. These stems, in turn, branch again to produce more slender stems, which are covered with tufts of small leafy shoots. The whole structure is usually very compact and low-growing, seldom rising more than a few centimetres above the ground and giving the appearance of a leafy cushion– for the branches are usually hidden from view by the densely packed tufts of leaves.

Both the rosette and the cushion habits are adaptations to difficult conditions often experienced on mountain summits and exposed, wind-swept ledges. The low growth habit protects the plants from fierce winds which, apart from physically damaging the plants, would have a serious drying-out effect by causing water to evaporate too quickly from the leaf surface.

Drought, indeed, is one of the major problems facing saxifrages living at high altitudes. For many months of the year the soil is covered with a deep layer of snow, and

Above: Starry saxifrage (*Saxifraga stellaris*), a rosette-forming species common on damp ground– particularly springs and stream sides–in many mountainous regions. The leaves of this plant are held semi-erect above the ground, probably to prevent them becoming waterlogged.

Right: Dovedale moss (*Saxifraga hypnoides*) overwinters as a cushion of tightly packed leaves, producing upright heads of white flowers from May to July. Also known as mossy saxifrage, it is one of our more widespread members of this group.

London Pride

Many saxifrages make excellent garden plants, one of the most commonly grown being a hybrid usually called 'London Pride', a reference to its ability to thrive in London's once-smoggy atmosphere. Occasionally escaping and becoming naturalised, this hybrid is a cross between two species, one being *S. spathularis*, an Irish saxifrage sometimes known as St Patrick's cabbage, and *S. umbrosa*, a saxifrage native to the central and western parts of the Pyrenees Mountains.

reams and soil-water may be frozen solid. such conditions it may not be possible for a xifrage to take up enough water through the oots to compensate for water loss through e leaves. Furthermore, summer comes late these areas, and it may be as late as June efore the last traces of snow have disppeared from the tops of the highest ountains. On sheltered slopes it may not ear at all. Also, much of the rain falling on a ountain is lost down the slope, and the

Above left: Yellow mountain saxifrage (*S. aizoides*) grows on wet stony areas and by stream sides.

Right: The flowers and ripening fruit capsule of Dovedale moss.

Below: Opposite-leaved golden saxifrage overhanging a stream.

stony soil high up receives very little. So, although the rainfall is usually high in mountain areas, the soil itself can often be dry.

Purple saxifrage One of the loveliest cushion-forming species is the purple saxifrage, whose rosy-purple flowers first appear during April in Scotland, and February and March in north Wales. This is often before the snows have melted away. The flowers of this species–in common with those of others in the genus *Saxifraga*–have five petals and five sepals. Within this outer ring are ten stamens, five of them opposite the petals and five alternating. In the centre are two styles. The flowers secrete nectar to attract flies and small bees.

The fruit of a saxifrage consists of a capsule with two diverging horns on top–these are the remnants of the flower's two styles. When ripe the fruit splits open along the top to release the seeds, which are gradually shaken

out as the capsule is blown in the wind.

The leaves of the purple saxifrage exhibit an interesting feature–their tips have a special gland called a hydathode which regulates the transpiration of water from the leaf. On dry days, when the rate of evaporation through this gland is high, the tissues immediately around the gland secrete lime. The lime is dissolved by the water in the gland, and the water evaporates to leave the lime behind as a deposit. This deposit builds up and the gland is eventually shut off, preventing any more water from escaping. During the night, or in colder weather when the rate of transpiration is low, some of the lime dissolves and the gland is opened up again.

Tufted saxifrage Another cushion-forming species, but one much rarer than the purple saxifrage, is the tufted saxifrage. This species grows only on the highest summits. It has small, usually three-lobed leaves which lack the lime-producing glands of the purple species. Its flowers are whitish and are borne,

one or two to a stem, from May to July.

The flower stems of tufted saxifrage are covered with short sticky hairs to prevent crawling insects from climbing up and stealing the nectar without pollinating the flower. In practice, although the plant produces abundant nectar, it is often not visited by pollinating insects and pollinates itself instead.

Two rosetted species A typical rosette saxifrage is the alpine saxifrage. The erect flowering stems bear three to twelve flowers clustered into a dense head. The petals are greenish-white but the surrounding sepals are often purplish, giving colour to the flower as a whole. At the base of the flowering stems is a rosette of leathery, egg-shaped leaves with toothed margins.

A much more common rosetted species is the starry saxifrage, found on many mountains in Scotland, Wales and Ireland. Its leaves have a thinner texture than the alpine species and, instead of being held close to the ground, are semi-erect. The flowers are pure white with two small yellow spots near the base of each petal. They are borne on leafless stems in heads of 12 or more.

Bulbil bearers Because the growing season is very short in mountainous areas, saxifrages are sometimes not able to complete their reproductive cycle and disperse their seeds before the onset of winter. Instead they may rely on vegetative reproduction, often by producing miniature bulb-like structures called bulbils.

An extreme example is the rare drooping saxifrage, which always reproduces in this way in Britain, never by seed. Its small, brownish-red bulbils are borne in the axils of the leaves and bracts, and also near the base of the plant.

Golden species The second group of plants found in Britain belonging to the saxifrage

family are different enough from the main body of species to be placed in a separate genus, *Chrysoplenium*. Commonly known as golden saxifrages, they differ from the true saxifrages in having flowers with no petals and usually fewer sepals and stamens.

Two species grow in Britain, the opposite-leaved and the alternate-leaved golden saxifrages. Both grow in wet places in woods, and along stream-sides, springs and wet rocks.

Their botanical name comes from two Greek words—'chrysos' meaning gold and 'splen' meaning spleen. The first half refers to the greenish-golden flowers which appear between April and June and the second half refers to the supposed similarity between the shape of the leaves and the shape of the human spleen. At one time an infusion of the leaves was prescribed against ailments of this origin.

Above: The purple saxifrage (*Saxifraga oppositifolia*) is one of the loveliest species, appearing early in the year, often before the snow has cleared away. It grows on damp rocks and soil-covered ledges of mountain cliffs, where its long roots penetrate far down through cracks and fissures in search of water.

Yellow marsh saxifrage (*Saxifraga hirculus*)

Drooping saxifrage (*Saxifraga cernua*)

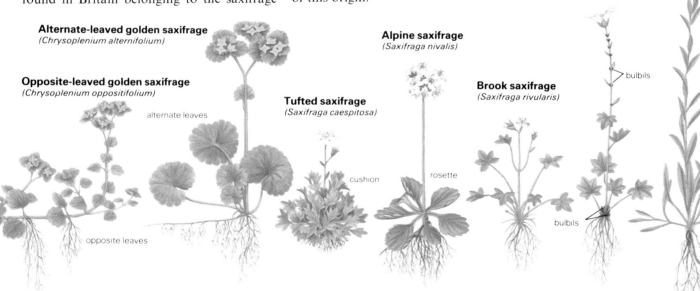

Alternate-leaved golden saxifrage (*Chrysoplenium alternifolium*)

Opposite-leaved golden saxifrage (*Chrysoplenium oppositifolium*)

alternate leaves

opposite leaves

Tufted saxifrage (*Saxifraga caespitosa*)

cushion

Alpine saxifrage (*Saxifraga nivalis*)

rosette

Brook saxifrage (*Saxifraga rivularis*)

bulbils

bulbils

Above: Our two species of golden saxifrage can be told apart at a glance just by looking at the way the leaves are arranged.

Above: The two growth habitats of saxifrage are cushion, as in the tufted saxifrage, and rosette, as in the alpine saxifrage.

Above: Both the drooping and the brook saxifrages reproduce by bulbils, the drooping saxifrage exclusively so in Britain.

PLANTS THAT EAT ANIMALS

Insectivorous plants sound as if they should be exotic and tropical, yet some species are quite common in Britain in areas where there are wet peatland bogs. Their fascinating insect-trapping mechanisms ensure that they obtain nutrients unavailable from the soil in their habitats.

here are three main species of insectivorous ant growing in the British Isles. They all otain essential nutrients, and amino acids d proteins, by the same method – trapping, gesting and absorbing small creatures (usu-ly insects) – although they differ in their apping mechanisms. Some of the essential trogen for this growth is supplied in this ay, and so insectivorous plants are able to ow in areas where conditions would other-ise have been unsuitable.

Bog moss plants Sphagnum bogs, in par-cular, are often colonized by insectivorous ants. The round-leaved sundew grows in the ssocks of bog moss, while the smaller inter-ediate sundew is found on bare peat or in

the drainage channels leading from raised sphagnum bogs. Both species are found throughout the British Isles, while the great sundew is more common in Scotland and Ireland. This species differs from the others in having leaves held in an erect rosette, whereas the leaf rosettes of the other two are flat and pressed to the ground. The leaves of all three are paddle-shaped and covered with tiny, glistening, pin-like hairs which shine like dew in the sun, giving the plants their name.

Glands on the tip of every hair and on the leaf surface, produce an abundance of sticky mucilage that looks like nectar; an insect attracted to the leaves is soon trapped in the 'glue'. Its struggles trigger off the movement

Above: The brilliant colour of this moorland pool is created by the sticky red hairs on the leaves of a carpet of sundews. Nutrients vital to the plants are obtained from animal tissue, in the form of insects. Each sundew plant can catch as many as 2000 insects on its leaves in one summer alone.

Below: Once trapped by a sundew, the prey is soon enclosed by digestive hairs.

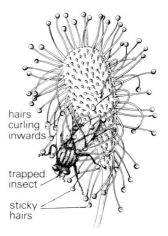

hairs curling inwards

trapped insect

sticky hairs

Above: The droplets on the tips of the leaf hairs of the round-leaved sundew (*Drosera rotundifolia*), glisten like dew in the sun. In fact, they are lethal plants and once an insect like this damselfly touches them it is trapped.

of the long, outermost hairs which wrap over the insect. Once it is enclosed by the hairs, digestion by the enzymes present in the mucilage can begin. When the liquefied remains have been absorbed, then the hairs re-open and the fly-trap is ready for action again.

Grasping leaves A similar trap is set by the common butterwort, which favours the same sort of habitat as the sundew–wet rocks, marshes, fens and peatland throughout Brittain (although nót on the sphagnum tussocks themselves). It has long-stemmed, violet flowers and distinctive yellow-green leaves which form a basal rosette. The hairs on the

leaves are microscopic and much more numerous than in the sundews–as many as 25,00 per square centimetre (160,000 per sq in Any insect landing on the leaf is trapped b the sticky hairs, while the leaf margins ro inwards to enclose it. A thick digestive flu is produced by the leaf to break down th insect's body so the plant can absorb th nutrients. The process completed, the leaf r opens.

Two other species, the pale butterwo (*Pinguicula lusitanica*) and the Irish butte wort (*Pinguicula grandiflora*) are also foun on these islands; the former grows on the ac moors of Cornwall, Devon and Hampshi

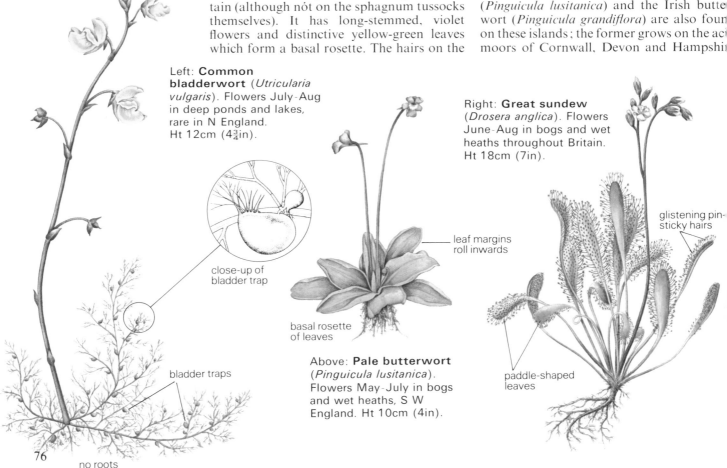

Left: **Common bladderwort** (*Utricularia vulgaris*). Flowers July-Aug in deep ponds and lakes, rare in N England. Ht 12cm (4¾in).

close-up of bladder trap

bladder traps

no roots

Right: **Great sundew** (*Drosera anglica*). Flowers June-Aug in bogs and wet heaths throughout Britain. Ht 18cm (7in).

glistening pin-sticky hairs

paddle-shaped leaves

leaf margins roll inwards

basal rosette of leaves

Above: **Pale butterwort** (*Pinguicula lusitanica*). Flowers May-July in bogs and wet heaths, S W England. Ht 10cm (4in).

he bladderwort trap

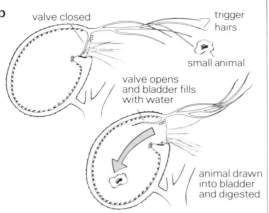

he circular mouth of the
adder trap is closed by
valve, and when a tiny
eature brushes by it
ctivates the special
igger hairs that open
e valve. The negative
ressure inside the trap
auses the water to rush
, carrying the animal
ith it. Here it decomposes,
d the remains are
sorbed, the waste
roducts being pumped
ut of the bladder.

valve closed

trigger
hairs

small animal

valve opens
and bladder fills
with water

animal drawn
into bladder
and digested

d the latter, as its name suggests, in Ireland.
Underwater traps The bladderworts form
other small group of native British insect-
orous plants, but their lifestyle is totally
ferent from the species already described.
ey are rootless water plants, and only the
mmon bladderwort is at all abundant,
owing in peatland pools throughout Brit-
. The leaves of the bladderworts are sub-
erged and, like the leaves of many aquatic
nts, they are finely dissected to allow easy
sorption of food for growth. Some essential
neral salts are lacking in this watery
vironment, but the plant obtains these
sential nutrients from living tissue in the
m of micro-organisms caught by its
adder traps. These are tiny, intricate traps,
2mm in diameter, which catch rotifers,
otozoans and small crustaceans. Male water
as (*Daphnia*) are quite commonly caught in
e traps, which, viewed from the side, bear a
semblance to other *Daphnia*. The males
proach the traps with the intention of trying
mate, and are immediately sucked in and
sorbed by the plant.
Deadly pitchers Pitcher plants are not
tive to Britain, although one of them, the
rple pitcher plant (*Sarracenia purpurea*),
s become extensively naturalised in the
hagnum bogs of central Ireland.
The leaves of the plant are modified to form
chers, or jug-like structures, which are
rtly filled with fluid. The pitchers of all
ese plants are brightly coloured, these
rticular ones being purple. This colour,
ong with the sweet scent of the nectar
nds at the top of the pitcher, helps to
tract insects. They alight on the lip of the
cher and crawl down into the depths of
e water below. Once there, they are pre-
nted from returning to safety by the scaly
les that prevent them obtaining a grip of the
cher, and by downward-pointing hairs.
The death of the insects is helped along by
e powerful narcotics that drip into the
ter from the nectaries. The bodies are then
gested by enzymes produced by special cells
the lining of the pitcher.
Many more carnivores? Insectivorous
ants are considered to be a rarity in the

Below: The bright, sticky
leaves of the common
butterwort, also known as
the bog violet, clasp any
insect that lands on them.
They enfold it and start to
digest it, very often while it is
still living.

plant world. The usual explanation for their
existence is that the insectivorous habit
evolved from a need to obtain protein, which
was lacking in their acid, nitrogen-sparse
habitats. In such areas they cannot synthesise
sufficient amino acids for their needs. However, one of the founders of modern biology,
Charles Darwin, thought that insectivorous
habits were much more widespread than
acknowledged today. He studied them widely,
publishing a book, *Insectivorous Plants*, in
1875. Despite his findings, and those of
many other studies since, few botanists
acknowledge the evidence that insects are
killed and may be digested by many species.
Plants such as the tobacco plant (*Nicotiana
tabaccum*) and potato plant (*Solanum tuber-
osum*) are all covered by a variety of hairs,
some of which are glandular. These, and
other similarly sticky plants, are often seen
with dead insects adhering to the hairs. In
the potato at least, enzymes capable of
digesting insects have been found in the
secretions from these glands.

BRACKEN: BEAUTIFUL BUT FATAL

Hillsides covered with golden bracken look marvellous in the autumn sun. But this species is a bane to farmers, causing disease and even death to livestock.

To a modern hill farmer, bracken is a formidable enemy. It spreads by means of long underground stems (rhizomes) that make it almost impossible to eradicate, and it contains several chemicals that are highly poisonous to horses and cattle.

Bracken is one of the most common plant species on heaths and uplands. It has been estimated that it grows over about one and a half million acres in the British Isles – about 10% of our total hill country, and when it is well established it covers the land completely.

Bracken is a tall, broad fern and, like other ferns, it grows larger and more luxuriant in sheltered shady places. The spore-bearing sori form a continuous line beneath the margins of the pinnules, and millions of spores are produced each year. The life cycle is similar to that of the male fern, but there is one difference – the mature fern does not form tufts or fronds (crowns). Instead, the fronds sprout at intervals from the rhizomes that creep in the soil.

Vigorous colonizer It was almost certainly man's influence that led to the spread of bracken, transforming it into a serious pest. In pre-Neolithic times when the British Isles was covered by forests bracken grew with other plant species in the forest undergrowth. As Neolithic man cleared the forests and more of the land was used for primitive agriculture, bracken spread into the newly opened areas and quickly invaded any abandoned arable land. Bracken still grows in woodlands all over the country, but it rarely dominates them as it does in more open places.

During medieval times bracken was apparently held in check for it was cut and used for a variety of purposes. Cutting provides a good method of control, especially if done in midsummer, for the vigour of the plant is then impaired. Late summer cutting leaves the plant susceptible to frost.

In the 18th and 19th centuries bracken began to spread once again. At that time many upland farmers started to keep sheep instead of cattle, as had been their previous practice. Cattle feed on some of the young shoots, damage others with their heavy

hooves, and crush mature fronds with their weight. But by contrast sheep avoid eating bracken and, as they are so much lighter than cows, they do not cause the same amount of damage to the fronds. Bracken therefore had an opportunity to become well-established.

During that period many upland areas suffered from depopulation as people migrated to the cities, where the industrial revolution was dramatically changing the lifestyle of the country. The arable land that had once been farmed provided an excellent environment for bracken – and rabbits. These animals, like sheep, do not eat bracken but feed on other plants that live in similar habitats. This eliminates potential com-

Above: In autumn bracken turns a beautiful shade of golden brown. It is a pioneer species, and quickly invades uncultivated land. Indeed, its name is thought to be derived from the German words *Brache* or *Brachfeld*, meaning uncultivated land. Medieval people used bracken as bedding for livestock, as a source of potash in the manufacture soap and glass, in treating wool for dyeing, in medicine as a fuel and as a compost

etitors and enables the bracken to spread even faster.

Depopulation of upland areas allowed the spread of bracken in other ways too. As long as people lived close to the land they could inspect it regularly and eliminate perennial weeds, such as bracken, before they became properly established.

Lack of inspection of marginal land has led to a renewed expansion of bracken during the first half of the 20th century when, during the world wars, labour was scarce and food production took priority. Many scientists think that the exceptionally warm weather during this time also contributed to the spread of the plant, since its susceptibility to frost ensures that it does not spread in cold periods. Spore counts from archaeological digs usually show an increase in bracken pollen in warm periods and a decrease in cold intervals.

Livestock killer Scientists and farmers are actively seeking ways to prevent any further contamination of grazing land. Bracken can be poisonous to cattle and horses. An enzyme in the plant destroys thiamine (vitamin B_1) in horses causing symptoms of unco-ordination, known as staggers, which progresses to convulsions, and eventually death. Steps can be taken to treat an affected animal once it is realised that the disease is due to a lack of this vitamin. In cattle other poisons in the bracken will destroy the bone marrow, and result in the lack of blood platelets essential for blood clotting. Poisoned animals haemorrhage throughout the body.

There are other poisons in bracken which cause even more dangerous symptoms, especially in cattle. Recent research has shown that there are powerful carcinogens in the plant which may damage the bone marrow and intestines of cattle. These cancer-inducing chemicals can also affect man: in Japan, the eating of young bracken fronds—considered a delicacy—has been linked with stomach cancer.

If our livestock are to avoid bracken poisoning, then the ever increasing spread of this fern into our farm grazing land must be halted. Perhaps they had the right answer in the Middle Ages when they continually cut the plants and used them for numerous purposes. If we found a use for this species then it would be harvested regularly, and this would help enormously in the fight for control.

Above: These young bracken fronds have sprung up just three weeks after a fire had burnt the vegetation to the ground.

Below: **Bracken** (*Pteridium aquilinum*) is common in woods, on heaths and grassland on acid soils, absent from limestone areas. Very common, spreads fast. Fronds may be up to 2m (6ft) long.

young fern with curled frond (crozier)

pinnules

underground stem (rhizome) can stretch for several metres, producing new fronds at intervals

RARE FERNS OF OUR UPLANDS

The often bleak and barren appearance of our mountains belies the fact that some of our rarest and most delicate ferns are to be found there.

Ferns are generally considered to be plants of damp places, so it is surprising to find them growing in the seemingly arid environment of a mountain. Nevertheless, the conditions under rocks and on some ledges can be damp enough to allow spores to germinate and ferns to establish themselves.

Delicate filmy ferns The most delicate mountain ferns are the filmy ferns, an apt name because the blades of their fronds are but one cell thick. They grow only in places where the humidity is constantly very high and so are found on rocks by shady streams and waterfalls, and on moist, shady rock ledges. The thread-like rhizomes of these ferns branch to form a network over the surface of the substrate, producing the delicate fronds at intervals.

In filmy ferns, the sori (which contain the spore capsules) are not found on the underside of the frond blades, as they are on most ferns, but at the tips of some lobes of the blades. The sori are protected inside the cup-like indusium. This is a flask- or bell-shaped structure containing a thin spike—the receptacle—on which the spore capsules are formed. The spores of filmy ferns, like those of the royal fern and the horsetails, are unusual in that they contain chlorophyll and may begin to germinate before being shed from the

Above: Parsley fern growing in the crevice of a Welsh mountain. The fronds with the thin inrolled margins are fertile; the other fronds, looking rather like leaves of the parsley herb, are sterile.

Below: Both the alpine woodsia (here) and the oblong woodsia are confined mostly to higher latitudes, being especially common in Scandinavia and northern USSR, though they also occur in mountainous areas in the rest of Europe.

capsule.

Rare Killarney fern Of the three species filmy fern found in Britain, the rarest is Killarney or bristle fern. This species is c fined to just a few localities, having been m extinct in many areas through overcollecti Fortunately, it is now protected by the Wi life and Countryside Act of Parliament; i now illegal intentionally to pick, uproot destroy the plant, and to collect spores from

The name bristle fern comes from its co spicuous receptacles, which project from sori. Its alternative common name, Killarn fern, reflects the fact that it was first noted the British Isles in this region of Ireland.

The fronds of the Killarney fern are abo 10-15cm (4-6in) long, though they may much smaller, and have a dark vein runni to the tip of each lobe. Its indusia are narr and bell-shaped. It is now found in a very f areas in Britain, though it is more common Ireland, especially the south-west. Althou it is found in mountainous regions in British Isles, it is not confined to this habit

Other filmy ferns Britain's two other spec of filmy fern—Wilson's filmy fern and Tunbridge filmy fern—differ most obviou from the Killarney fern in their receptac Unlike those of the Killarney fern, they not protrude beyond the end of the indusia

The two species are easy to distinguish fr each other when fertile, for the Tunbridge irregularly toothed indusial lobes, where the Wilson's has smooth-edged indusial lob This difference can be clearly seen with a hand lens.

When the plants are not fertile they can still be distinguished, after a little practice. The Tunbridge filmy fern is blue-green with flat-spreading fronds; Wilson's filmy fern is a darker olive green with fronds that curve over the tips and margins.

Wilson's filmy fern, named in honour of a famous Victorian botanist, reaches the northernmost limit of its European distribution in the British Isles. It is found in Ireland and the west of Britain.

The Tunbridge filmy fern was long thought to be the same species as Wilson's. It was first recognised as a separate species from specimens growing near Tunbridge Wells in Kent—hence its name. Yet it grows in just a few places in south-east England, occurring mostly in south-west England, Wales, Scotland and Ireland, though even in those areas it is not common.

Protected woodsias Two other ferns of acidic uplands found in the British Isles are the alpine woodsia and the oblong woodsia. Both are extremely rare and, like the Killarney fern, are protected by law. They grow in damp rock crevices high up on mountains, the oblong woodsia in north Wales, northern England and Scotland and the alpine woodsia only in north Wales and Scotland.

The two species are very similar, both growing from a short branching rhizome that produces only a few fronds at a time. These are usually 5-10cm (2-4in) tall and lance-shaped in the oblong woodsia, with oblong pinnae (the branching divisions of a frond) which usually have between seven and thirteen deep lobes. The alpine woodsia has oblong fronds 3-15cm (1-6in) long, with egg-shaped or triangular pinnae bearing three to seven shallow lobes.

Less rare ferns There are several other ferns to be found in the acid mountainous regions of the British Isles which, though not as rare as the filmy ferns or the woodsias, are nevertheless still uncommon.

The parsley fern is usually found on scree slopes, walls and bridges. This fern is unusual in that its fertile fronds are often twice as tall as the sterile ones, reaching 30cm (12in). The young sori lie hidden under the unrolled margins of the pinnae.

The alpine lady fern is very similar to the common lady fern except that it is a smaller plant with circular sori. It is found only on rocks and screes in the Scottish mountains. Another species, the alpine buckler fern, is found in rock crevices in mountain areas of Scotland, the north of England and Wales, but it is so difficult to distinguish from its close relative, the broad buckler fern, that no one is sure of its distribution. The dwarf male fern, another mountain species, resembles the common male fern, but is smaller.

above right: Wilson's filmy fern (*Hymenophyllum wilsoni*), a species that in this country reaches the northernmost point of its European distribution. In the British Isles it is confined mostly to Ireland and the western parts of Britain. It is very similar to the Tunbridge filmy fern, especially when sterile, though the Wilson's fern is a darker olive-green colour, whereas the Tunbridge is blue-green, and its fronds curve round the tip and sides.

Mountain ferns

1 Killarney or bristle fern (*Trichomanes speciosum*) showing receptacle on sorus.
2 Tunbridge filmy fern (*Hymenophyllum tunbrigense*) with sorus.
3 Oblong woodsia (*Woodsia ilvensis*).
4 Alpine woodsia (*Woodsia alpina*).
5 Parsley fern (*Cryptogramma crispa*) showing sterile frond and pinna.
6 Parsley fern showing fertile frond with pinna and sori.

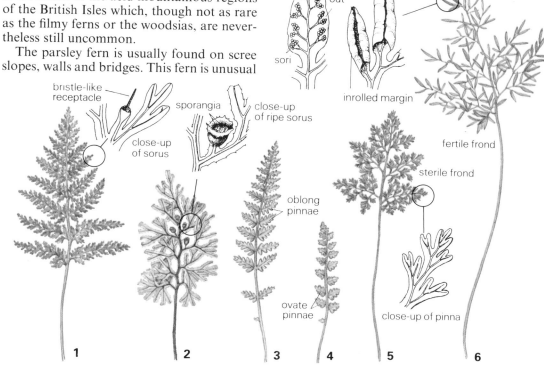

ANCIENT AND MODERN CLUBMOSSES

All too often overlooked as 'just another moss', the clubmosses are not in fact related to mosses but linked instead to the giant trees existing millions of years ago.

During the Carboniferous period 280 million years ago the vegetation was dominated by large trees, such as the giant *Lepidodendron* tree ferns. These massive plants, which often reached 92m (300ft) in height, had large trunks and branches that were divided into two, each branch ending in a huge cone. Pieces of these branches particularly the stem with its characteristic overlapping scales, are still found today as fossils.

Tiny descendants It is rather a shock to find that the living descendants of these plants actually look more like mosses, rarely growing above 15cm (6in) in height. These plants are called clubmosses but, despite their name, they are not actually mosses.

They contain woody tissue, and well-defined structures for conducting water, mineral salts and food material, which are not found in mosses. Clubmosses are usually allied with ferns, but they are not really closely related to these either. The clubmosses differ in having leaves and spore cases which grow on the upper side, rather than the underside of the leaves. They really have more in common with the horsetails.

Structure Clubmosses, which are green all year round, are usually creeping plants, although the fir clubmoss is upright. Most have branched stems, densely packed with small pointed leaves but alpine clubmoss has broader leaves that clasp the stem like overlapping scales. Each leaf is a simple structure, with a single vascular strand running down the middle, giving support and conducting water. Creeping clubmosses root at several points as they grow along the ground. The plant branches regularly, usually forming two equal-sized branches at each point. Both, or only one, of the branches can grow, resulting in either a creeping mat, or in the plant growing in more or less a straight line.

Cones of spores In the summer, the clubmoss bears small cone-shaped organs of reproduction. These may be held aloft on modified stems, or borne along the ground. Clubmosses share with ferns and horsetails a process known as alternation of generations.

Above: Fir clubmoss (*Huperzia selago*) grows in damp mountainous areas of Scotland, northern England, Wales and Ireland. The spores, which are ripe from June to August, form a very fine yellow powder. Reproduction takes place asexually, when small buds formed on the leaves fall off and grow into new plants.

Opposite: Alpine clubmoss (*Diphasiastrum alpinum*) prefers mountainous areas above 610m (2000ft). It has square branched stems that creep along the ground, anchored by strong wiry roots. Clumps of erect branches are produced at intervals, with yellow cones containing the spore cases developing at the tips of some of them. The yellow spores are produced from June to August.

his means that the plant has two distinct
hases of reproduction, sexual reproduction
iking place in the second phase. During the
rst phase the plants produce cones that
re actually specialised structures of closely
acked leaves. On the upper surface of these
aves, there is a box-shaped spore case,
hich bursts in the summer to liberate many
pores. These spores are borne on the wind;
' they land in moist and shady conditions
ey produce a small structure, the pro-
allus, which develops underground. This
where the sexual stage of reproduction
kes place.

Fertilisation occurs when male sperm
vim across the water film on the prothallus,
ntering the neck of the female organ and
rtilising the egg. The embryo thus formed
arts dividing and growing into a new plant,
bsorbing nourishment from the prothallus
ntil the new leaves are able to photosynthesise.

Looking at clubmosses Fir clubmoss is an
pright, bushy plant, looking very like a
nall fir tree with its long, narrow, dark green
aves. The spore capsules in this species
o not accumulate in cones, but are borne in
ie angle between a leaf and the stem. The
lant is characteristic of high moorland areas,
rowing in crevices on wet rocks and heath.

Interrupted clubmoss is also to be found in
iountainous areas, as well as on moorland.
is a semi-upright plant with stiff bristly
aves growing around a stem that appears
onstricted or interrupted at intervals. The
ines, which are borne singly, are made up of
aves that are different in shape and colour
om those of the main stem.

Lesser clubmoss, found on wet rocks in
iountainous areas of the British Isles, differs
om the other species mentioned so far in
iving two kinds of spores – microspores and
iegaspores – borne in separate spore cases.

Above: Stag's horn clubmoss
(*Lycopodium clavatum*),
shown with paired cones,
takes its name from its
resemblance to the branched
antlers of deer. The stems
creep along the ground,
rooting at intervals, and
are thickly covered with
leaves which have long
hair-like tips. The kidney
shaped spore cases growing
in cones produce a bright
yellow powder, lycopodium
powder. This formerly had
uses ranging from coating
pills to making fireworks.

Right: The creeping stems
of lesser clubmoss
(*Selaginella selaginoides*)
produce numerous upright
branches with narrow
pointed leaves. Large
yellow-green megaspores
appear in the lower parts of
the large-leaved cones
at the top of the plant.

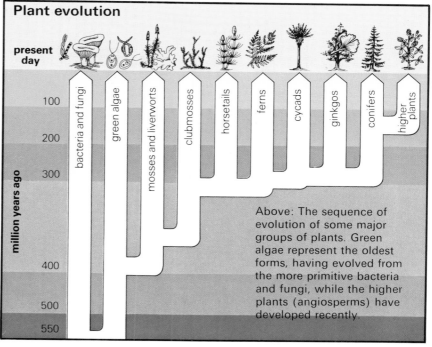

Plant evolution

present day

million years ago

100
200
300
400
500
550

bacteria and fungi
green algae
mosses and liverworts
clubmosses
horsetails
ferns
cycads
ginkgos
conifers
higher plants

Above: The sequence of
evolution of some major
groups of plants. Green
algae represent the oldest
forms, having evolved from
the more primitive bacteria
and fungi, while the higher
plants (angiosperms) have
developed recently.

PEAT-FORMING SPHAGNUM MOSSES

Sphagnum moss, often unnoticed but actually one of the most prominent bog plants of our countryside, is the prime constituent of the peatlands that cover an astonishing 93 million acres of the earth. It has a number of unique and specialised features.

Above: Sphagnum moss growing in a stagnant pond. The Sphagnum gradually encroaches on the pool by absorbing large amounts of water to create a bog. Peat is eventually formed from the accumulation of decayed tissue that collects there.

The world's peatland resources are to a very great extent made up of the living members – and dead remains – of a large genus of mosses called Sphagnum, an important and interesting group of plants. There are a number of different species to be found in the British Isles, in marshy areas, on wet moorlands and on fenlands.

The Sphagnum bog mosses have a numb of unique features which make them easy distinguish from the other sorts of moss, all stages of their complex life cycle.

Habitat Sphagna are only found growi in wet places and usually where the ground permanently waterlogged. They also gr as epiphytes–that is, stuck on to the trun and branches of trees–in the woodlands the wetter western coasts of Ireland, Wa and Scotland.

Structure The plants have very weak a brittle stems and cannot stand up on th own, hence they are always found growing dense carpets, or often as swelling hummoc their packed stems providing mutual suppo A close look at a single stem reveals th the branches arise in whorls, several spro ing out at each level, the separate branc themselves being covered by overlappi leaves.

Closer inspection, using a good lens microscope, shows that each leaf (thou made up of a single layer of cells, as in mosses) consists of two distinct sorts of ce

compact covering of thread-like outgrowths around their lower stems. The individual threads are known as rhizoids and the whole covering is the tomentum. The tomentum varies in both colour and extent from species to species. It probably functions like a wick, drawing water and nutrients up the leafy shoot. In *Aulacomnium palustre* the tomentum is reddish-brown and often thick, while *Polytrichum alpestre* has a white tomentum which, to the naked eye, resembles a thin coating of damp cotton-wool. A red tomentum is often produced among the bristle-like leaves of *Campylopus paradoxus*.

Spore dispersal Bryophytes propagate themselves by means of spores, which can be dispersed over a great distance. The spores are produced in a capsule borne on the end of a long slender stalk called the seta. When the capsule is ripe the lid falls off and the spores are released through the mouth of the capsule, which in most cases is ringed with teeth. By opening or closing, these teeth are able to regulate the release of the spores, allowing them to leave only during the dry breezy conditions most favourable for their dispersal.

The setae of bog mosses often grow several centimetres long, enabling the mature spores to be released above the humid, still air that lies close to the surface of a bog. In partially immersed mosses, a long seta may be essential to carry the capsule clear of the water. *Drepanocladus exannulatus*, for example, produces setae that grow to a height of 4-7cm (1½-2¼in) above the small curved leaves of its creeping branches.

Leafy liverworts Of the two major groups of liverwort–leafy and lobed–the leafy are most commonly found in *Sphagnum* bogs. In leafy liverworts the spore capsule develops from a fertilised female sex organ called the archegonium, enclosed within in a protective sheath of modified leaves called the perianth. When fully developed the capsule is elevated upon a rapidly elongating seta. (In mosses, the seta grows before the capsule develops.) Among the spores inside the drying capsule are long narrow cells called elators with peculiar spiral-shaped thickenings on their walls. As these cells lose water, they writhe about, increasing tension in the wall of the capsule. Eventually the capsule violently splits into four petal-like segments, which flip backwards exposing the spores to the air.

In many bog liverworts the chance of successful cross-fertilisation is reduced by the fact that the male and female sex organs grow on different shoots. Such is the case for *Kurzia pauciflora* and *Odontoschisma sphagni*, which are often found growing together scattered among stems of *Sphagnum*. In both plants, sex organs and therefore spore capsules very rarely occur. *Kurzia* has minute, slender, dark green shoots adorned with claw-like leaves while the shoots of *Odontoschisma* have two rows of round, overlapping leaves.

Above *Pleurozia purpurea*, one of the most conspicuous liverworts of *Sphagnum* bogs. Common only in the moorland bogs of the western Scottish Highlands, its stems resemble a cluster of large rearing caterpillars.

Below: Four bryophytes of *Sphagnum* bogs. Notice how the leaves of *Polytrichum alpestre* have a series of lamellae (parallel longitudinal walls of green cells) partially covered by the inrolled leaf margins.

Mylia anomala, another liverwort with this sexual arrangement, may reproduce asexually by means of microscopically small structures called gemmae, produced along the margins of its leaves. These can become detached and give rise to new plants. Some bog liverworts have organs of both sexes on the same stem, although in spite of this only a few species frequently produce spore capsules. As in *Mylia*, gemmae often contribute to their proliferation.

Many of these bog bryophytes are rare and seldom found outside *Sphagnum* bogs. Yet this unique habitat is slowly being destroyed under the combined effects of pollution and commercial drainage schemes.

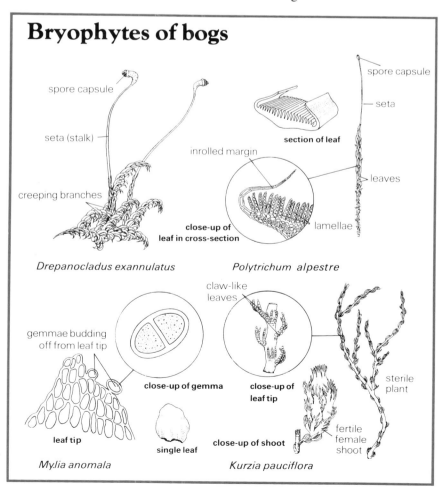

Bryophytes of bogs

spore capsule

seta (stalk)

creeping branches

Drepanocladus exannulatus

spore capsule

seta

leaves

section of leaf

inrolled margin

close-up of leaf in cross-section

lamellae

Polytrichum alpestre

gemmae budding off from leaf tip

close-up of gemma

leaf tip

single leaf

Mylia anomala

claw-like leaves

close-up of leaf tip

close-up of shoot

sterile plant

fertile female shoot

Kurzia pauciflora

Cold-blood creatures of mountain and moorland

Besides the more obvious birds and mammals of the mountains, there are a whole host of less obvious animal groups, including the fishes, insects and other invertebrates which, altogether, comprise many hundreds or even thousands of species. Despite being less obvious to us, their role in the mountain ecosystem is vital – they are predators, prey, parasites, herbivores or omnivores – and their presence is ubiquitous.

Mountain waters impose their own limitations on wildlife, in that they are cold, nutrient-poor and often acid, and frequently fast-moving. There are, however, compensations: they generally have more oxygen than lowland waters; they are only rarely polluted; and they are more cushioned against temperature extremes than the surrounding high altitude land habitats. Several groups of animals have taken readily to mountain waters, especially the mayflies, stoneflies, caddisflies and some of the true flies; and a few fishes such as the charr and brown trout are resident, feeding mostly on insect prey, while the salmon and sea trout use the higher reaches of rivers as spawning grounds. Dragonflies – perhaps the ultimate in insect predators – are a rare sight in the uplands, though a few hawkers and the golden-ringed dragonfly are common enough in lower mountain areas, and there are two or three arctic specialists that occur in Scottish hill waters.

Life for the larger flying insects is hard in the mountains, as many of them need at least some sunshine and warmth, and not too much wind to fly and breed. The mountain ringlet is our only really specialised mountain butterfly to survive at high altitudes despite the cold and wet conditions. Like some other mountain invertebrates, it is dark in colour to absorb whatever warmth is on offer, and it carries out most of its active life in the short mountain summer, though it is badly affected by unusually cold or wet summers and never reaches high densities. Moths do rather better, perhaps because they are less dependent on sunshine, and such species as the northern dart are real high altitude specialists.

Left: Although it may often seem that the only insects to be found on our upland moors are biting mosquitoes, some others do exist there. Both the mayfly (left) and the damselfly (right) can be seen near upland streams and ponds.

CHECKLIST

This checklist is a guide to some of the cold-blood creatures you will find on mountains and moorlands. Although you will not see them all in the same place, you should be able to spot many of them throughout the changing seasons. The species listed in **bold type** *are described in detail.*

Blackflies
Caddisflies
Charr (fish)
Common lizard
Golden-ringed dragonfly
Grayling (fish)
Ground beetles
Large heath butterfly
Mayflies
Midges
Mountain ringlet butterfly
Mosquitoes
Northern dart moth
Salmon
Scotch argus butterfly
Spiders
Stoneflies
Trout

Left: The spectacular golden-ringed dragonfly is fairly common in lower mountain areas but cannot survive on mountain tops. It is easily recognisable with its strong flight and bold colour.

91

SILVER-BLUE SALMON

No fish is more handsome than the silver-blue salmon, whose colour reflects the hues of the ocean where it feeds. Its deep red flesh makes it the prize quarry of fishermen.

he Atlantic salmon (*Salmo salar*) is a migratory fish found in the temperate and Arctic regions of the Northern Hemisphere. There are w fish that have such a fascinating life cycle. he salmon uses the gravel in the streams and vers for the protection of its eggs and the esh waters themselves for the nursery stages f its young. Then, when the young are 0-15cm (4-6in) long, and able to cope with onditions at sea, they leave the rivers in their ousands to feed voraciously in a rich marine nvironment, growing to a weight of several ounds in the same period of time that it took em to reach only a few ounces in the river.

The mystery of migration The ocean currents undoubtedly play a part in this fascinatg journey as, quite probably, do the stars, e moon and the sun, for salmon travel in the urface waters and so may be able to navigate y them. Once the fish approach the coast on eir return journey, and are close to the vers where they hatched out, new influences ke over. One theory is that the charactertic odour or 'taste' of the salmon's parent ver is recognised by the returning fish. ecent research suggests that the salmon etects the secretions or 'pheromones' exuded y the young fish of its own breeding stock the river.

Life in the river Salmon return to their river f origin throughout the year, even though ney do not spawn until late autumn or early inter. Some spend two or three years feeding the sea before returning to the river, while thers spend only a little over a year at sea efore coming back to spawn. These earlyturning fish tend to be smaller and are iven the name 'grilse'.

After the salmon has been in fresh water or a few weeks, it loses its silver coloration. he male gradually assumes a red and ottled appearance and develops a thick pongy skin, an enlarged head and a welleveloped hooked lower jaw known as a ype'. The changes in the female are not so ramatic. She becomes dark brown or purple d grey underneath. By the time she reaches e spawning grounds, she is unable to egotiate obstacles in the river, as the large range eggs make her body too heavy.

The long fast It is believed that salmon do not feed in fresh water, but this makes it difficult to explain why they are caught by anglers using artificial flies, minnows and fresh garden worms as bait. The actual point in their return migration at which food intake is reduced is not known but salmon taken in nets along the coast frequently have stomachs full of sandeels. On entering the river the salmon's stomach shrinks and the only food it can swallow consists of soft-bodied organisms such as worms, which can be digested with the minimum expenditure of energy. Very occasionally, young salmon have been found in the stomachs of male salmon on the spawning grounds, probably taken while chasing away intruders. The fast can be very long and the fish do not start feeding again until their return to the sea early in the following year.

Spawning time As autumn approaches, the smaller streams with their clean beds of siltfree gravel and cool, well-oxygenated water are gradually occupied by the ripening adults. By early November spawning starts and, with the appearance of late-comers, may continue well into December.

When the female is ready to spawn, she tests the gravel, cutting a well-defined, saucershaped depression to see if it is suitable for her nest. She does this by turning on her side and producing a vigorous flapping of her tail, alternately bending and straightening her body and dislodging the gravel which is carried downstream by the current. As the saucer-shaped depression gets deeper, a mound of gravel appears on the downstream edge. When the nest, or 'redd' as the depression is called, is to the female's liking she 'crouches' in the gravel prior to shedding the eggs. The male fish, always in attendance unless chasing away other males or young salmon, darts forward. Then, as the female bends her body and ejects the eggs, the male

Right: A male salmon in breeding colours. One characteristic for which the salmon is famed is that of jumping. Salmon have been recorded jumping successfully over vertical falls as high as 4m (13ft). The female fish (below) becomes brown or purple, with grey underparts, when she is ready to spawn.

Salmon migrations
It is only in the last thirty-five years or so that the sea feeding grounds of the salmon have been located. Most salmon appear to congregate in the rich seas off Greenland and the Faroe Islands. They may spend anything from one to three years feeding at sea before undertaking the long migration. From here they migrate to the northern and eastern coasts of North America, southern Scandinavia, northern Scotland and the Bay of Biscay. Here they will seek the same small river or stream in which they were born, and then spawn in shallow gravel beds. Details of the navigational aids used as they migrate to, and find their way back from, the rivers in which they were hatched, is still something of a mystery.

adult male
in breeding
colours

adult female

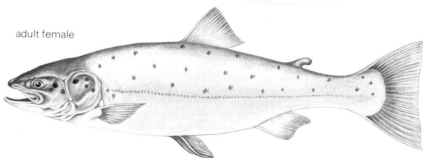

93

starts to shed his milt. The female covers the fertilised eggs with gravel as she moves up-stream and excavates another redd.

All fish that have just finished spawning are referred to as kelts until such time as they reach the sea. Some kelts return to the sea shortly after spawning, while others do not leave the river until March, April or even May, and only 3-5% return to spawn a second time in later years.

The young stages Throughout the long winter months the large, orange, yolk-filled eggs lie under 15cm (6in) or more of gravel and are washed over by cool, well-oxygenated water. The eggs develop 'eyes' by late January as the salmon embryos grow, the rate of development depending on water tempera-ture. By the end of March the young salmon or alevins break out of the egg and at first bear little resemblance to a fish, owing to the large yolk sac suspended from their 'stomach'. After a few weeks, their yolk sacs disappear and they become miniature fish, ready to feed.

The term 'fry' is given to salmon during their first year of life, at the end of which time they are called 'parr'. An interesting aspect in the life of the parr is that some of the males became sexually mature in the autumn. The testes of these fish develop fully and the milt from them is capable of fertilising the eggs shed by the adult female.

River departure The transformation from the parr to the 'smolt' stage starts in the spring when those parr which have reached a length of 10cm (4in) or more develop a silvery coat-ing on their scales and their tail fins become black, so that they look very much like miniature salmon. Many factors trigger off the downstream movement of smolts, in-cluding a rise in water temperature, and an increased river flow as a result of rain. It seems likely that smolts need some time to become acclimatised to the salt water, as they often remain in the estuary for a short time before entering the sea.

Enemies and diseases Like most fish, the salmon has a number of enemies. During its river life the main predators are pike, cormorant, goosander, red-breasted mer-

Stages of salmon growth

fry

parr

Fry is the name given to salmon after the alevin stage, up to one year old. Only 3-5% of fry reach the smolt stage, and only 6-10% of the smolts return to the river as adult salmon.

Parr are 1-3 year old salmon, easily recognised by the distinctive 'thumb' marks on their side, each separated by a red spot. The parr become silver in colour as they grow.

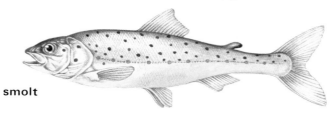

smolt

The smolt is the final stage in the development of the young salmon. The parr marks disappear, the markings of the silvery smolt now resembling those of the adult salmon. Smolts move downstream and feed in the estuary for a while, before entering the sea where they grow rapidly. Male fish have reached a length of 1.5m (59in), with a weight of 36kg (79lb), during their lifespan of 4-6 years.

ganser, heron, mink and otter. All these e parr and smolts; the pike and the goosand having the most serious effect on the stock young salmon. Only the otter regularly ki adult salmon, although cormorants have o occasion been recorded taking small salmo chiefly grilse. The most serious predator salmon at sea is the grey seal, which eats much as 7kg (15lb) of fish a day. Until viral epidemic hit the seal population 1988 attempts were made to control se numbers by annual culls of pups. This metho has always met with strong opposition, ar licensed culling is at present prohibited.

The two most serious diseases affectir salmon are furunculosis and ulcerative derm necrosis, or UDN for short. The former is bacterial disease which affects salmon durir the low water conditions of summer drough when the water temperature is high and t fish are concentrated in the rivers in lar shoals. It is not known for certain wh causes UDN, and although scientists hav studied the disease the organism responsib has not been found. Some believe it to be virus, while others suggest that it may l caused by sensitivity to solar radiation as result of some food they have consume Whatever the cause, the symptoms it pr duces are most unpleasant. Salmon are mo susceptible to such diseases as they a weakened by the efforts of their migrato journeys, and many fish die each year.

Below: Four day old alevins, their yolk sacs clearly visible. The eggs hatch after anything from 70-200 days, and the egg's yolk then nourishes the alevin for about six weeks, during which time it stays in the gravel and moves around very little. After this time the young salmon, now known as fry, start to feed on plankton.

THE TROUT: A FISH FOR ALL WATERS

The bewildering variety of colours, markings, sizes and habitats of the trout once led naturalists to recognise over ten separate species. Today it is regarded as a single species with two main forms: the non-migratory brown trout of rivers and lakes and the sea trout which migrates to sea and returns to spawn in the river in which it hatched.

Brown trout vary in colour from bright silver in lakes to very dark in muddy pools. This fish has adapted its colour and markings to its surroundings.

e brown trout favours fast-flowing rivers, eams or lakes, where the water is clean and s a reasonable amount of oxygen. Access to table spawning sites, which are usually in llow water with small sized pebbles form- the river bed, is also important.

In Britain the brown trout is therefore only turally scarce in the lower reaches of large land rivers. Otherwise it is a hardy fish viving even in the harshest moorland oks where other species would perish. Its ic colour is a greenish-brown on the back, h lighter sides and a paler yellow belly. The es also have black and red spots, some of ich may be circled with white. The trout ng in large lakes (sometimes called lake

trout) and rivers tend to be even lighter in coloration and larger than the brightly col-oured trout living in small streams.

The sea trout has the same general body shape but its colouring is strikingly different. Its back is silvery blue and the sides and belly brilliant silver, with a sprinkling of dark spots on the upper sides. It does not have the red spots which are so typical of the brown trout. The sea trout also tends to be very much larger. As its name implies, it is found in most of our coastal waters, particularly around estuaries, and in rivers.

Migration Brown trout are thought of as non-migratory, but even these trout move down river (ie migrate) from their nursery

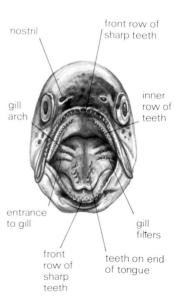

nostril

front row of sharp teeth

gill arch

inner row of teeth

entrance to gill

front row of sharp teeth

teeth on end of tongue

gill filters

streams, and others travel further into lakes. Sea trout, as their name implies, migrate to sea. Some trout, however, never leave the stream in which they were hatched. Those that move downstream do so between one and four years after hatching, in search of more food.

The young brown trout move downstream from the nursery area into large brooks. The fish have up to nine dark oval blotches (parr marks) on their flanks and at this stage are known as parr.

By tagging young trout it is possible to trace their movements; after migrating to lakes and larger rivers the mature trout return each year to their nursery streams to spawn. Sometimes large trout move up streams only deep enough for them to swim in for a few hours after heavy rain. Trout probably learn the chemical 'fingerprint' of their home stream soon after hatching and return to it because they know it is a place where successful spawning can take place. A few trout must, however, go astray or they would never be able to colonise new streams.

The young fish that migrate to sea are known as smolts; they are brilliant silver in colour. If you were to catch one at this stage you could rub off the silvery pigment with your fingers and the parr marks would be visible underneath. The smolts migrate in spring down rivers. They then spend several years in coastal waters before returning to

their native stream to spawn in successive years. One sea trout is known to have spawned 12 times and reached a size of 13kg (28lb).

Colour variations Essentially, all kinds of trout vary their colour to blend in with their environment by altering the proportions of pigments in their skin, a process which happens automatically as a result of the information the eyes receive about the colour of the fish's background. The colour of brown trout can vary dramatically depending on their surroundings; many trout in lakes are silvery whereas trout in peaty brooks can be almost black. With sea trout, should the young be prevented from migrating to sea, perhaps because of a man-made dam or an inflow of pollution, they remain in the river and stay indistinguishable in colour from the non-migratory brown trout.

Feeding The brown trout's diet contains many bottom-living organisms, but also includes aquatic animals drifting in midwater and on the surface. Some flying and land insects, which have fallen into the water or have been washed in during heavy rain, are also consumed.

Trout eat an enormous variety of invertebrates, including freshwater shellfish such as shrimps, pea mussels and water boatmen. In spring and summer they favour surface food and winged insects which alight on the water's surface. These include many species of caddis fly, mayfly and midge and it is imitations of

Above: Sea trout grow fas are larger and travel farthe than brown trout. The trou growth rate depends on th type and quantity of its fo Growth also depends on temperature. The sea trout (shown here) may attain a length of 1.4m (55in) and weight of 13.6kg (30lb). Brown trout in small brool will probably not grow lar than 23cm (9in), and thos which pass all their lives in the acid waters of larger Scottish lochs, where ther very little food, grow very slowly indeed, many takin six to eight years to reach 35cm (13in).

However, at the other extreme, in some shallow water lochs, trout turn to fish-eating at an early age, feeding on the land-locke shoals of arctic charr. Thes 'ferox trout' have been known to weigh as much 10kg (22lb) and live for between 15 and 20 years.

The life of the trout

adult brown trout 25cm (10in) long

Above: In autumn the female excavates a nest (redd) in a clean stream. By violently flexing her tail, the fish disturbs and shifts the gravel, leaving a saucer-like depression.

black and red spots on back and sides

male

female

clouds of sperm (milt)

eggs

eggs 4mm (1/8in) wide

Left: Males compete for the right to join a female by the redd, after which eggs and sperm are shed at the same time.
After spawning, the female fish moves upstream and covers the eggs to a depth of 5-10cm (2-4in with gravel (below); in so doing she excavates another redd—a process which is continued until all the eggs have been shed. Clean, oxygen-rich water passes through the redd and over the eggs, which take 60-150 days to develop

low: The rainbow trout is
t native to British waters,
t huge numbers are now
sed on fish farms, and
ny have also been
troduced to our lakes and
eams for the benefit of
glers. They feed on insects
d insect larvae, snails and
ariety of crustaceans. They
n attain a size of 1m (39in)
d a weight of up to 15.9kg
5lb).

these that the angler uses to catch trout. Adult trout also feed on many smaller fishes, even young trout and salmon. The sea trout feed on small fishes and crustaceans, and are themselves a target for larger fish such as cod and even seals. On return to fresh water they often bear scars left by unsuccessful predators.

The type of food eaten by trout makes a difference to the colour of the flesh. Brown trout which have fed heavily on crustaceans such as freshwater shrimps have orange coloured flesh, due to the presence of a carotene pigment in the shrimps. This is the reason why sea trout flesh is usually orange-red (as marine shrimps and prawns form a large part of their diet).

The over use of agricultural fertilizers and the discharge of treated sewage effluents into lakes has resulted in a form of pollution by enrichment which makes them less suitable for trout and more so for their fish predators and competitors. In rivers such pollution can blanket the trout's spawning grounds with silt.

As a result of these pressures rivers and lakes are often stocked with brown trout from hatcheries, in which the fish are artificially reared. Stocking takes place where trout would be unable to spawn naturally, for example in reservoirs, or to increase the number of trout in waters where they do occur naturally. Reservoirs are often stocked with quite small trout, whereas in rivers they will usually already be large enough for the angler to take. During the first few weeks after stocking these trout will be far easier to catch than the native fish because they are less wary and in the hatchery have become conditioned to feeding exclusively at the surface.

Rainbow trout Many still and running waters are stocked with the exotic rainbow trout (*Salmo gairdneri*) which was first introduced from the west coast rivers of the United States. It is easily distinguished from the brown trout by the prominent pink or mauve band along its flanks; and it is valued by anglers because it grows very quickly. The rainbow also has a seagoing form known as the steelhead.

e trout (*Salmo trutta*)
two main forms, chiefly
tinguished by their life
tory, the brown trout and
sea trout.
e of brown trout varies
h habitat, from about
cm (8in) in small streams
80cm (31in) in big lakes;
a trout generally larger).
eight of brown trout
ges similarly from 225g
b) to 2kg (4½lb); (sea
ut generally heavier).
espan 4-6 years on
erage.

Territorial fish Trout are territorial and the largest, dominant trout will occupy the best position or 'lie'. Favoured lies in rivers will be where a good food supply is brought down by the current and where it is sheltered, for example where the river bank has been undercut or where the fish is hidden by overhanging vegetation. When an angler catches a good sized trout from a lie it is often soon reoccupied by a smaller, previously subordinate fish.

Stocking Trout live in a hard world. Those which are not caught by anglers or taken by predators, such as mink, otters, herons or cormorants, face a range of threats from pollution and other man-made problems.

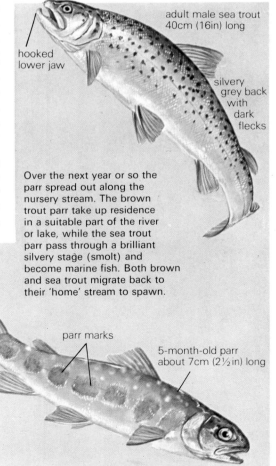

adult male sea trout
40cm (16in) long

hooked
lower jaw

silvery
grey back
with
dark
flecks

Over the next year or so the parr spread out along the nursery stream. The brown trout parr take up residence in a suitable part of the river or lake, while the sea trout parr pass through a brilliant silvery stage (smolt) and become marine fish. Both brown and sea trout migrate back to their 'home' stream to spawn.

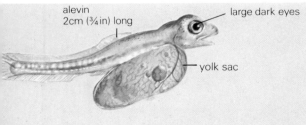

alevin
2cm (¾in) long

large dark eyes

yolk sac

Above: Newly hatched trout (alevins) feed on their yolk sacs for 2-4 weeks. When about 2cm (1in) long, the yolk being almost used up, the young trout must leave the redd and seek food such as water fleas.

Right: Young trout (parr) have thumbprint-like marks on their sides. Parr are highly territorial and defend an area a few centimetres across.

parr marks

5-month-old parr
about 7cm (2½in) long

THE CHARR: STRANDED LAKE FISH

The colourful charr, one of the migratory fishes we know was left behind after the last ice age, has adapted successfully to its 'prisons' in the mountainous lakes of Britain.

The charr is a member of the same family as the trout and salmon and its general features resemble those of its relatives. Its slender, streamlined body is covered with scales, its fins lack spines and it has the characteristic rayless, adipose (fatty) fin on its back just in front of its tail fin. The most obvious difference between the charr and the trout and salmon, however, is that the charr has very much smaller scales.

Brilliant colour Although relatively little known, the charr is probably the most brilliantly coloured fish in our fauna. The back is usually olive or brownish and the belly silvery white, orange or even crimson (the deep red colour being typical of males in the breeding season). Pink or orange spots are scattered along the sides and the fins, while the ventral fins are reddish with the leading edge white in contrast. Colouring may differ from lake to lake with the seasons and as the fish grows; and males in the spawning season (winter or early spring) are almost unbelievably bright.

It is in recognition of this coloration that the Welsh name for charr (which live in Llyn Perris and Padarn) is *torgoch*, meaning red belly. Even the name charr may be derived from its red underside, since in Gaelic *ceara* is red and *cear* blood.

Trapped in lakes The charr is widely distributed in the mountain lakes of northern and western Britain. In Wales it is found only in lakes close to Snowdonia, and in England only in the Lake District, while there are large numbers of Scottish lochs, mainly in the Highlands, with charr in them. It also occurs on the Hebridean island of Lewis, and on Shetland. In Ireland it is found mostly in the west coast loughs. The charr's origin in the hundred or so lakes in which it occurs is of some interest, for it is believed that each population was isolated some time after the last ice age.

In Iceland and along the Norwegian coast, as well as Greenland and Canada, the charr is migratory, feeding in the sea but returning to fresh water to spawn – just as the salmon does.

During the ice ages charr were forced further south than where they are found today and it can be assumed that they were migratory off the British coast, passing from the sea into rivers to spawn. As the ice retreated further north, some are presumed to have lost their migratory habit and spent the whole of their lives in the rivers and adjacent lakes, until changes in the level of land relative to the sea trapped them in individual lakes or river systems.

This happened between 8000 and 10,000 years ago. Since then, each population has adapted to the ecosystem within which it lives. Some lakes are food-poor; some are rich in potential food. Some are deep; others are shallow. Some are acid; others, on account of the rocks around them, are alkaline. These, and other factors, have all had an effect on

Above: All native charr in Britain live in lakes in mountainous regions. In Wales the fish is found onl in the lakes close to Snowdonia, such as here a Llyn Idwal. The charr has managed to exist in its ofte food-poor lakes for thousands of years, but its survival is precarious.

e charr, which have had to adapt to survive
1 the surroundings in which they found
iemselves.

As a result, fish from one lake may look
omewhat different from those of other lakes.
o great are the differences, in fact, that in the
arly 20th century as many as 15 different
pecies or subspecies were recognized in the
ritish Isles, many of which could only be
identified if one knew in advance which lake
hey came from. The modern practice, how-
ver, is to ignore all the different names and
eat the British charr as part of the species
alvelinus alpinus, which occurs across much
f northern Europe and northern North
merica.

Smaller in lakes One of the most striking
eatures consequent upon living in lakes is the
mall size of the charr. Few lake charr grow
onger than 12in (30cm) and only in ex-
eptionally rich lakes do they attain a weight
f more than 3lb (1.3kg). In contrast, in those
arts of the world where the charr migrates to
ie sea, it grows to a length of 39in (1m) and
p to 27lb (12.2kg) in weight.

Spawning seasons Lake charr spawn in
inter or early spring. In Lake Windermere
e winter spawners lay their eggs in water
3-10ft (1-3m) on gravel shallows in Nov-
mber and December, while the spring
pawners shed their eggs in 66-96ft (20-30m)
water between February and March. Some
her lakes have two spawning races, but
ost have just one or the other.

Their eggs are relatively large (4-5mm in
ameter) and are buried in the gravel,
veloping slowly until they hatch in the
ring. Growth rates vary enormously from
ke to lake. In Windermere charr spawn at
 age of five to six years, while in food-poor
kes they may be 10 or 12 years old before
ey mature. In the Scandinavian Arctic lakes
imature fish of 20 years have been found.

Charr tend to eat whatever suitable food
ey can find in their home lake. In Britain
is means their diet, especially when young,
 confined to copepods and crustaceans
ater fleas) and insect larvae, particularly
idges, and freshwater shrimps. Large charr
ay eat other fish, but in general these tend

to be scarce in the lakes inhabited by charr.

Fight for survival Unfortunately, for all
their beauty charr are always on the border-
line between survival and non-survival. Several lakes known to have contained them no
longer do so, among them Lough Neagh in
Ireland in which they became extinct in the
early 1800s.

Many of man's activities are detrimental to
the survival of charr. Possibly the most harmful is the discharge of domestic or farm sewage
into the lakes, this enrichment causing a
change in the fauna detrimental to this fish.
Another serious hazard is the introduction of
other fish species to their lakes. Among these,
the pike, perch and trout are obviously
harmful as predators, while other fish compete
for food. Acid rain, due to pollution, has also
affected the delicate balance of alkalinity in
some lakes and is particularly serious in
Scandinavia. Water storage systems and
hydro-electric schemes may pose another
threat. Llyn Peris in North Wales is now used
to generate electricity; though this does not
appear to have affected the local fauna.

All over the northern hemisphere the survival of populations of the charr is under
threat. Although the species as a whole is not
threatened, many lake populations are. As
each of these has evolved in genetic isolation
for thousands of years, the loss of any one is
significant bringing the charr just a little
bit closer to extinction.

Above: The colourful charr
(*Salvelinus alpinus*). There
has been some disagreement
about the spelling of the
fish's common name. When
Francis Willughby first
described the populations in
Lake Windermere in his
Historia Piscium (1686), he
spelt it 'charre'. In the 19th
century it was corrupted to
'char', but is now spelt
'charr'.

Below: The charr shows
some similarities with its
relatives, the trout and
salmon. Apart from having
much smaller scales,
however, it also has no
teeth on the mid-line of the
roof of its mouth. It does
have distinct and sharp
teeth on the front of its
palate, as do the trout and
salmon which also have a
staggered double row of
teeth in the middle of the
palate.

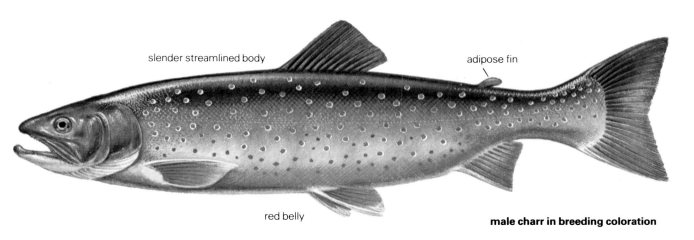

slender streamlined body
adipose fin
red belly
male charr in breeding coloration

THREE MOUNTAIN BUTTERFLIES

The mountainous regions of Britain–barren and inhospitable tracts of land–are the home of three attractive species of butterflies: the mountain ringlet (renowned for the effective way it protects itself from hungry predators at all times), the scotch argus and the large heath.

The mountains of Europe, endowed with rich alpine meadows, support a wide variety of plants and insects – a claim we cannot make in Britain since the chief characteristics of our uplands are poor quality grasslands and bogs. Nevertheless three species of British butterflies do manage to thrive in these bleak and inhospitable conditions. They are the scotch argus, the mountain ringlet and the large heath. All are 'brown' butterflies, members of the family Satyridae, and are only found in northern Britain.

Scotland's mountain butterfly As its name implies, the scotch argus is found throughout Scotland, although it also occurs in three localities in Cumbria in northern England.

Within Scotland it is often found on marshy hillsides in mountainous areas, and in sheltered, rough grassland. Here the adults can sometimes be seen flying in the sunshine, but at other times they remain deep down in the grassy tussocks.

From a distance these dark brown butterflies appear rather drab, but a closer look reveals their rich deep velvety-brown colour, shot with reds and purples, which contrasts with rust-red marginal bands with prominent black and white eye-spots. These bands are particularly conspicuous on the paler females.

The female lays her relatively large eggs singly on the larval food-plant – purple moorgrass. In common with all the 'browns', the

Left: Since flowers can be few and far between on the poor mountainous terrain where the scotch argus (*Erebia aethiops*) is found the adults feed on a wide variety of plants – this butterfly is drinking nectar from a bramble flower. The caterpillars are more particular, however, feeding entirely on purple moorgrass, a plant which grows abundantly on mountain slopes in Scotland.

The mountain ringlet's extra 'eyes'

The eye-spots are arranged on the wings so that the attention of birds is always deflected away from the vulnerable body.

a)

When in flight – and therefore exposed to predators – the eye-spots on the upper wing surfaces are conspicuous.

b)

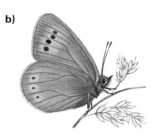

On landing (a) the upper wing surfaces are briefly displayed. The wings are then closed (b) to reveal the under-forewing spots.

c)

If unmolested after a further few seconds, the forewings are folded inside the hindwings (c) to leave a camouflaged exterior.

Colour variation—north to south

The large heath butterfly varies in wing colouring according to where it lives—a phenomenon known as 'clinal variation'. The butterflies from most of Scotland are poorly marked and pale, those from the Scottish borders, northern England, the Western Isles and Ireland are slightly darker with more eye-spots, while specimens from Lancashire and Wales are heavily spotted and the darkest. The causes of this are uncertain, but it may be a response to climate and 'predation pressure'—the higher altitude butterflies with less spots are exposed to fewer insectivorous birds.

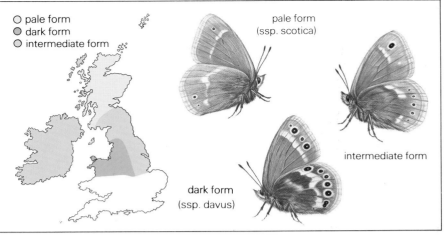

○ pale form
● dark form
◐ intermediate form

pale form
(ssp. scotica)

intermediate form

dark form
(ssp. davus)

---

erpillars are shades of green or light brown h pale longitudinal stripes. They feed ring the summer nights, and then crawl ep down into the turf in October to hiber- e for the long harsh winter.

On waking up the following spring, they ume feeding and are fully grown in July, en they form chrysalids in loose cocoons the ground. The adults finally emerge in e July and can be seen flying around in ny weather until late September.

Solo alpine species The small mountain glet is our only true alpine butterfly since is rarely found below 550m (1800ft), and restricted to the mountains of Cumbria, gyll, Inverness and Perth. Despite inhabit- some of the wettest places in Britain, with re than 5100mm (200in) annual rainfall, s species is a sun-loving butterfly, and s only when the sun is out. It is therefore narkable that the butterflies manage to oliferate when cold mists may shroud the lsides for weeks during their mating son.

Adult mountain ringlets are a rich deep own colour, appearing almost black when shly emerged from the pupae. Their dark louring maximises heat absorption when ey bask in the sun—a process necessary to se their body temperature and enable them become active.

During these fleeting sunny spells, the ults channel their energies into finding a

Right: The large heath butterfly (*Coenonympha tullia*) is found on damp boggy moorland. Sadly its numbers are dwindling in England as a result of land reclamation and drainage schemes—in the past it occurred as far south as Derbyshire, but nowadays it is found in only a few localities in Cumbria, **Northumberland, Yorkshire, Shropshire and Humberside. However, in Scotland the large heath butterfly still thrives on the lowland areas of blanket bogs. It also has a wide distribution in Ireland, and occurs in a few sites in North and Central Wales.**

Below: Despite inhabiting some of the wettest parts of Britain, the small mountain ringlet (*Erebia epiphron*) is a sun-loving species, flying only in bright sunshine. A cloud only has to pass across the sun to make this butterfly disappear.

mate and laying eggs. The males avidly seek out females, flying low over the turf to avoid being blown away from the colony site by strong winds. The eggs, which the females lay on mat grass, are large to provide the young caterpillars with sufficient food reserves when they hatch into the hostile environment. Like the caterpillars of the scotch argus, they feed during the summer and then hibernate from the end of August until the following March, eventually completing their development by June.

Bog butterfly The final species associated with upland Britain is the large heath butter-fly. While it has been recorded as high as 760m (2500ft), it is generally found at all altitudes on wet ground. A characteristic plant of this terrain—cottongrass—is thought to be the foodplant of the large heath cater-pillars.

Like the other two mountain species, the caterpillars hibernate over the winter and take one year to complete their life-cycle. The adults appear any time from June to August, depending on how far north or south the population is.

MAYFLIES & STONEFLIES

Throughout the summer you can see mayflies flying over rivers, lakes and some ponds. Stoneflies have a more limited range, but you can find them near fast-flowing upland streams in the north and west.

Adult mayflies and stoneflies–both groups of aquatic insects–have in common a very short lifespan. Mayflies, referred to by the poet Shelley as creatures 'gathered into death without a dawn', often live less than a day, while stoneflies live perhaps a week or two. This brief existence is, however, compensated for at the nymph stage. Many mayfly nymphs take about a year to complete their metamorphosis, while others, such as *Ephemera*, take two or more years. Stoneflies spend one to three years at the nymph stage, depending on the species. In both groups of insects, metamorphosis is incomplete, with no pupal stage.

Mayflies mainly frequent lakes, streams and rivers, but a few occur round ponds. Stoneflies, on the other hand, prefer clear, fast-flowing streams or the wave-washed shores of lakes, although a few species are found in still or reedy water. In the British Isles there are 47 species of mayfly, and 34 species of stonefly.

Adult life Adult mayflies can be recognised by their two or three long tails (cerci), short bristle-like antennae and large, delicate forewings. Their hind wings are much smaller than the front pair, and a few have none at all. Mayflies always hold their wings upright over the body, even when at rest as they are unable to fold them.

It is rare to find mayflies far from water. Their flight is weak and, unless blown by the wind, they stay close to the stretch of water from which they hatched. The males are famous for their 'dancing' or nuptial swarms. They emerge from their nymphal stage in late May to September and congregate over the water in huge numbers, rising and falling in a spectacular dancing flight. The females join them and mating, lasting a few minutes, takes place in the air.

Like mayflies, many stoneflies possess long tails, but they have only two, never three. Their antennae are long. They have two pairs of heavily veined wings, the hind pair being shorter and wider than the fore pair. The position of the wings at rest distinguishes stoneflies from mayflies. The wings fold flat over the body, or roll tightly round it, giving

Above: Subimago of the mayfly *Ephemera danica*. It will moult one final time t become fully adult. This species reaches 15-20mm (¾in) in size (excluding tails Fishermen call the subimag a dun and the adult insect a spinner.

Left: Egg clusters of a *Baeti.* mayfly under a submerged stone. A female can lay hundreds of eggs in a day.

Right: Mayfly nymph *Ephemera vulgata* – note the three long tail filaments.

102

neflies their typical long slender appearance. The males of some species are almost ~~n~~gless, or have short wings, and therefore not fly. Even the fully winged females are ~~rel~~uctant to take to the air, having a weak, ~~un~~steady flight. Both male and female prefer ~~to~~ crawl among stones on river banks or lake ~~sh~~ores–hence their common name. Mating ~~ta~~kes place on the ground.

Adult mayflies do not feed–there is little ~~ne~~ed since they live for so short a time. Some ~~ad~~ult stoneflies do not feed either, while ~~ot~~hers may occasionally take flower pollen or ~~pe~~rhaps algae scraped from stones.

The female mayfly lays her eggs after mating ~~in~~ the nuptial swarm. The method she uses ~~va~~ries from species to species: some drop the ~~eg~~gs straight into the water, others settle on ~~th~~e water, dip their abdomen in and release ~~th~~e eggs, while yet others crawl down a water ~~pl~~ant and deposit the eggs on a submerged ~~st~~one or other object.

There are a variety of different forms of ~~ma~~yfly nymph. In still water habitats some are ~~bu~~rrowers in mud or sand–such as species of ~~Ep~~*hemera* which have shovel-like fore-legs ~~an~~d dagger-shaped upper jaws for digging. ~~Ot~~hers, streamlined in shape and agile, ~~cl~~amber about in the vegetation (*Cloëon* for ~~ex~~ample); members of yet another group– ~~Ca~~*enis*–live on the bottom. In fast streams or ~~riv~~ers some, such as *Ephemerella*, inhabit ~~m~~oss and other plants, while others, *Baetis* ~~fo~~r example, are active swimming types.

The nymphs can be distinguished easily by ~~th~~eir three long tail filaments. In some ~~sp~~ecies, the middle filament degenerates at the ~~fin~~al moult, and the resulting adult insects ~~ha~~ve only two tails. All the nymphs have ~~tr~~acheal gills situated on the abdominal seg-

ments of the body. In some species these can absorb oxygen directly from the water, whereas in others the gills serve only as paddles which maintain a constant flow of water over the body–respiration taking place through the 'skin'. The nymphs feed mainly on plant material, especially algae on stones.

The creature that emerges from the nymphal skin is not a fully developed adult (imago) but a winged 'subimago' which moults to give a true adult. This moulting of a winged stage is unique to mayflies. The whole body of the subimago, including the wings, is covered in a transparent skin which dulls the colouring. After a few hours this skin is moulted and the full colouring and glistening wings are revealed.

Most stonefly nymphs require clear, unpolluted lakes or fast-flowing streams with stony, gravelly bottoms for successful development.

The adults emerge and mate mainly between March and August. Stonefly eggs, 'glued' together with a sticky substance, are attached in a mass to the tip of the female's abdomen and she runs along the water or dips the abdomen into it so that the egg mass breaks up and the eggs sink to the bottom. The nymphs hatch in anything from three weeks to three months, depending on the species, and they live under stones, in vegetation or in the sand or gravel at the bottom of the stream.

These nymphs can be distinguished by their two long tail filaments and by their slow, creeping, rather sluggish movement when disturbed. Smaller species are mainly herbivorous, while larger ones tend to be carnivorous.

In larger species of stonefly–*Perla* and *Dinocras* for example–the nymphal stage may last for three years, but in smaller species this stage lasts a year. When the nymph is ready to emerge, it crawls out of the water up a plant stem, stone or perhaps the support of a bridge. Its skin splits down the back of the head and thorax, and the adult insect draws itself out slowly and laboriously.

Above: Adult stonefly *Dinocras cephalotes* with empty nymph case. The adult is about 15-20mm (¾in) long. The nymph, known as a creeper, crawls about on the river bed.

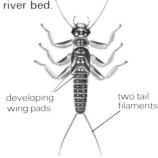

developing wing pads
two tail filaments

Above: Stonefly nymph *Perlodes microcephala*, about 20mm (¾in) long, lives in stony rivers and streams.

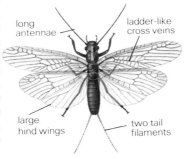

long antennae
ladder-like cross veins
large hind wings
two tail filaments

Above: Adult female stonefly *Perlodes microcephala* with wings outspread. By contrast with the female, the male has no wings and cannot fly. The female, however, is reluctant to take to the air and has a weak flight.

Birds of mountain and moorland

For the birdwatcher mountains are marvellously exciting places because the birds, though often sparse, are unfamiliar, most of those occurring being of exceptional interest or beauty.

For many years, up until recently, our large mountain birds of prey have been declining in numbers for a complex variety of reasons, including pesticides, persecution, egg-collecting and changes in agricultural practice. At last, though, there are signs of a revival – though it is not all one way – and more liberal and sensible attitudes are beginning to prevail. Our most magnificent bird, the golden eagle, has recently started to colonize the mountains of northern England; the osprey has been a success story, building from the first pair in 1959 to over 50 pairs regularly breeding now; peregrines have returned to their pre-war levels; hen harriers have spread southwards dramatically; and white-tailed eagles have now begun to breed in the wild as a result of a re-introduction programme. At the same time, several less obvious species are beginning to re-establish themselves in the highlands, among them the wood sandpiper, snow-bunting, redwing and Temminck's stint, and possible re-colonizers include such Arctic species as the Lapland bunting and long-tailed skua.

Smaller birds occur at higher densities than the predators, for some insect and plant food may be abundant for a short period. The meadow pipit is probably the commonest bird overall, but such birds as twites, linnets, skylarks and ring-ouzels all do well.

Inevitably, though, the bird world is dominated by those species managed by man, particularly the red grouse, and this one species has a strong influence on the appearance and land use of many upland areas, especially in eastern Scotland.

Left: A pair of merlins — note that the female is somewhat larger than the male. Our smallest bird of prey, the merlin dwells in the far north and west of the British Isles, flying low over open, hilly moorlands in search of prey.

CHECKLIST

This checklist is a guide to some of the birds you will find on mountains and moorlands. Although you will not see them all in the same place, you should be able to spot many of them throughout the changing seasons. The species listed in **bold type** *are described in detail.*

Black grouse
Buzzard
Chough
Dotterel
Golden eagle
Golden plover
Greenshank
Grey plover
Hen harrier
Lapland bunting
Linnet
Meadow pipit
Merlin
Osprey
Peregrine falcon
Ptarmigan
Raven
Red grouse
Redwing
Ring ouzel
Rock pipit
Skylark
Snow bunting
Snowy owl
Temminck's stint
Twite
Wheatear
White-tailed sea eagle
Wood sandpiper

Left: The golden plover —
here seen in all the glory of
its breeding dress — frequents
southern coastal marshes and
inland fields in the winter,
but in spring heads for our
upland hills and moors to
breed among the heather.

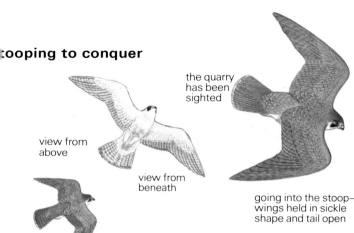

ooping to conquer

the quarry
has been
sighted

view from
above

view from
beneath

going into the stoop—
wings held in sickle
shape and tail open

the tight stoop—tail and
wings closed and flight
starting to level off

PEREGRINE: PRINCE OF BIRDS

Among all the birds there is none to rival the peregrine falcon in its powers of flight nd devastating speed when it hunts its prey.

erything about the peregrine falcon con-
ys strength and power. It has powerful
oulders, a short neck, broad chest, large
es, immensely strong legs and dispropor-
nately large feet armed with formidable
ons. The dark eyes, framed in a bright
low orbital ring, are of enormous size,
cupying a large part of the skull, and give
e peregrine visual acuity at least four times
sharp as that of humans. The slate grey
perparts of the adults, and the bold black
oustachial stripe, contrast with the pale,
ely barred underparts.

t is on the wing, however, that the full
jesty and speed of the peregrine has to be
n to be fully appreciated. In silhouette
m below, as you would normally see it, it
sickle-shaped and heavily built, with a
ort tail and neck. In level flight it has the
oid wing-beat shared by other falcons such
kestrels and merlins, but it also soars and
des high above the hillsides and sea cliffs
ere it lives.

n its famous 'stooping' dive, in which the
regrine attacks its quarry (principally other
ds), it has been estimated that the bird
y reach speeds of between 150 and
Omph, depending on the angle of descent.
level flight the peregrine can attain 60mph
more, with short bursts of speed up to
mph. But whatever the hunting method it
ploys—whether it is the stoop or a strike
wards from below—the passing silhouette

Above: The peregrine feeds almost exclusively on other birds up to the size of a grouse or pigeon, catching them on the wing by sheer force and speed. The most dramatic technique is the stoop, in which the peregrine, having gained height above the quarry, closes its wings and accelerates at breathtaking speed in a stooping dive of several hundred feet or more to hit the unfortunate prey with its talons in a bone-shaking flurry of feathers.

Peregrine falcon (*Falco peregrinus*); resident bird of prey haunting cliffs and mountains. Male 38cm (15in), female 46cm (18in).

Below: An immature female peregrine; it lacks the adults' black 'moustache' and slate grey upperparts.

the catch and lift-off—
the quarry is killed with
a blow from the hind toe

these chemicals responsible for killing ma~~~ song birds, their persistent nature was al~ affecting predatory birds higher up the fo~ chain. Other birds of prey – sparrowhawk~ barn owls, kestrels – were also affected, b~ it was the peregrine decline that warned of t~ grave consequences of the extensive use ~ these chemicals. Government action led ~ a reduction in the use of the most damagi~ poisons and slowly the population, by no~ reduced to a shadow of its former leve~ levelled off and then began a slow upturn.

Through the 1970s this increase speeded ~ and the remarkable resilience of the peregri~ has been demonstrated by its recent recove~ in Britain to its pre-war numbers. Ov~ wide areas of its northern range, howeve~ both in Europe and North America, t~ peregrine has virtually disappeared. It ~ listed as an endangered species and t~ British population assumes an ever great~ international importance. At present the~ are over 800 pairs breeding in Britain.

Cliff and mountain dweller Essentially t~ peregrine is a bird of open country. By t~ nature of its hunting methods it is ill-equipp~ to deal with birds that can take refuge in t~ cover of woodland or elsewhere, and it nee~ to fly down its prey where there is the le~ chance of losing it once the hunt is under wa~ Much of Britain is therefore suitable count~ for the peregrine, but the bird's distributi~ is restricted for much of the year by the ne~ to find nesting ledges on steep rock faces – ~ is almost exclusively a cliff-nesting species ~ Britain. Its breeding strongholds are t~ mountains and cliff-bound coasts of Scotlan~ Wales, Ireland and the south-west peninsu~ of England. Here there are nest sites ~ abundance and an endless supply of small ~ birds as prey.

Nowhere is the peregrine more at hor~ than in the mountains and cliffs of the w~ and north of our islands. Both inland and ~ the coasts, pigeons, especially stray homi~ birds, are the favoured prey, but the ran~ of species taken is very much wider, includi~ birds as large as the shelduck and malla~ and as small as house martins and finches.

Many individuals stay in the vicinity ~

of the predatory peregrine casts a feared shadow on the ground. It can induce panic in flocks of wildfowl or waders, occasionally putting them into the air to fly at great heights, sometimes for hours on end, and on the ground, nesting grouse, plover and lapwing crouch motionless as the lethal sickle shadow passes over.

Decline and rise The story of the peregrine falcon has not been one of unrestricted success, especially in recent decades for, in the 1960s, it became clear that there was something seriously amiss with the British population.

Ironically, the first signs of this were picked up when a national survey of peregrines was carried out in 1961, following a petition to the Home Office by pigeon fanciers who claimed that increasing peregrine numbers were making serious inroads into their homing pigeon stocks. The evidence from the 1961 survey showed clearly that there was in fact a serious reduction in pairs and that, in southern Britain, but less so in the north, peregrines were in headlong decline. By 1962 the number of breeding territories occupied was a mere 56% of the total at the beginning of World War II.

As investigations continued, attention focused on the presence of several synthetic agricultural chemicals being used in seed dressings, principally DDT and the related dieldrin group of pesticides. Not only were

Above: A peregrine family at their cliff-ledge nest. The female is on the left, the male on the right, while the chick, which has not yet lost its grey downy covering, is furthest from the edge. Occasionally peregrines choose to nest in strange places. Some have recently prospected Salisbury Cathedral in Wiltshire, but failed to find a suitable ledge.

Below: The peregrine can look pretty untidy when it is moulting.

eir breeding cliffs throughout the winter, rtainly for as long as the flow of food mains, but others, perhaps predominantly ung birds, wander further afield and turn in river valleys and coastal marshes well ay from the breeding area. Here they take daily toll of the flocks of wildfowl and ders and can often be found using regular rches on flood-drifted logs or fence posts.

Pairs and breeding As in most birds of ey, the female peregrine is markedly larger an the male—as much as 15% in some cases. is sexual size difference means that the nale, measurably the more powerful of the ir, is better adapted for taking the largest od items, although the male (called the rcel) is quicker and more agile.

Peregrines normally pair for life and they d their descendants use the same nest ledge r a series of alternative sites) with great elity generation after generation. Some es have been used for many hundreds of ars and a remarkable fact was that, after ds began to return to the areas from which ey had been wholly eliminated in the 1960s,

Above: A peregrine in flight —the essence of aerial power and majesty, and awe-inspiring to watch.

Below: A female peregrine feeding her chick. A brood of three or four chicks is usual for peregrines.

the re-establishing pairs began to occupy the same ledges that their forebears had always used.

Once winter is on the retreat, by late February, occupation of the breeding cliff becomes more regular and the pairs increasingly hunt together in the early morning to satisfy their daily food needs. Successful hunting is often followed by spectacular display flights by the tiercel, careering, speeding, twisting and plummeting over and in front of the breeding cliffs. Mutual chasing often takes place and can be breath-taking in its speed and agility. As in many other bird species, the male feeds the female at this period as part of the process of strengthening the bond between the pair.

Mating takes place three weeks before the laying of eggs, and the first eggs appear in the south of Britain before the end of March. Incubation, predominantly carried out by the female, especially in the early stages, begins around the time when the third egg is laid. A full clutch is usually three or four eggs, occasionally five. They are normally laid at intervals of two days, and are mottled and spotted in different shades of reddish brown.

Incubation takes about 30 days and the newly hatched young are tended with great attention by the female peregrine. During the 40-day fledging period the young birds grow rapidly, passing through a grey downy stage when they appear ungainly and immobile. Over the last two weeks of fledging they develop the brown juvenile plumage. The young males leave the nest first.

The contribution of the female to hunting is small at this time and it is the male who provides for the female and the growing brood on the cliff ledge, although from the third week onwards the increasing demands of the young require the female to hunt.

Prospects The future of the peregrine in Britain at present is bright, and this is one of the few areas of the world where the peregrine population has actually increased over recent years. Nevertheless both here and in the rest of the world, the potential problems of human robbery, persecution and toxic contamination remain.

The sport of Kings

Falconry has been practised for over 4000 years and it is reasonable to guess that trained peregrines would have featured from early times. In Britain the Middle Ages were the golden age of falconry, and in the hierarchy of the sport the peregrine was at the very pinnacle, valued above all other birds for its lordly powers of flight and for the size of prey to which it could be directed. Game birds were its principal quarry. The birds were taken to the field hooded and tethered (right). Falconry still has a minority following today and many falconers have a deep knowledge of peregrines in the wild.

OSPREYS: HIGHLAND RARITIES

The osprey has suffered from ruthless persecution by egg collectors and gamekeepers but, since the return of the first breeding pair in 1959, numbers are now increasing.

e osprey is supreme among those birds of y that hunt fish; it hunts and breeds cessfully in many parts of the world and is l equipped to find all its food in water.

Plunging for prey The bird has a striking pearance: the white undersides of its body 1 wings contrast sharply with its rich wn upper plumage; and its length of 60cm t) is dwarfed by enormous angular wings ich, when fully spread, measure 145cm t). It is capable of catching and carrying ay fishes of several pounds in weight, but arely seizes the larger ones: most frequently akes fishes between ½lb and 1lb (230-450g). The osprey's plunge-dive is an awe-inspir- sight. It searches slowly over the water for table prey and when it has found a likely tim it banks, circles and hovers. Basking surface-swimming fishes of many species, h as pike, perch, trout or carp, are all en by the osprey. Quickly it enters a ceful plunge, at the end of which it takes selected victim in its talons. Often the dive airly gradual, but sometimes it is almost tical; and often the osprey plunges from ghts of 16m (50ft) or more.

As the bird strikes the water, it thrusts its ons forward to take the fish (at the same e they help to absorb the impact of hitting water). The osprey holds its wings high as nters the water. It is thought that the bird dom dives deeper than 1m (3ft), and usually es a far shorter distance below the surface. most immediately it rises from the water in for, provided that the dive has been formed well, the bird has little difficulty in aining the air.

Terrible talons The feet of the osprey are cially adapted to assist it in seizing and aining such slippery prey as fishes. The t and legs are particularly large and power- ; the claws are strongly curved, and the dersides of the feet are equipped with spiny les that grip the body of the fish. Perhaps st remarkable of all is that one of the four s is completely reversible – the osprey can n it either backwards or forwards. With toe pointing back, alongside the true hind , the osprey can hold a fish securely by two ws in front and two behind. Once it has

risen from the water, the osprey turns the fish so as to hold it in a fore-and-aft position and carries it away to eat it at leisure. Ospreys digest even the bones of fishes without difficulty.

From the edge of extinction In the late 1980s over 50 pairs of ospreys were known to be breeding in Britain, all of them in the Scottish Highlands. For over 40 years in the first half of this century, this splendid bird was extinct as a breeding species – a result of ruthless persecution, mainly by egg collect- ors. The eggs were considered a great prize by enthusiasts, whose determination to build up their collections led to the disappearance of the species from Britain.

Another major cause of the decline of the osprey in Britain over the past 200 years was the fact that it depends on fishes for its living. Gamekeepers and water bailiffs assumed that this made the osprey a serious competitor with man for the fishes in Britain's rivers and lakes. The latter part of the 19th century was a particularly ruthless period of game pre- servation and unbridled destruction of any

Osprey (*Pandion haliaetus*). Rare summer visitor, the 1980s have seen an increase to over 50 pairs. Breeding in the Highlands of Scotland. Two or three eggs, richly marked in reddish brown or chocolate colour. Length 60cm (2ft), wingspan 1.4m (5ft).

distinctive white underside of body and wings

fish carried head-first in flight

soaring in search of prey

Opposite: The large nest is made of sticks and a typical site is in the top branches of a Scots pine or other tree. Ospreys have been known to build nests on tall buildings or high cliffs. The two birds seen in this nest are juveniles.

plunge-dive may be nearly vertical

wings raised and talons lowered as bird nears water

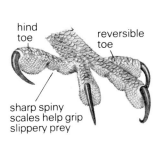

hind toe

reversible toe

sharp spiny scales help grip slippery prey

115

Above: A female feeding her young. At first only the male fishes, but later both parents are needed to find food for the growing family.

Below: Mating begins soon after the female has arrived in the nesting area.

wildlife that seemed to threaten stocks of game fishes such as trout and salmon.

Even today, following its return to the Highlands, the osprey has not been slow to learn the attractions of modern fish farms, and has sometimes caused losses to the owners of these enterprises. However, fish farmers normally have no difficulty in scaring off the ospreys, while many are prepared tolerate the presence of these beautiful a rare birds, provided their visits are reasona short.

After its period of extinction, the osp quite unexpectedly made its appearance Scotland in 1955, visiting but not breed during four successive seasons. Then in 19 a pair of ospreys raised a brood at a site in RSPB reserve at Loch Garten in Speysi in Scotland's Highland region. The RS set up a visitor centre at Loch Garten, that while the ospreys regularly breed in safety of the reserve, thousands of visit each year have the chance to see th majestic birds without causing them unc disturbance. The centre has become one the most exciting wildlife facilities provic for the public in Britain.

Summer in Scotland The Highlands Scotland are the only part of Britain wh ospreys breed. Here, a multitude of fre water lochs and an unlimited choice of si able nesting sites are available. Typically osprey's nest is built on top of a Scots pi but other species of tree and different sites sometimes chosen. Some of the legend Scottish sites in the last century were ruined island castles. In coastal areas, nest is sometimes on a cliff or an offsh pinnacle of rock.

In the Highlands, ospreys may tra several miles from one water to another

d better fishing if the need arises. Although
e British population is essentially a fresh-
ter one, ospreys in some other parts of the
rld are exclusively coastal birds, and feed
sea and in shallow estuary waters.

The Scottish birds return from wintering
early or mid April–the older, more ex-
rienced birds arriving first. Once a pair of
preys has settled at the nesting site–the
le sometimes arriving a few days ahead of
e female–they start to breed. The male
dertakes all the fishing, while the female
nains close to the nest. A spectacular sight
this time is the male's thrilling aerial
play of soaring, swooping and undulating
ht, which he accompanies with shrill calls.
ating occurs frequently up to the start of
ubation, and begins from the first days
er the female's arrival. Two or three eggs,
ich are marked with rich brown or choco-
e coloured flecks, are laid; they are in-
oated for five weeks, and the young hatch
intervals corresponding with the two or
ee day interludes between laying.

World-wide species The osprey is one of
e most widely distributed birds in the
rld, breeding all across the temperate
itudes of the northern hemisphere. There
e some coastal populations of ospreys in
Mediterranean and North African region
d in many parts of the Far East as well as
stralia. In North America, where there are
th coastal and inland populations, a highly
ccessful method of attracting ospreys to
st in a given neighbourhood has been
veloped. Osprey wheels–usually cartwheels
re set up on top of poles, and the birds soon
gin to settle on them.

The northern breeding birds are strongly
gratory and, as the fishes move deeper
ow the water surface with the arrival of
tumn, the ospreys set off on the long flight
West Africa. Recoveries of ringed birds–
eral of these proving to be the victims of
nters–indicate their route through Iberia
d north-west Africa to Mauritania and the
mbia. Ospreys en route for the south are
quently seen in many parts of England
d Wales (presumably some of these are
andinavian birds), and they are also seen
ing north on the return journey in April and
ay. In between these times, the birds while
ay the winter months in the easy fishing of
rm tropical waters.

Over 50% of ospreys, as in the case of most
er birds of prey, die in their first year, due
various factors including the poor ability
the young birds to feed and defend them-
ves. Those lucky enough to be still alive
nain in their tropical habitat until the
rd year, by which time they are in breeding
dition. At this stage, they are also ready to
dertake the long flight to the north. Pair-
takes place while the birds are still in
rica. By the time the female reaches Scot-
d, the male will have found a good site
d perhaps begun to build the nest.

Above: Supervised from
overhead by the mother, a
young osprey makes its
first flight. The father is often
away from the nest, either
finding fishes or, if he has
already brought enough for
the day, sitting quietly on a
favourite perch near the
nesting tree.

Left: A young osprey, in
the typically hunched
attitude of the bird at
rest. The sharply hooked
beak is useful for tearing
and eating fishes, the only
food of ospreys.

BUZZARDS: RUGGED BIRDS OF PREY

Buzzards, usually seen wheeling and soaring, gained an early reputation for laziness, although patient waiting is part of their efficient hunting strategy. They are not agile, relying mainly on a silent planing approach to catch their varied prey.

Three buzzards occur regularly in Britain, the common buzzard, the much scarcer rough-legged buzzard and the unrelated, but equally scarce, honey buzzard which is a similar sized bird to the other two but belongs to a separate genus of the family.

The common buzzard (pictured left) is a familiar bird of prey in Wales, south-west England, the Lake District and Scotland, although it is absent from much of lowland England. It is the British bird which, perhaps, comes nearest to the familiar conception of what a bird of prey really looks like. One of the most obliging features, for the bird watcher, is that this bird is so conspicuous. Perched, it has a slightly hunched attitude, and its compact, robust features are clear; in flight, its broad wings, short tail and soaring habit, often with wings rigid and upturned, immediately proclaim it as a bird of prey. In sunny weather it spends much time in the air, wheeling and circling above woodland or open hillside, often calling loudly with a plaintive and characteristic mewing.

Although it is predominantly a brown plumaged bird, relieved only by the bright yellow of its feet, legs and cere (the fleshy covering at the base of the bill), individuals are very variable. The wings can be the whole range of colours from blackish brown through all shades of blotching and streaking to almost white in some birds.

In population terms the buzzard qualifies as a successful bird in the British Isles. There are about 30,000 individuals, although they are by no means universally distributed. In upland areas where the buzzard is now concentrated numbers may be prodigious. Although buzzards are numerous in the south-west, slightly less so in the Lakes and Scotland, they are nowhere more numerous than in Wales. Here on a sunny day in April you may see up to 100 individuals in a day's travelling, with pairs breeding at intervals of half a mile or so. The densest buzzard populations are in Wales and south-west England where there can be as many as a pair to each 100-150 acres.

Diversity of habitat appears to be the key to the buzzard's success. Over extensive areas of

Right: **Rough-legged buzzard** (*Buteo lagopus*), 55cm (22in) from beak to tail. Breeds in Scandinavia where it is at the mercy of fluctuating populations of small mammals for food.

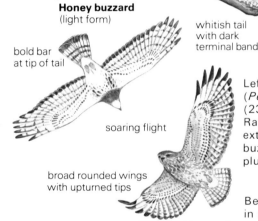

legs feathered to toes

dark belly patch

whitish tail with dark terminal band

Honey buzzard (light form)

bold bar at tip of tail

soaring flight

broad rounded wings with upturned tips

Common buzzard

Left: **Honey buzzard** (*Pernis apivorus*), 58cm (23in) from beak to tail. Rare summer visitor in the extreme south. (Common buzzard also shown for plumage comparison).

Below: Some buzzards nest in crags or cliffs; pairs move to a new site annually.

mountain, moorland or forest numbers are relatively low, but in valleys where broken countryside is studded with trees and copses, old hedgerows and small fields, breeding pairs can be numerous. Here the variety of countryside and rough vegetation guarantees high numbers of the small mammals which form the bulk of their prey, and buzzards are in their ideal habitat.

Chequered history The buzzard has had a chequered history in the British Isles, intimately bound up with its relationship with man. The clearance of woodland by the Middle Ages opened up much suitable country and the bird was certainly common by the 15th century. Thomas Pennant, writing in 1776, regarded it then as the commonest hawk in Britain, although it was already suffering from lack of food because of vermin control. This campaign intensified throughout the 18th, 19th and early 20th centuries, latterly in the name of game preservation. By the First World War the buzzard was very rare; it was absent from lowland England and found only in the more mountainous western areas. With the rapid decline of gamekeeping at the outbreak of World War II the buzzard reoccupied some of its lost ground; and the slightly more enlightened attitudes since that time have enabled the recovery to continue, albeit within limits.

In the mid-1950s myxomatosis, which killed thousands of rabbits, had an instant effect on the buzzard with widespread decreases in breeding reported, especially in southern England. But within only a few years the numbers had readjusted to somewhat lower levels and then stabilised as those individuals which had exploited the plague populations of rabbits in some areas divers-

Common buzzard

Above and below: **Common buzzard** (*Buteo buteo*), 55cm (22in) from beak to tail. Our most common large bird of prey, found in wooded valleys, and on hillsides of western areas of England and Scotland. Small rabbits and other mammals form an important part of the varied diet of buzzards.

Killer poisons

It is well known that in addition to the legal control of some pests, widespread illegal destruction of protected birds and other animals still occurs. The most worrying aspect of much of this illegal killing is the use of poisons on meat baits or injected into eggs and laid in the open. The most common poisons are strychnine, phosdrin and the narcotic drug alphachloralore. They are used to protect game stocks or reduce predation by crows and foxes on lambing flocks, but as they are non-selective, they account for a tragic catalogue of deaths. Apart from target species, buzzards, ravens, magpies, hedgehogs, badgers, farm dogs and other species are regular victims, and, more serious still, rare birds such as the carrion-eating red kite, golden eagle, goshawk, peregrine falcon, marsh harrier and hen harrier. It is not only the range of species that causes concern, but also the actual numbers of birds and mammals killed in one year are horrifying.

distinguished by a smaller head and slim neck, and bold barring on the tail and under-wings. This is a secretive bird, most at home in a mosaic of mature deciduous woodland and open glades. Honey buzzards winter in wooded country in equatorial Africa, migrating to Europe from early April; some of the crossing points over the Mediterranean are characterised by spectacular concentrations of the birds. A very small breeding population clings to a toe-hold in southern England where they are carefully protected. The best place to see a honey buzzard is the New Forest.

The birds are largely dependent for food on the nests, larvae and adults of various species of wasps and bees, often found by following the flying insects to their nests. These are dug out with the use of strong feet; the stings are nipped off before the insect is swallowed, and the bird's resistance to stings is enhanced by scale-like feathers on the forehead and lores (the area between the eye and upper mandible).

ied their feeding. At present the population probably stable.

Nesting Most buzzards make substantial ests in trees close to the main trunk. They se sticks, twigs and heather, and line the est with green foliage before laying. Two or ree eggs are a normal clutch, although it is nusual for all to be successful. In areas where uzzards are already numerous, one fledgling oung is the normal product of a nesting air. Eggs are laid every few days, and both arents incubate for 33-35 days. The young e on the wing about seven weeks·after tching, so most have left the nest by early ly.

Varied diet A large part of the buzzard's ccess can be attributed to its resourcefulness d catholic choice of prey. Its most import-t food items are mammals–small rabbits, les, mice, shrews and others; it also eats nphibians, insects, soil invertebrates, par-cularly earthworms, and fledgling birds–eir immobility makes them relatively easy ey for the slow and somewhat ponderous zzard.

Buzzards are not agile like kites, sparrow-wks or harriers. They patiently sit on a nce or post, carefully scanning a favoured nting area to find food which they then ke by a straight, silent, planing flight from eir perch. They also soar over open ground d can hover well or hang in the wind, strel-like. They also spend much time lking around fields, picking up beetles and her large insects, and all kinds of other vertebrates such as earthworms.

The rough-legged buzzard is superficially nilar to the common buzzard, but it is ly a winter visitor appearing in small mbers, most frequently to the east and rth. It is a slightly bulkier bird, with deeper ng beats and a larger, markedly patterned l. A dark belly patch, rare in the common zzard, is an aid to identification. Its legs e completely covered with feathers. It is a rthern breeding bird, nesting in high itudes, mainly in open tundra areas, well the north of the range of common buzzards.

The honey buzzard is also superficially nilar to the other two, although it is

Above: Buzzard chicks in their nest. The young are cared for by both parents.

Below: The honey buzzard, as its name suggests, is largely dependent on bees, and wasps for food.

MOORLAND MERLINS

Our smallest British falcon, the merlin inhabits the lonely moorlands of the north and west, where it is noted for its speedy, agile flight and fearless character.

Where larger birds of prey such as buzzards, peregrines and kestrels search for prey in a high soaring flight, the merlin lives and hunts in the lowest band of air space just a few feet above the ground. The male merlin is no bigger than a mistle thrush and has a slate grey back and wings and black-banded tail. As with other birds of prey the female, at about 210g (7½oz), is markedly larger and heavier than the male. Her plumage is more uniformly brown and she may justifiably be

confused with a female kestrel. Both sexes of merlin have strong, yellow legs and feet, which are disproportionately large for the size of the birds.

Moorland hunter Merlins are northern birds, inhabitants of the zones in latitudes and altitudes lying beyond the tree line. They occur throughout Eurasia and North Amer-

Above: A female merlin perched on her lookout roc The merlin is the classic lov level hunter of open moorland, pursuing its prey just a few feet above the heather. The bulk of its foo is taken from ground-nestin species, most of which are small birds weighing less than 50g (2oz), although ring ouzel, mistle thrush an fieldfare—all considerably heavier birds weighing up 140gm (5oz)—are also take

Opposite page: Merlin country — open, hilly, heath moorland in northern Scotland, well above the tr line.

Left: The remains of a meadow pipit—a merlin kill. During the breeding seasor the male plucks the prey ar presents it to the female.

birds each day. The reason it has to eat s[o] much is that it expends a great deal of energ[y] in hunting: its striking rate is not particular[ly] good, only 5-15% of attempts resulting in [a] successful kill.

Although merlins prey mainly on bird[s] they do not spurn smaller animals and, whe[n] summer brings a bounty to their moorlan[d] breeding areas, they profit from the larg[e] numbers of day-flying moths such as the oa[k] eggar, fox and emperor, as well as dragonfli[es] and other large winged insects.

Unusual associations On the open hills, th[e] merlin has a very strong affinity with heathe[r] an association which, although well marke[d] is poorly understood. Heather gives goo[d] cover for nesting and contains ample supplie[s] of meadow pipits, yet moorlands withou[t] heather often hold considerably great[er] numbers of pipits and other suitable pre[y] birds, but they consistently remain unused b[y] merlins.

Another unusual association is that be[-] tween certain nesting pairs of merlins an[d] neighbouring pairs of hen harriers. Why som[e] merlins should choose to nest so close to he[n] harriers is not clearly understood. However, [it] is possible that the small merlin derives som[e] protection from this association. Certainl[y]

ica; indeed, their most southerly European breeding grounds are the British Isles, where the species is therefore at the very limit of its breeding range.

Skylarks, meadow pipits, ring ouzels and whinchats are frequently preyed upon by the merlin. All are birds that share the same open, hilly moorland, a habitat in which bird populations, both in terms of species (with the possible exception of meadow pipits and skylarks) and numbers, are low and food supplies therefore scarce. Consequently, the merlin–in common with other moorland predators–is forced to rely on large and wide-ranging territories.

For such a small bird, the merlin eats an impressive amount of food, a single individual being known to kill and eat more than two

Above: Three merlin chicks, one at 18 days old and two at 17 days. In a few days' time they will begin to tear up their own food, instead o[f] having it done for them, and the mother will then join he[r] mate in hunting.

Left: The same chicks eight days later. Soon they will take to the wing.

Right: A male merlin incubating the eggs, a task done mostly by the female while her partner hunts prey for her and later their brood

Merlin distribution

Above: The distribution of merlins in Britain and Ireland in the early 1970s. During the last decade its numbers have declined alarmingly: it is now virtually unknown as a breeding bird on Dartmoor or Exmoor, or in the Peak District.

Opposite left: Its large powerful feet are a merlin's principal weapons of attack.

the merlin–fast and bold though it may be–is no match for larger birds of prey and it is known to be attacked by peregrines and probably also goshawks when they come up from the lowlands to hunt the open moors for grouse and waders. Nesting in the shadow of a large and aggressive harrier (which does not attack merlins) gives the smaller predator a degree of protection that it would lack in a solitary site. It is also likely that merlins prey on small birds flushed out by the flying activities of the harrier, though this does not explain why they should choose to nest near by.

The breeding season Merlins return from their wintering grounds to the hills for breeding by April, often using the same sites year after year. Display flights take place on warm sunny days with both the cock and the hen birds participating, though these are mostly inconspicuous affairs; unlike other birds of prey merlins do not have a notable display.

In most of their British sites, merlins nest on the ground among heather, and sometimes bracken. Towards the southern end of their British range, however, the majority of pairs make use of old nests of crows or magpies in isolated hawthorn or rowan trees.

brown upperparts

blue-grey upperparts

black-tipped wings

yellow feet and legs

banded tail

Merlin (*Falco columbarius*). Resident bird of prey; Britain's smallest raptor, length 27-33cm (10½-13in), the female being noticeably bigger. Wingspan 52-69cm (20½-27in).

Merlins breed late, not laying until well into May in most areas, so that the young hatch at a time when there is a surplus of newly fledged (and therefore easily caught) young birds of other species. The four or five beautiful red-brown eggs–beguilingly tempting to generations of egg collectors–are laid at intervals of two days and hatched mainly by the female. The female alone tends the young and feeds them with items provided by the male. It is a time of great activity for him, for he has to bring in four or five kills a day, ready plucked for the female to feed to the chicks.

Four weeks after hatching the young are taking to the wing. They become independent a month after fledging, but family groups may well keep together for a while longer.

In autumn and winter some merlins hunt in the farmlands surrounding their moorland breeding sites, though they are most at home at this time of year on the marshes of our major estuaries. The majority of British estuaries have several merlins resident throughout the winter, some of which are Icelandic birds wintering here. British birds do not move much more than about 100km (60 miles) from their birth place, though young merlins regularly travel as far as western France during their first winter after fledging.

The merlin is now a scarce British bird but in days when it was more numerous, for example in the first half of this century, it bred quite commonly in areas away from its traditional open hills. Pairs used to breed regularly in sand dunes and on undulating heathery headlands on western clifftops. Since then the merlin's fortunes have been mixed.

Tracking techniques

To discover how serious is the merlin's decline, the RSPB in Wales has used a technique called radio telemetry in which a minute radio transmitter is attached to two of the tail feathers of adult birds. This allows the RSPB to monitor the movements of the birds as they hunt in the surrounding countryside. By this experiment the RSPB hopes to learn exactly what percentages of different habitats a merlin needs in the vicinity of its nesting site in order to sustain a viable population.

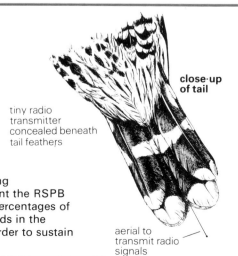

close-up of tail

tiny radio transmitter concealed beneath tail feathers

aerial to transmit radio signals

THE SNOWY OWL: A RARE VISITOR

Owls are an almost universally successful group of birds. Few of the world's terrestrial habitats have not been exploited by this adaptable family, and one owl species, the snowy owl, even lives in the Arctic wastes. This species has also bred in Shetland.

Below: A captive female snowy owl poses for the camera. High quality insulation is provided by the dense plumage, the heavily feathered legs and feet, and the long feathers of the facial disc, which partly conceal the strong black bill.

Snowy owls are very rare birds in Britain, although they have long occurred in small numbers during winter, usually as part of the post-breeding season dispersal of some of the population in northern Scandinavia and other Arctic regions. The Shetland Islands, far to the north of mainland Scotland, are the nearest part of Britain to the snowy owl's regular breeding grounds, and it is here

that individual vagrant birds, normally male have been seen with comparative regulari since the early 1960s.

Large, white owl The male is much t whiter of the two adult birds, often with markings other than a few dark flecks on t wings and back. The female, noticeab larger, with a wingspan of up to 1.5m (5ft) more heavily barred on the upperparts ar slightly less so on the underparts. Th barring, which acts as camouflage for t female when incubating on the nest, tends become less marked as summer advanc because of wear and tear. The chicks, thick insulated with grey down, resemble t adults by the end of their first summer. barely needs saying that body insulatic needs to be of the highest order for a bi which spends so much of its life in a devasta ingly cold and hostile climate. This requir ment is amply met by the bird's thick ar fluffy plumage at all ages.

The Arctic habitat The true home of t snowy owl is on the inhospitable tundr frozen solid and buried in a blanket of snc for more than half the year. The tundra is flat, empty expanse of land, but in the bri Arctic summer it is far from being a barre desert, for once the days lengthen and t strengthening sun thaws the snow and ic this landscape pulses with life. Migrant bir and mammals return to breed in the boun of plant, insect and aquatic life, and with the come the inevitable predators, which susta themselves at the expense of others – arct fox, gyr falcon, skuas, glaucous gull ar snowy owl.

Breeding on the tundra Snowy owls have circumpolar breeding distribution, nesti on the tundras around the coasts of t Arctic Ocean, as well as on most of t archipelagoes. In a few areas, they bre further south, for example in Iceland and t mountainous snow-covered spine of Sca dinavia. Wherever they are, however, t breeding grounds of the snowy owl are amo the most inaccessible and desolate places which any birds choose to nest. Observatio suggest that these remarkable birds stay the same range through the icy cold of t Arctic winter as well.

A diet of lemmings In its Arctic and su Arctic home in summer, the snowy owl fee mainly on lemmings, and to a considerab degree the cycles of both brown and collare lemming populations determine the abu dance or scarcity of the owls themselve The number of lemmings normally rises to peak every four years; at peak times the ow thrive, rearing large broods. After the pea summers, as the supply of lemmings wane numbers of snowy owls tend to move sout and in winter these 'emigrants' are seen areas where the species is not normal encountered. This is the background of a the sightings in Shetland.

If lemmings form the bulk of the diet, hov

, they are by no means the only prey of snowy owl. Willow grouse and arctic [hare]s are taken, and in summer a variety of [sma]ller birds – waders (especially their chicks), [sno]w buntings and occasionally young wild-[fow]l. In winter the main birds taken are [ptar]migan and seabirds.

[S]hetland discovery In the spring of 1967 [the] RSPB's Shetlands Officer, Bobby Tulloch, [obs]erved a female snowy owl several times [on t]he island of Fetlar, and on 7th June he

Snowy owl (*Nyctea scandiaca*). Arctic species of owl visiting Scotland as a vagrant, mainly in Shetlands. Length: males 53cm (21in), females 60cm (24in). Wingspan of female 1.5m (5ft).

Below left: A snowy owl chick on the typical low vegetation of its habitat.

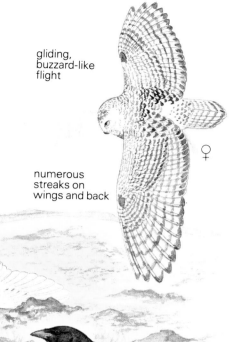

gliding, buzzard-like flight

numerous streaks on wings and back

♀

defence posture

a few dark flecks on wings and back

♂

intruder – raven looking for eggs

[Abo]ve: A female snowy owl [sit]ting on a limestone [outc]rop. Her plumage is [heavil]y barred with brown, [espe]cially on the back and [wing]s. This is good [cam]ouflage at breeding time [in th]e Arctic, when the [back]ground often consists of [brok]en patches of snow.

[Righ]t: The long feathers of [the f]acial disc of a male [snow]y owl. He lacks the [barr]ed crown of the female. [The] eyes of both sexes are [liqu]id golden yellow.

came across a nest with three eggs on the hill of Stakkaberg on the northern slopes of the island. This was the first time on record that the snowy owl had come to nest in Britain. The nest scrape, in a grassy patch on rocky ground, was on the slopes of this windswept hill, where low vegetation all round was reminiscent of the prostrate plant cover typical of the bird's Arctic breeding grounds.

In Shetland, the low hill on Stakkaberg gave a wide view of the surrounding area, giving some warning of any approaching danger. Although lemmings do not occur on the Shetlands, there are rabbits in plenty, and these formed the major part of the food of the birds that lived there, and later their young. Other birds breeding in this part of the island were also taken – arctic skuas, oystercatchers and other waders. In 1967 the Shetland pair produced seven eggs, and eventually in August five young successfully flew.

Fetlar is much visited by birdwatchers, and from the outset in 1967 it was clear that the secret could not be kept.

In 1968, to the delight of the many bird-watchers among whom word had gone round about this exciting phenomenon, the original pair of snowy owls were still on Fetlar and reappeared on the breeding site. During the seven years from 1968-75, these two parents raised a further 14 young. In 1975 the same male, mated with a different female, reared four young. The following winter the old male snowy owl disappeared and, having previously driven off all the young males, left the females without a partner. In 1989 an exhausted male, rescued from a ship in the North Atlantic, was released on the island and a possibility of future breeding now exists.

SNOW BUNTINGS: ARCTIC VISITORS

The snow bunting's breeding range extends north of the Arctic Circle, and even in summer it is seen amid ice and snow. A few pairs breed in Scotland, but many snow buntings winter in the British Isles, even occurring as far south as Kent and Sussex.

Buntings on the beach The first indication of the presence of snow buntings on a desolate winter beach is one of its calls, a far carrying 'teu'. At closer range, the flock can often be heard to maintain a fluting, musical twitter. The species is essentially a ground-dwelling one: the birds run rapidly across the beach rather than walk. When they leave the ground their flight is undulating, and both individuals and flocks often fly high; when landing, the entire flock drops quickly but then characteristically skims the ground for a few metres before alighting.

The winter diet of the snow bunting is typical of that of many other buntings, consisting mainly of seeds of various grasses, plantains, docks, samphire and many other plants. The snow bunting also eats cereal grains, sand-hoppers and insects in winter but, like many shorebirds, its diet in summer switches to the insects that abound in the Arctic and also in parts of Scotland—notably midges, mosquitoes and their larvae.

Scarce in summer Watching the snow buntings in summer is a different experience altogether. In British ornithology, the bird holds an important and prestigious position, for it is one of the rarest breeding birds. It is restricted to a few mountain tops, usually over 1000m (3000ft), Scotland being its southern-most breeding area in Europe. We do not know how many pairs breed each year, for no systematic bird census has been carried out in the remote peaks of the Cairngorms. It seems likely that the breeding population can rarely number more than 10 pairs, but even then studies in the Cairngorms indicate that the number of breeders can vary considerably from year to year. In poor years females may be absent, and unmated males may be the only indication of a resident population.

The scarcity and isolation of breeding birds means that few birdwatchers are familiar with the full glory of the male's breeding plumage. His back, wing tips and central tail feathers are black and the remainder of his plumage pure white. His bill and legs are black. The female is less striking: she has white under parts but her head and back are greyish brown, the latter with black flecks.

The majority of British birdwatchers encounter the snow bunting as a winter visitor, mainly between October and March, on coasts and on inland hills. It is highly gregarious, and can occur in spectacular flocks, containing 500 birds or more. It often associates on coastal flats with a variety of other finches and buntings such as linnets, twites, corn buntings, and the much rarer Lapland buntings, as well as skylarks, meadow pipits and sometimes shore larks. Such massed flocks are naturally attractive to predators, and it is thought that merlins and sparrowhawks actually single out snow buntings from mixed flocks, possibly on account of their conspicuous black-and-white plumage.

Above: A male snow bunting in summer, proclaiming his territory. The song is a loud, fluting trill, and birds are therefore easily located, by both their song and their brilliant plumage.

Right: A male snow bunting in winter, photographed in grass close to the coast of southern England. It is rare for a snow bunting to occur inland in the south, while in the south-west it is seen only as a bad-weather migrant, even on the coast.

Snow bunting plumages

faint white stripes

dark wing

faint white outer edge of tail

mottled brown back

chestnut nape

dark crown

white rump

white inner wing

Winter

dark outer wing

Juvenile

brown cheeks and crown

mottled brown back

Winter ♀

nt white ng stripe

light brown head and nape

mottled brown back

white wing stripe

faint white outer edge of tail ♀

white head and nape

Summer

black back and outer wing

white inner wing ♂

vivid white outer edge of tail

Snow bunting distribution

Above: The summer range of our resident population of snow buntings, breeding in Scotland. The range of the wintering birds has not yet been charted with the same precision, but they are regularly seen in every county of Scotland. In England their range is mainly on the east coast, extending inland only to the Pennines and Northumberland Moors. They also occur on the south coast, while small numbers visit the Kent and Sussex Downs.

Snow bunting
(*Plectrophenax nivalis*). Small resident population restricted to mountains of northern Scotland. Larger wintering population. 16.5cm (6½in).

Below: Snow buntings in the snow. Despite the small size of the Scottish breeding population, flocks like this are seen in spring after a fresh fall of snow. The birds temporarily abandon their territories and congregate where food is most easily available.

Both sexes become duller after the autumn ult. The underparts of the female become ty white, and the male develops chestnut rkings on the head while his back becomes ttled brown. He retains the brilliant white tches on his wings, however, and these can e the impression of snowflakes against a udy sky. Before winter migrants depart in arch and April, some males may begin to ain their breeding plumage by losing the own head markings and developing a black ck and a black, rather than yellowish bill: s is the best chance that most of us have of ing this beautiful breeding dress.

Display and breeding The few snow bunting irs that breed in Scotland begin their sting activities late in comparison with most our more familiar birds, for eggs are not d until late May or early June.

The male establishes a large territory, often several hectares, advertising his presence by song flight, in which he rises about 10m ft) with fluttering wings and spread tail, ply displaying the contrasting black and ite of his plumage. He then glides down th his wings held in a 'V' shape, a position t is held when the bird lands. Snow ntings also sing from prominent perches h as rocks, and where the birds are undant in the Arctic, some visitors to these ions have noted that each large boulder has attendant singing male.

Males generally arrive first in the breeding

areas, and later attempt to attract females to their territories. In his courtship display, the male walks slowly away from his mate, spreading his wings and tail to display his black and white patterning. When he is about 2m (6ft) away, he closes his wings and runs back to the female's side.

The nest, built by the hen but usually with the male nearby, is constructed of grasses, mosses and lichens but lined with finer materials such as hair and feathers. Between four and six eggs, occasionally more, are laid. Incubation, mainly by the female who is fed on the nest by her mate, takes 12 to 13 days, and the young leave the nest about a fortnight later. Females sometimes rear second broods.

GAME BIRDS OF OUR MOORLANDS

The red grouse and ptarmigan are much prized game-birds of the uplands. Estate owners, keen to attract wealthy hunters, have done much to conserve the birds' moorland habitat.

The red grouse and the ptarmigan are in fact both grouse. The ptarmigan lives further north and at higher altitudes than the red grouse, being confined to Scotland where it is a bird of barren, rocky mountain tops, generally above 800m (2500ft). The red grouse on the other hand, has a more widespread distribution covering Scotland, England, Wales and Ireland. It is a bird of upland heather moors, although it also lives in peat bogs and even on heather covered sand dunes at sea level in parts of Scotland. The current population of red grouse is a little under 500,000 pairs, while that of the ptarmigan lies between 1000-7000 pairs.

Distinguishing features The two birds are very similar in shape: the ptarmigan is slightly smaller than the red grouse, and in both species females tend to be slightly smaller than males. Although you can distinguish the birds by their plumage differences, there are considerable variations within each species.

Ptarmigan undergo three moults during the year and their plumage therefore varies considerably from season to season. But there is one striking feature that can always be used to separate them from red grouse, which is that the ptarmigan has a white belly and, more noticeable to the fell-walker who may disturb one, white wings. The male (cock) red grouse is usually dark reddish-brown while the female (hen) is paler. However, the casual hill

Above: The female ptarmigan lays six to nine eggs in one of several scrapes selected by both adults. Ptarmigans lay their eggs from May to July. The red eye wattle is particularly evident on this bird.

Below: The red grouse female lays the same number of eggs as the ptarmigan, but earlier—in late April to early May, and in a scrape she makes herself. Like the female ptarmigan she alone incubates the eggs for about 22 days.

walker rarely sees grouse on the ground, details of the plumage can be difficult identify. The most common sight of r grouse is as they fly swiftly with bursts of rap flapping, alternating with spells of gliding markedly down-curved wings. As they ta off, with an explosive burst of wing beats, th often utter a gutteral 'kok-kok-kok' 'gobak gobak' call and on landing they usual run forward a few paces.

Pairing and nesting Pair-formation ar courtship are similar in the two species. Ea has a song-flight, or 'beck', that is also use by males establishing territories. The bi flies ten metres or more, planes for a bri period, then parachutes to the ground wi shallow wing-beats. The red grouse gives t becking call 'aarr' followed by several 'k ka-ka' calls on the ascent, while the ptarmig makes the same sounds on the desce Courtship includes a variety of postures i volving strutting, often with tail fanne wings drooped and the head shaking.

The nest, a simple scrape that is usua lined with grasses and leaves, is made by t female red grouse alone; but both sexes of t ptarmigan make several scrapes, one of whi is eventually chosen for the eggs.

Newly-hatched chicks leave the nest as so as they are dry and are brooded by the fem during the first six days but, even during t period, they feed themselves under t watchful eyes of both parents. Although th

e not fully grown until they are over thirty
ys old, they can usually fly short distances
the twelfth day.

Reliance on heather In Scotland heather
nstitutes the main food of the red grouse
roughout the year. Although the ptarmigan
es above the moors, heather is nevertheless
so a dominant plant in its diet, together
th bilberry and crowberry. With heather
vering such vast areas of moorland, you
ght suppose that food would never be in
ort supply. However, both the red grouse
d the ptarmigan are highly selective and
y old heather will not do. The birds eat the
ost nutritious parts, usually the young
owing shoots. These are particularly im-
rtant during the breeding season; and it
s been discovered that the ability of chicks
survive their first few weeks may be deter-
ned to some extent by the quality of the
od that the hen is able to eat while she is
anufacturing her eggs.

Territory with food Since food quality is
erefore of paramount importance for suc-
ssful breeding, the acquisition of suitably
tritious food is one of the main aims of
ck red grouse when they fight for territories
the autumn. In areas of moor that have
nty of high quality heather, the territories
ablished by males are smaller than where
ather quality is poor, and so the highest
nsities of breeding grouse are to be found
ere the heather best meets their requirements.

Territory acquisition is vital for males, not
only to allow them to breed, but also for their
own survival, for those that fail to obtain a
territory are forced by the dominant territory
owners to leave the moor. These unsuccessful
birds are almost invariably doomed to perish
over the winter through predation and starvation. Although foxes, golden eagles, buzzards and crows may take some grouse, an
important predator in winter is, of course,
sporting man.

Disease depredations The artificial maintenance of high densities of game-birds for
sportsmen frequently increases the birds'
susceptibility to disease. The red grouse is

Ptarmigan (*Lagopus
mutus*), 35cm (14in) from
beak to tail; slightly smaller
than red grouse. Distribution
Scottish barren mountain
peaks.
Plumage undergoes three
moults a year. In summer
upper parts, breast and
flanks are brown with pale
barring on feathers; in
autumn bird is greyer. Hens
are generally yellower, but
in winter both sexes turn
white, apart from the black
outer tail and black between
the cock's bill and eye.

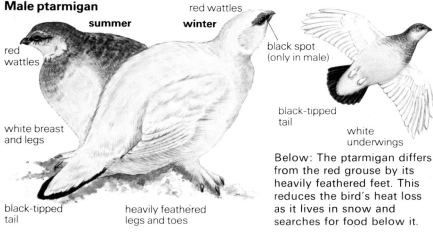

Below: The ptarmigan differs
from the red grouse by its
heavily feathered feet. This
reduces the bird's heat loss
as it lives in snow and
searches for food below it.

often infested with parasitic worms inside the body, and large numbers of sheep ticks may attach themselves to the skin of the birds to suck their blood. In addition, these ticks carry and transmit a virus, louping ill, that kills sheep as well as grouse, and can produce unpleasant symptoms in man.

In the past, disease was regarded as such a serious threat to grouse stocks that an investigation, the Grouse Disease Enquiry, was instigated in the early years of this century in an attempt to discover how best to maintain high grouse numbers. More recently, an exhaustive study of the red grouse and ptarmigan biology has been undertaken by scientists in Scotland in order to find what regulates the numbers of birds.

Moor management These studies have given us our present-day knowledge of what is important to game birds and, as a result, what features should be encouraged to maintain a 'good grouse moor'. So powerful an incentive has this been that the maintenance of high quality heather, through periodic burning of old heather to stimulate new growth, is one of the factors that preserves so much of this upland habitat in its present state.

Both the red grouse and the ptarmigan are extremely hardy birds. They remain in the hills in the severest weather and both species burrow into snow to reach buried food. High winds and drifting snow seem to present them with no hardship, since these conditions always leave some areas blown free of snow. An even cover of deep snow, on the other hand, renders food plants unavailable and then both species move to lower altitudes – the red grouse even to farmland – returning to the moors when the weather improves.

The ability of the red grouse and the ptarmigan to attract the rich hunting man's attention is so great that much of our upland countryside is shaped primarily for them – something not matched by any other British bird. Nor have any other birds had the doubtful distinction of being shot, flown south and dropped by parachutist to the lawn of a Surrey pub, so that they could appear on the table on the 'glorious' twelfth of August – the opening of the grouse shooting season.

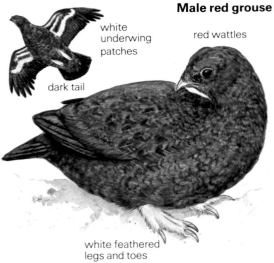

Male red grouse

white underwing patches

red wattles

dark tail

white feathered legs and toes

Above: The red grouse's eggs (like the ptarmigan's) are about 4.5×3cm (1½×1 and blotched with dark brown. The eggs are yellow than the ptarmigan's pinkis brown eggs.

Red grouse (*Lagopus lagopus*), 40cm (16in) fro beak to tail. Distribution heather-clad moorlands. Plumage varies from almos black to pale barring becau moulting occurs year-roun Cock dark reddish brown, wings blacker, legs and to white. In summer pale and heavily barred; in autumn growing feathers are darke red-brown. Hen always pa resembling late summer co

Camouflage – cryptic plumage

Birds need to be seen by others of the same species, particularly when breeding, but often the same birds have to merge into the background to avoid predators. The trick is done by camouflage or cryptic coloration (birds have colour vision). Incubating birds are reluctant to fly off leaving the eggs to chill, so the better camouflaged sex incubates – usually the female, as with red grouse and ptarmigan. Like this ptarmigan (right), the female may 'freeze' on the nest, hoping to be overlooked. Immature birds, including waders, rely on their camouflage to crouch motionless and unseen by predators.

BLACK GROUSE

Although not a common gamebird, the black grouse is exciting to watch, with its ritual contests and matchmaking in the arena or 'lekking' ground.

he British Isles boast few birds that occur owhere else in the world, but the race of the ack grouse that occurs here is unique. This is bird of moorland or heathland with scat-red clumps of trees or open young conifer-us or birch woodland—it prefers the margin tween woodland and moorland. This kind habitat is locally widespread, and the black ouse used to occupy such areas in southern d eastern counties of England. However, it

can no longer be seen in Surrey, Sussex, Dorset, Hampshire, Norfolk or Lincolnshire, and even where it still occurs its numbers are much smaller than in the late 19th century.

Attempts to reintroduce the black grouse to areas where it has declined or disappeared have not succeeded. Black grouse do not occur in Ireland and all attempts to introduce them into that country have failed.

Second largest gamebird Black grouse are fairly large gamebirds. With a body length of 40-55cm (16-22in) they are larger than red grouse and partridges, but smaller than the capercaillie. The male, called the blackcock, is unmistakable with his glossy blue-black plumage, long outwardly curving tail feathers and white wing bar and undertail feathers. A white spot at the base of the leading edge of each wing is made conspicuous during dis-play, as is the red wattle above the eye. The female, or greyhen, is a much duller bird, the colour of her plumage being designed for camouflage. Above, she is a warm brown, while her belly is greyer, but all of her body is spotted and barred with black. Juveniles are

Above: The adult male black grouse, or blackcock. These normally begin breeding at three years old, while the females (or greyhens) start earlier. For a large bird, the species is short-lived—the oldest ringed bird being only five years old.

Black grouse distribution

Above: A greyhen broods her newly hatched young. She has not yet had an opportunity to tidy away the egg shells (which might attract attention) for it is rainy and her first priority is to keep the downy chicks dry and warm. She continues to brood the chicks at night and during rain for ten days. For safety, she may move away from the nest within a few days, to a distance of half a kilometre or more. At a fortnight old the chicks can fly short distances.

various berries such as bilberries, and the nutritious growing shoots of heather, constitute the preferred foods.

This vegetable diet supplies the full-grown birds with all their needs, but the extra protein requirements of rapidly growing chicks are met by a mainly animal diet. Insects, predominantly ants, are the main constituent of the food of very young chicks, but after a day or two they also take increasing numbers of berries and fruits.

Tending the young The black grouse normally nests on the ground, but occasionally makes use of old nests of other birds in trees. The nest is a shallow depression and is fashioned by the greyhen, who lines it with grasses and other fine plant material. She lays between six and eleven eggs, at 36 to 48-hour intervals during May and June, and incubates these for 25 to 27 days. The nest is usually well hidden under a tussock of grass or in scrub, and the eggs themselves are protectively coloured, being buff with brown spots.

Although hens are solitary nesters, probably as a protection against predators, black grouse are nevertheless gregarious birds, especially the blackcocks, which form their own flocks in winter. The hens and first-year males form mixed flocks, and they rarely associate with the blackcocks.

Breeding behaviour The most intriguing aspect of the black grouse's social life, however, is what is known as 'lekking' behaviour. This can occur around dawn and dusk throughout the year, but does so especially during autumn and spring, with the most intense and prolonged bouts in spring. Within the range of a group of grouse, the blackcocks assemble each day at an open piece of ground, termed the 'arena', where they display or 'lek'.

similar to hens until their first winter, when young males resemble adult males, though their backs still show signs of barring and the tail feathers are shorter.

Mainly vegetarian Black grouse are essentially a vegetarian species, though the birds do eat some insects in the summer. In spring, summer and autumn they feed mainly on the ground, but in winter they feed in bushes and trees: this explains their requirement for a mixture of open ground and woodland.

The winter habit of feeding in trees can lead to forestry damage, for the buds and shoots of conifers are sometimes eaten. Pine needles and cones, birch catkins, heather and grasses also contribute to the winter diet. In summer,

Gamebird habitats

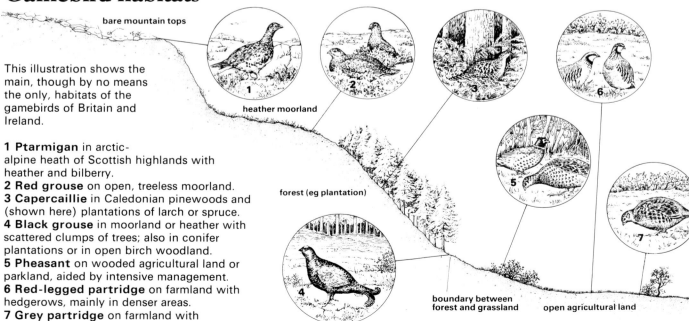

This illustration shows the main, though by no means the only, habitats of the gamebirds of Britain and Ireland.

1 Ptarmigan in arctic-alpine heath of Scottish highlands with heather and bilberry.
2 Red grouse on open, treeless moorland.
3 Capercaillie in Caledonian pinewoods and (shown here) plantations of larch or spruce.
4 Black grouse in moorland or heather with scattered clumps of trees; also in conifer plantations or in open birch woodland.
5 Pheasant on wooded agricultural land or parkland, aided by intensive management.
6 Red-legged partridge on farmland with hedgerows, mainly in denser areas.
7 Grey partridge on farmland with hedgerows.

Arenas are traditional lekking sites, and some are known to have been used as such for over 50 years. Within the arena, the males establish territories. Each territory averages about 100 square metres and the territories may be visited by intruding non-territorial birds, who are usually driven out, and also by hens. The number of territory-holding blackcocks varies from arena to arena, but a dozen or more individuals may be involved – all competing strongly against each other.

The arena is the area where most copulations occur, and from the male's point of view it is important to hold a territory near the centre of the arena, for central males achieve more copulations than do peripheral ones. Thus the arena, with its associated lekking behaviour, gives the males an opportunity to display their prowess, and the females to choose the best males with which to mate.

The chief reason why the males are able to find so many females to mate with is that the black grouse as a species does not form a pair bond between breeding partners. The birds are highly promiscuous, and males attempt to mate with any females that land or walk through their territories. Females are particularly attracted to fighting and copulating males.

The intriguingly complex social behaviour of the lek must have evolved as a means of ensuring that sufficient young are produced to maintain the black grouse's population. In this, the species seems to have failed during the present century, doubtless due largely to a variety of man's influences. Attempts at managing the land for black grouse are less enthusiastic than with other British game because black grouse are described as 'determined and unpredictable' birds on the shoot – in short, they are not very sporting!

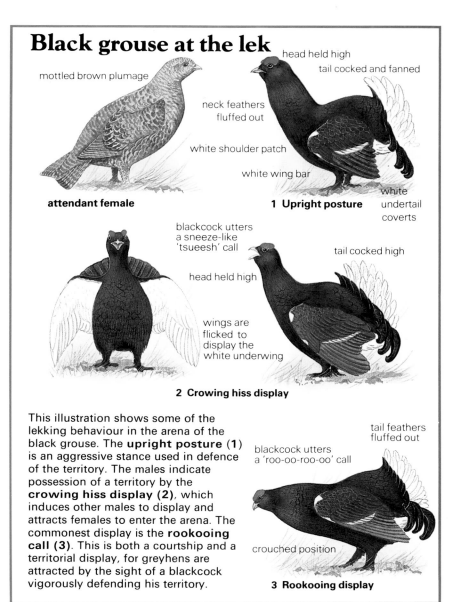

Black grouse at the lek

mottled brown plumage

attendant female

head held high

tail cocked and fanned

neck feathers fluffed out

white shoulder patch

white wing bar

white undertail coverts

1 Upright posture

blackcock utters a sneeze-like 'tsueesh' call

head held high

wings are flicked to display the white underwing

tail cocked high

2 Crowing hiss display

This illustration shows some of the lekking behaviour in the arena of the black grouse. The **upright posture (1)** is an aggressive stance used in defence of the territory. The males indicate possession of a territory by the **crowing hiss display (2)**, which induces other males to display and attracts females to enter the arena. The commonest display is the **rookooing call (3)**. This is both a courtship and a territorial display, for greyhens are attracted by the sight of a blackcock vigorously defending his territory.

tail feathers fluffed out

blackcock utters a 'roo-oo-roo-oo' call

crouched position

3 Rookooing display

Left: Three blackcocks sorting out a territorial dispute in the arena. If a dispute breaks out between two birds near the boundary of a third territory, the occupier of this territory is likely to join in and ensure that the matter is not settled at his expense. Confrontations like this involve much use of the upright posture, as well as frequent bowing, but actual fighting is uncommon. In nearly all cases a decision is reached without violence – one bird surrenders, adopting a submission posture with wings trailing, and is chased off.

Black grouse (*Lyrurus tetrix*). Large gamebird resident on moors and heaths in Scotland, England and Wales. Length 55cm (22in).

UPLAND PLOVERS

Three wading birds famous for the beauty of their plumage can be seen in Britain at different times of the year. They are the dotterel and the grey and the golden plovers.

Above: The plaintive, bell-like calls of the golden plover are one of the most evocative sounds of our upland heathery hills and moors in the summer.

Opposite right: The dotterel in autumn plumage. Autumn is a good time to see these rare birds here as they pass on to southern Europe.

Below: The few breeding pairs of dotterel in the British Isles are protected under the Wildlife and Countryside Act.

The dotterel and the grey and golden plovers are closely related, showing the classic characteristics of the plover family. They are small, plump-bodied wading birds with short legs. Silent by nature for much of the year, they are solitary (or loosely colonial) on their breeding grounds but gregarious on passage and on their wintering grounds. They frequent areas of open mud, tundra or short turf, for they are not probing birds like most waders, but find their food by surface feeding, running quickly over short distances and picking small invertebrates from the bare ground; they are also adept at extracting earthworms or ragworms with their short bills.

The ringed plover and the lapwing are probably the most familiar British representatives of the family, but the dotterel and the grey and golden plovers are notable for their extraordinary migrations, beautiful

plumage and the aura of discreet mystery th surrounds them – probably engendered by t wild and remote places to which they resc for breeding.

Seasonal movements The dotterel is a mi rant and rare summer visiting bird in Britai a few arrive each year to breed on our desola northern mountain-tops and fells, but mc just pass through to winter in the Medite ranean basin and as far east as the Persi Gulf.

There are two races of golden plover; o own breeding population (the southern rac is resident here all year round, nesting on t lonely moorlands of northern Britain. T northern race, distinguished by certain plu age differences, is an uncommon migrant a also a winter visitor to Britain and Irelan it breeds in Iceland, northern Scandinav and Russia.

The grey plover, breeding in high latitud on the coastal tundra of the Arctic basin, is passage migrant and winter visitor to Britai moving south in late summer to the shores every Continent; few suitable coastlin throughout the world do not see grey plove at some time or another.

Spectacular summer plumage The gr plover (or silver plover as it is more evocative called in Europe) and the golden plover a similar in size and shape, but with the obvio difference of their silver and gold colourin In their full breeding plumage both are ma nificent birds, with jet black bellies and throa edged broadly with white. The golden plov is spangled with gold and black speckles the upperparts, the grey plover with silver a black. When the sunlight catches their bac as they move, the gleaming of the golde yellow and silver-grey is like a surface jewelled droplets.

In autumn and winter the birds lose the black underparts, but the spangled upperpa still distinguish them from each other. The are also easily separated by the fact that t grey plover feeds exclusively on intertid

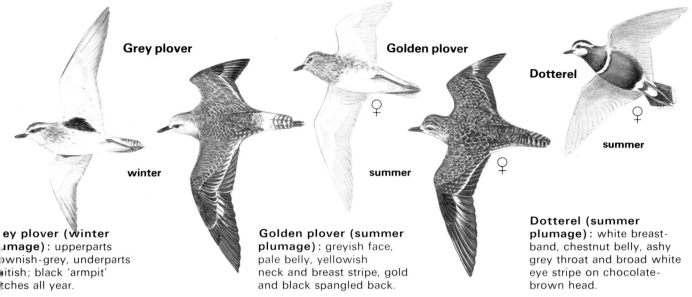

Grey plover

Golden plover

Dotterel

♀ winter

♀ summer ♀

summer

ey plover (winter
umage): upperparts
ownish-grey, underparts
itish; black 'armpit'
tches all year.

**Golden plover (summer
plumage):** greyish face,
pale belly, yellowish
neck and breast stripe, gold
and black spangled back.

**Dotterel (summer
plumage):** white breast-
band, chestnut belly, ashy
grey throat and broad white
eye stripe on chocolate-
brown head.

idflats around our shores while the golden
over frequents lowland fields and marshes.
Different dotterels The dotterel, so similar
the golden and grey plovers in shape,
ght and feeding methods, is wholly different
other ways. In breeding plumage it is a
iking bird, not to be confused with any
her. Bold white eye-stripes meeting at the
ck of the neck in a narrow V separate the
ocolate-coloured crown from the ashy grey
oat and upper back. Another narrow rib-
n of white separates the grey throat from
bright chestnut breast; when the birds are
oving fast over the mountain mosses and
hens on their bright yellow legs they are
nspicuous, but they blend with the terrain
soon as they stop moving.
The female is slightly larger than the male
d has distinctly brighter plumage—clues

which alert one to the fact that in this species
many of the sexual roles are reversed, with the
male caring for the young while the hen produces a second brood from a mating with
another male. This male in turn incubates the
eggs. So fixed are these roles that the cock
regularly drives away the hen if she approaches the unfledged young, probably ensuring that the chicks do not suffer unneces-
sary competition for food at this crucial stage.

The development of these reversed roles
probably derives from the need to free the
female from the constraints of nest protection, incubation and brooding so as to maxi-
mise her opportunity for producing and replacing eggs in the short, harsh mountain-top
environment.

In the British Isles only the highest mountain-tops, notably the Cairngorms in Scotland, support small breeding populations of
dotterel. From time to time a few pairs try
to nest in Snowdonia and the Lake District
but the whole British population rarely
exceeds 100-150 pairs a year.
The plover breeding season In spring, as the
grey plovers leave Britain for the far north,
heading for the narrow coastal band of tundra

A beautiful baby

yellow-black
mottling on
upper parts

greyish-white
down

The golden plover chick
has golden-yellow and
black speckled upperparts.
Tended by both parents,
it stays in the nest
for a month.

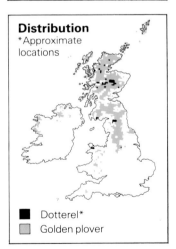

Distribution
*Approximate
locations

■ Dotterel*
▨ Golden plover

Grey plover (*Pluvialis
squatarola*). Passage
migrant and winter visitor to
our coasts and estuaries.
Length 28cm (11in).

Left: About 20,000 grey
plovers are found in the
British Isles at their
January winter peak.

137

on the shores of the Arctic Ocean, the golden plovers are also on the move. Our resident golden plovers re-populate the hills and moors of upland Britain, while the northern race aim for Iceland and Scandinavia.

From April to July the cries of our breeding golden plovers can be heard on the hills. Their eggs–buff, with blotchy dark brown markings–are laid on the ground in a clutch of four, perfectly camouflaged against the dark heather stems and peaty soil. The golden-brown chicks, which hatch after about four weeks, are among the most beautiful in the world.

Golden plovers share their upland home with only a few other bird species – red grouse,

Above: The southern form of the golden plover, which breeds here; it is joined in winter by the northern race from Iceland and Scandinavia.

Golden plover (*Pluvialis apricaria*). Resident (southern race) and winter visitor (northern race). Nests on hills, moorland. Length 28cm (11in).

Dotterel (*Eudromias morinellus*). Migrant and rare summer breeding visitor. Length 21cm (8½in).

Above left: The male dotterel's distraction display, aimed at drawing attention away from the nest and chicks. The male bird looks after the young. In the picture below a male is carefully turning over the eggs.

the ubiquitous meadow pipits and skylar scavenging crows and ravens, and the ev present predatory peregrine, merlin and l harrier. The other principal wader wh keeps them company on the rolling mo lands is the small, dapper dunlin–a co panion so constant that it has earned nick-name of 'plover's page'.

Much further north, the grey plovers arr singly on their breeding grounds, strang ignoring the vast wastes of Greenland a Spitzbergen which seem perfectly suitable, breed only on the moorland coastal tund of Arctic Canada, Alaska and Siberia. He as winter retreats and the short intense bea of the Arctic summer bursts, the grey plov pair, mate, nest and rear their young. Th cannot linger; time is short and each year n present difficulties. In a season when the th is too late or conditions bad, breeding n be an impossibility and the adults will retu south early. Even in a good year a seco brood is out of the question.

Winter populations Autumn brings all th different plovers on passage through British Isles. The dotterel, small 'trips' them faithfully stopping on traditional rest sites on mountain-tops, headlands or lowla fields, pass on southwards. The grey plove hugging the coastlines of western Euro spread themselves over favoured estuari and the golden plovers distribute themsel on inland and coastal pastures.

Our own breeding golden plovers (southern race) are joined by those from I land and Scandinavia. These northern bi have bolder, more extensive black bellies o the breeding plumage develops in late wint The total number of golden plover winter here is probably 600,000 or more, 25% them on estuary marshes and the remaine inland. Any congregation of lapwings seen fields at this time of year is worth checking the presence of the dumpy, less conspicuo forms of golden plover among them.

Although many golden plover are prese in winter, they are a declining and contracti breeding species on the southern fringes their range in Britain and Continental Euro This is probably due to habitat loss.

Left: A fully grown young raven on a crag: the species is associated with the rocky coastlines of northern and western Britain, the wilder coasts of Ireland, and the more craggy mountainous regions inland. In such places, ravens frequently occur together with choughs, on the same length of cliff or at the same inland quarries or crags.

Bottom: Ravens lay 4-6 eggs, which take 18-19 days to hatch. Fledging takes 5 weeks.

Raven distribution

Chough distribution

RAVEN AND CHOUGH:TWO CLIFF BIRDS

The raven and chough differ from the other, more commonly seen birds of the crow family, for they belong to the wild places of the north and west.

The raven is a large bird, biggest of the whole crow family, measuring some 64cm (25in) in length and having a wing span as large as a herring gull's. Its legs, feet and bill are jet black. Size difference alone is a sure way to distinguish ravens from other members of the crow family if they are seen together, but when the comparison cannot be made it is not immediately easy to distinguish between the raven and the carrion crow. The most useful features then are the massive proportions of head and bill in the raven and, in flight, the gradually tapered tail as compared to the square-ended tail of the crow. Also helpful is the fact that ravens are vocal birds, calling frequently. Their deep, resonant croak is an almost legendary characteristic, which instantly draws attention and distinguishes the species from all others.

Powers of flight Ravens are notable acrobatic performers on the wing. At any time of year, but especially in late winter and early spring as the breeding season approaches, ravens, which pair for life, often indulge in exciting display flights. The two ravens fly side by side, often at a great height, and one of them—most often the larger male—suddenly rolls upside down and continues gliding in this position for a short distance before righting itself again. Similarly, one of the pair may suddenly close wings and nose-dive through the sky with impressive power.

Carrion feeder The raven is predominantly a carrion eater, taking advantage of the ready supplies of meat afforded by this food source. Ravens often assemble in large numbers where a surfeit of carrion is available. In Wales, where it is a common bird, the presence of up to a hundred together is not infrequent at refuse dumps or when severe weather has caused local kills of sheep. There have also been reports of up to 800 congregating at the carcases of whales in the Shetland Islands.

Not relying on carrion alone, ravens otherwise take small mammals, eggs of other birds if the opportunity arises and frogs, reptiles or any other available form of meat. Sheep farmers in the hills view the raven with some suspicion, and accuse it of attacking the eyes of ewes in labour and of killing new-born lambs and sickly sheep. Such fears do from year to year result in illegal persecution of the species (which is fully protected by law) although in the areas where ravens occur the numbers are generally fairly large and they weather such local persecution reasonably well.

International range The raven is an immensely successful bird throughout the northern hemisphere, absent only from the lowlands

of Europe and the eastern United States. It is a denizen of the frozen north, and equally an opportunist of the desert areas of the southern United States, the Sahara, Arabia and of the whole of central and eastern Asia and of most places in between. It is one of the world's most successful bird species, profiting–as vultures do–from the inevitability of death in the animal kingdom and further benefiting from surplus waste produced by man.

Devon, Cornwall, Wales and the western and northern islands of Scotland are the

Above: A raven nest–possibly a few years old, but still in use–in a tree. Nests are built in traditional sites, and are enlarged a little each year. Ravens are a strictly resident species in Britain, and are among the earliest breeders in the year. Nest building is well under way in many areas by the end of February, and adults incubate solidly through the very worst of late winter weather.

Left: The chough has suffered from the reduction in the area of short-grazed turf and windswept coastal heathlands, which contain an ample supply of its invertebrate food.

strongholds of ravens in Britain, and in the areas their numbers are large. In Wales, n sites are often at regular spacings of 4km (miles) or so, but there is a considerable n breeding population to add to this. The to number in Britain is unlikely to be in exc of 5000 pairs and is declining, though th general unfamiliarity is due to the remoten of the regions they inhabit.

Captivating choughs How different from t raven is the chough: apart from being bla belonging to the same family and oft sharing the same wild cliffs, the two have lit else in common. Of all members of the fami the chough is the most popular, most captiv ing and indeed the only one which at no ti can be said to conflict with man or his intere in any degree.

The chough is a lightly built bird, sma than the crow or rook, and possibly mc likely to be confused with the jackdaw, w which it readily consorts as these two spec

w: A chough family at approach of fledgling. ugh nest sites tend to be ngly traditional, like those he raven. Unlike ravens, vever, choughs nest deep ck fissures in cliffs, in roofs of sea caverns or, as e, in roof spaces of rarely ted buildings. In these es they are safe from ost all forms of predation ept for determined egg ectors. The stick nest is constructed on a ledge n a cleft of rock and ply lined with wool.

often share the same cliff-top feeding areas and nest sites. Choughs can, however, readily be distinguished, both in flight and on the ground. Their outline, and especially the widely fingered flight feathers, give them a unique silhouette on the wing, and on the ground the bright red legs and bill–the latter being slender, long and decurved–are striking features which instantly distinguish the chough. Added to this is the fact that the chough, like the raven, is a vocal bird with a highly distinctive call–'tchay, tchay'–which immediately draws attention to it above the cacophony of jackdaws, breaking seas and seabird calls.

In flight, the chough is light and buoyant, a master of the close encounter, dashing and

responsible for its widespread decline and local demise in the face of the agricultural change which has transformed rabbit-grazed turf to arable land and pasture.

Choughs are invertebrate feeders, digging in soft turf with the long, curved bill and probing among rock crevices and the base of grass tufts for beetle larvae, moth caterpillars and other similar invertebrates. They also feed successfully on sandy beaches along the strandline, or in pastures by chiselling open cowpats.

Distribution of choughs The modern distribution of the chough in Britain is well defined. It is predominantly a bird of the western coastal cliffs with strongholds in Ireland (about 680 pairs) and Wales (about 140 pairs). The Isle of Man has a stable population of 50 to 60 pairs, and in Scotland it is restricted to 60-70 pairs in the Western Isles; with a few other small populations on nearby coasts. Since 1968 it has been absent from Cornwall, one of the traditional homes of the so-called Cornish chough. In other areas, for example north Wales, it has actually expanded its numbers a little and taken advantage of inland quarries and sheep-grazed hillsides.

In former days, when the land was less intensively cultivated and short turf was plentiful, the chough was a far more numerous and widespread bird, occurring round much of the coastline of England. It also bred inland across northern England.

ven (*Corvus corax*). ident in coastal areas of north and west, and in ggy mountains. Length m (25in).

ough (*Pyrrhocorax hocorax*). Resident in ote coastal areas of and and west Britain. gth 39cm (15½in).

careering wildly about the sea cliffs with breathtaking agility and abandon. It loves to wheel, dive and rise with closed wings, turn on its back as ravens do, or perform steep upward arcs, calling continually.

Small prey Compared to the raven, the chough's feeding habits are wholly refined, as it is a highly specialised and selective feeder. In fact it is probable that the bird's very particular feeding requirements have been

und-up of the crow family

black bill

Raven
64cm (25in)

black legs

red downcurved bill

Chough
39cm (15½in)

red legs

Jay
34cm (13½in)

agpie
cm (18in)

Jackdaw
33cm (13in)

Carrion crow
47cm (18½in)

Hooded crow
47cm (18½in)

(a sub-species of the carrion crow)

Rook
45cm (18in)

RING OUZEL: A MOUNTAIN BLACKBIRD

A hardy relative of the blackbird, the ring ouzel is a summer visitor, breeding each year on mountains and moorlands in the British Isles.

The ring ouzel is very much the 'mountain blackbird', an upland species keeping to mountain, moor and fell. Although blackbirds are found just as far to the north and west as ring ouzels, in all areas the blackbirds are the birds of the valleys, with plentiful bush or tree cover, while ring ouzels are birds of high-altitude, open landscapes or exposed, almost treeless areas nearer to sea level in the far north.

Differences from blackbirds The black plumage of the ring ouzel has a sooty, non-reflective tone, unlike the velvet blackness of the blackbird. As well as the vivid white crescent on the upper breast–known as the gorget–there are also smaller, pale crescent markings on the body, and some brownish overtones. The beak is yellow, unlike the strong orange colouring of the male blackbird's beak. The closed wings appear grey rather than sooty black, and in flight the grey contrasts strongly with the body: this is a useful field identification feature.

The female is browner, and her gorget is

Above: A female ring ouzel incubates her eggs. As in the blackbird, the female ring ouzel is a browner version of the male. Often the gorget is less pure white than in this case.

Left: Ring ouzels are unusual in having a higher rate of hatching success than most birds.

Below: Breeding distribution matches the pattern of mountains–except, mysteriously, in Ireland's mountainous south-west.

Ring ouzel distribution

often buff-coloured or an indistinct wh
The young pose something of an identifi
tion problem if seen in the absence of adu
They are brown-backed and have grey-bro
wings, but they also have a white throat (a:
some female blackbirds) not a collar or g
get. The breast is cinnamon, with bc
thrush-like dark blobs. After moulting
autumn they resemble their parents.

Spacious territories Ring ouzel territor
are usually far larger than those of blackbir
presumably reflecting the difficulties the bi
have in finding adequate food supplies
their harsher environment. Upland pa
usually choose stretches of land with
casional crags and isolated trees (often row
or mountain ash) that serve as song posts
the male, and with some sheltered cwms a
gullies in which to build the nest.

Although often conspicuous in this habit
especially since they choose prominent si
ing perches, they are far shyer in the prese
of man than their lowland cousins. On
ground, they have the same jaunty g
scampering over the grass, then paus
briefly to look and listen for food, flicking
wings and tail and occasionally cocking
tail high, especially immediately after la
ing.

Whistling song The usual first clue to
presence of ring ouzels is either the song
the call. The song is a disjointed series
remote-sounding, penetrating whistles, sor

142

nes single, sometimes double-phrased.
s simplicity adds to its penetrating power
d range in the boisterously windy weather
evalent at high altitudes. There is a piping
ntact call, and a quietly scolding 'chuck,
uck', very like the call used by the female
ackbird to keep her young under control.
ore characteristic, both on the breeding
ounds and when flocks form in autumn, is
harsh, laughing 'tchack-tchack-tchack'.

Mediterranean migrants Our ring ouzels
e migrants. It is thought that most of them
nter in the Mediterranean basin. In autumn,
en the southward journey lacks the urgency
spring migration and when numbers are
ollen by the year's generation of young
rds, ring ouzels may occasionally be found
most anywhere in lowland Britain where
nditions are suitable for migrant thrushes.
ey choose sites where there is a plentiful
pply of berries including elder, hawthorn,
se and rowan.

Ring ouzels of a Continental race are seen
casionally in autumn among the passage
grants recorded at the bird observatories
ound our coasts. These are Alpine ring
zels, from the mountain ranges of central
rope, and they are characterised by a much
ore scaly, almost silvery body.

Because their migration is a relatively short
e, ring ouzels are among the earliest of our
mmer visitors to return, many reaching the
uth coast bird observatories early in March,
d arriving at their breeding grounds a few
ys later. Passage, including birds passing
rough Britain on the way to Scandinavia,
ay continue until early May. Return mig-
nts begin to gather in flocks to meander
uthwards in late August and September,
d a trickle of migrants often continues into
ovember. There are also numerous reports

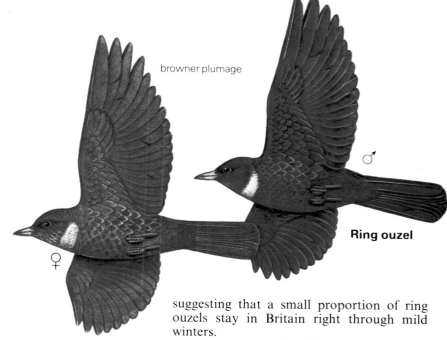

browner plumage

Ring ouzel

Above: Ring ouzels resemble
blackbirds in size and shape.
Their flight, however, is
swifter and more direct,
with wings beating almost
continuously.

Ring ouzel (*Turdus
torquatus*). Summer visitor
resembling a blackbird with
a white gorget. A few birds
winter in lowlands. 24cm
(9½in).

Below: The plumage of the
male is sooty black, in
contrast with the velvet
blackness of the blackbird.
The most striking feature
is the white crescent on the
upper breast.

suggesting that a small proportion of ring
ouzels stay in Britain right through mild
winters.

Finding a nest site Once back on their
breeding grounds, the ring ouzel pairs quickly
set about the establishment of a territory,
which is loudly proclaimed by the male from
his song posts, and fiercely defended by both
birds calling harshly and 'dive-bombing' intruders, be they crows, stoats, foxes or even
innocently straying humans or mountain
sheep. The nest is made of coarse grasses,
heather and a good deal of mud; and it is
lined with soft, fine, dry grass. It is most often
built in a crevice or on a rock ledge on a small
crag or fall of scree. Almost as common are
nests in low vegetation (below 46cm/18in),
and some are even built directly on the ground.

One feature common to most ring ouzel
nests is that they command a wide view of the
surrounding countryside for the sitting bird
to survey, and another is that they often have
an overhang close above, offering some protection from inclement weather. Occasionally birds use crevices in deserted barns or
mine buildings as a substitute for crags, and
there are several descriptions of nests actually
below ground level in old mine shafts, the
lowest being 5m (15ft) down. In contrast,
very few nests indeed are reported more than
1m (3ft) above ground in trees, the maximum

Spot the difference

orange bill

large white crescent
on upper breast

yellow bill

small crescent
markings

blackbird

ring ouzel

Left: During the breeding season, much of the ring ouzel's food consists of earthworms, insects and their larvae, and small snails. Fruits of various plant species become a more important food source when autumn approaches.

Below: The rushing burn above the Corrie Bhrodain waterfall in Inverness-shire. Here in the Grampian mountains the ring ouzel is at home. In the far north a few pairs nest at lower altitudes, even down to sea level; but over 80% of nests found in one recent study were between 230 and 530 (750-1750ft). The highest nest recorded was at a staggering altitude of 1140m (3750ft) in the Cairngorms.

on record being 3m (10ft) up in a tree.

Raising the brood The first eggs are laid in mid-April, with a distinct peak in egg production at the end of April and early in May below 450m (1500ft). Above this altitude, egg laying seems to occur later (as would be expected for climatic reasons)–perhaps by a week or ten days. There are indications that while first clutches lost are replaced, true second clutches are not common. Accurate timings of incubation and fledging periods are hard to obtain, perhaps not surprisingly in the light of the remoteness of most ring ouzel nests, but the indications are that each may last about a fortnight.

The great majority of clutches are of four eggs, pale blue in ground colour with a peppering of bold dark brown and lavender spots. Some clutches of three or five eggs are reported each year, but six is most unusual. Egg losses tend to be either single ones that prove to be infertile, or whole clutches lost either because of desertion or in the raids of predators.

Declining numbers It is clear from Victorian bird books that in the last century ring ouzels were both more numerous and more widely distributed than they are today, and that in some areas there has been a considerable decrease. Reasons for the decline are not obvious: certainly the ring ouzel seems well able to tolerate the relatively limited intrusions by man into its habitat. There has been a suggestion that the increase of the blackbird during this century has adversely affected the ring ouzel, possibly with the additional influence of a milder climate–favouring the blackbird and reducing the area of the ring ouzel's montane habitat. The most recent estimate puts the population at between 8000 and 16,000 pairs.

THE WHEATEAR: BIRD OF THE OPEN SPACES

Despite its name, the wheatear does not eat ears of wheat, nor does it usually live near cereal fields; in fact it eats insects and lives in open, grassy places. However, its name does have some meaning, since it derives from the Anglo-Saxon for 'white rump', which is the bird's most conspicuous feature.

Wheatear distribution

e wheatear is a little larger than the robin, d not dissimilar in shape and feeding haviour. Like the robin, it feeds from the ound, hopping some distance and then nding bolt upright to survey the grass, en flicking its wings and tail in a distinctly rt and ready-to-pounce fashion. It makes l use of raised points such as hummocks boulders, since these give a wide field of w. Adult and larval insects form the main ey, but other invertebrates such as snails, llipedes, spiders and worms are also taken. me insects are even caught in mid-air if ey fly close enough.

The plumage of the male wheatear is full sharp contrasts: black wings and eye ask' stand out from pale grey upperparts d whitish underparts, and black tips to the tail feathers highlight their white bases and the white rump. This white rump is the most conspicuous feature of wheatears of both sexes. On most males, the throat and breast are pale buff, fading gradually to pure white on the undertail coverts, and there is also a white stripe above the eye 'mask'.

The female's plumage is less contrasting: black is replaced by dark brown, and grey by paler brown. Thus, for example, her facial markings are not at all conspicuous. Beneath, she is buff coloured, with little trace of white. Nevertheless, she does have the white rump, so that identification is normally easy.

Open habitats Several other species of birds have white rumps, including the bullfinch, jay, brambling, house martin and several waders, but these all live in quite

Above: Wheatears are commonest on sheep-grazed uplands, coastal headlands, shingle banks and islands.

Below: The chicks hatch 14 days after the last egg is incubated. After only 15 days in the nest they are able to fly, and not long after that they are fully independent. These three juveniles have just fledged; at this stage, they are particularly attractive, being heavily speckled. The growth of these young birds is so rapid that both parents have to collect food for them.

different habitats – at least during the summer when wheatears are here – and have very different patterns of behaviour. A small bird with a conspicuous white rump, feeding on open ground, is almost certainly a wheatear. The species is also characterised by constant activity – flitting from one place to another – so the birdwatcher rarely has to wait long for one to alight nearby, giving a good view.

In spring and autumn, when they are on their way to or from their breeding grounds, wheatears are seen in most open habitats – beaches, grassland, ploughed fields, waste land, coastal headlands and rough tracks – but such birds are merely passing through, and usually move on after a day or so when

Above: On the breeding grounds, wheatears (this is a female) blend marvellously into the background, their grey, white and black plumage looking just like lichen-covered rocks. But listen for their alarm calls as you approach. 'Chack-chack' is the usual call, or 'weet-chack-chack

Below: The male wheatear is instantly distinguished from the female by his black eye-stripe and bold colours.

they have found sufficient food to last throu their next flight.

In the breeding season they are mo particular. At this time, short turf seems to the major requirement, since it supports t insect population on which they feed. Shee grazed upland is ideal and many wheatea live on the hills and mountains in the nor and west, even at altitudes of over 1000 (3300ft). Windswept coastal headlan shingle banks and even small islands provi suitable habitats in which wheatears thrive

However, in southern and eastern Englar wheatears have become quite rare. Until t turn of the century, chalk downland a heathland used to hold quite large popu lations. Roast wheatear was commonly eat as a delicacy, and shepherds used to s wheatears which they caught on the dow without any significant impact on the bree ing numbers.

It was the decline in sheep farming whi seriously affected the wheatear populatio since the grass then grew long and scr invaded, rendering the land quite unsuitab A reduction in the number of rabbits as result of myxomatosis made things wor and today relatively few of the traditio wheatear breeding sites are occupied.

Assortment of tunnels Wheatears also sho a strong preference for areas with dry sto walls, scree slopes or abandoned buildin This is because, unlike many birds of op grassland areas, wheatears require more th a simple tussock in which to place th nest. The ideal nest site would be a shelter hollow at the end of a rocky 'tunne perhaps several feet long – easily reached the birds but totally inaccessible to prec tors such as the fox. Where rocks are available, interesting alternatives have be recorded. For example, at Dungeness Kent, where wheatears breed on shing nest boxes, drain pipes and even discard ammunition boxes have proved adequate. (downland, old rabbit burrows provide reac made tunnels for some wheatears.

Breeding wheatears The male defends t territory by means of song and displa Although delivered with great enthusias the song is not particularly tuneful. It d contain some melodious warbling notes, these are mixed with harsh scratchy soun in a short, rather jumbled sequence.

Meanwhile, the female builds the ne collecting dry grass stems first for the ma structure and then feathers, wool or hair a smooth warm lining. In neither nest-bui ing nor incubation does the male give h much help. Later, when the chicks ha hatched, he comes to her assistance, for t young develop rapidly and the work of bo parents is needed to sustain their growth.

Migration schedule On the south coast England, the first wheatears usually arri from their African wintering grounds in ea March. Most of them arrive about a mor

Wheatear recognition features

autumn juvenile

black 'mask'

ttled pattern
head, back
underparts

autumn adult

♂

black 'mask'

brown 'mask'

buff
underparts

♀

inverted 'T'

black 'mask'

♂

black wings

white rump

pale grey
upperparts

inverted 'T'

summer adult

white eye-stripe

brown upperparts

brown wings

♀

er. Some lay eggs in mid-April and there-
re have young in May. For others, es-
cially those breeding further north or in
ountainous regions where snowfalls are
ll likely, May is the egg-laying month and
ne is the time for young. Only those that
eed early seem to lay two clutches regularly,
e second brood fledging in July.

August and September are the main
parture months, though some wait until
ctober. Before they leave, all the adult
rds moult into their winter plumage, grow-
g a whole new set of feathers in just a few
eeks. The young birds, too, grow new head
d body feathers. Males, females and young
rds look very similar at this time: all
semble females in summer plumage.

Marathon migrants Wheatears breed
roughout most of Europe and northern
sia, but also in the extreme north-western
d north-eastern parts of North America.
is distribution, and the fact that all
heatears migrate to tropical Africa for the
nter, suggests that the species originated in
e Old World and only spread to America
recent years. For example, no wheatears
nter in South America.

As a result, some wheatears fly phenomenal
stances during their migration. Those from
reenland have to make a 3200km (2000
le) sea crossing over the North Atlantic to
eland, Britain or Spain – a remarkable non-
op flight for so small a bird. Needless to
y, such birds must build up large reserves of
ergy-rich fat in their bodies before setting
f; there is no chance of refuelling on the
y, and certain death results if the supply
ns short. Those that reach dry land arrive
ed and hungry, and only two-thirds of
eir starting weight.

The Greenland wheatears These are slightly
rger than British wheatears, and they tend
stand more upright. They perch in tall
es much more frequently than ours do,
d, at least in spring, they have more richly
loured underparts. Finally, the Greenland
rds tend to pass through this country
ther later than our own, both in spring
d summer. Their peak passage months are
e April/early May, and September/October.

Wheatear (*Oenanthe
oenanthe*). Summer visitor
to upland grazing land and
other open habitats.
Greenland race is slightly
larger but difficult to
distinguish. Length of
British birds 15cm (5¾in).

Right: Seven unmarked, pale
blue eggs are the usual
clutch, but both the colour
and the number vary. Thus,
some eggs have dark spots,
and some females lay up to
eight or nine eggs –
especially those in the far
north of the breeding range.

Below: A pair of wheatears
at the entrance to a
tunnel – probably an old
rabbit burrow that the birds
have taken over. The female
(holding a grub) has more
buff-coloured underparts and
the male's are whiter.

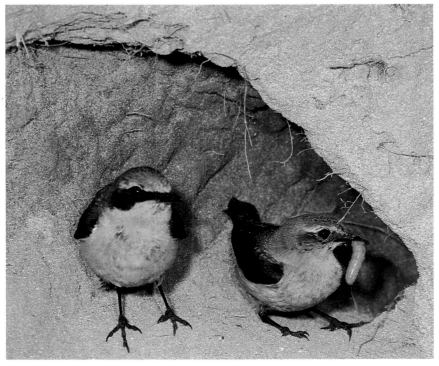

147

PIPITS OF MEADOWS AND ROCKY COASTS

The meadow pipit is the most conspicuous small bird of moorland, and is often seen in upland meadows, especially when performing its high-flying display in spring. The rock pipit looks similar, but its habitat is the rocky coastline.

As every experienced hill-walker knows, the most numerous bird at altitudes of 500-1000m (1500-3000ft) is almost always the meadow pipit. In spring and summer, the moors and rough, sheep-grazed grassland in Wales, the Pennines and Scotland seem alive with these small, streaked birds. And well they might, for Britain and Ireland can boast a population of some three million pairs of meadow pipits, at densities which sometimes exceed 50 pairs per square kilometre.

An insect hunter At 14.5cm (5¾in) in length, the meadow pipit is of similar size and build to the dunnock. As would be expected of an active, ground-feeding insectivore, it has long legs and toes and a finely pointed bill. The

Above: A meadow pipit seen against the open sky. In its exposed habitat, the species is particularly prone to attack by raptors.

Meadow pipit (*Anthus pratensis*). Present all year, some birds wintering overseas. Sexes alike. Length 14.5cm (5¾in).

Rock pipit (*A. spinoletta*). Resident. Sexes alike. Length 16.5cm (6¼in).

Right: A rock pipit chick, at fledging age.

hind toe carries a very long claw.

The majority of meadow pipits live in op upland habitats, but many can be found more accessible places. Heaths, sand-dur and saltmarshes all provide suitable feedi and nesting sites, and even intensively cul vated farmland may hold a few pairs if one two grassy banks or field corners rema undisturbed. The only large areas witho meadow pipits are in central and south-ea England, and comparison with geologic maps suggests that one reason for this mig be the presence of heavy clay soils in the regions. The soil itself is unlikely to be important factor, but the invertebrate fau associated with it may not be suitable for t birds.

As autumn approaches, and especia when snow returns to the mountains, ma meadow pipits are forced to congregate valleys and lowland areas. In winter, loc flocks are found in almost any open habit mixing freely with finches, buntings and sk larks.

Recognition features The meadow pipit c be distinguished from similar birds by combination of streaked plumage, white ou tail feathers, fine bill and a running gait opposed to a hopping one. The pluma provides excellent camouflage, the hea back, wings and tail being generally brown in colour, often with a greenish tinge. T underparts are creamy white, boldly mark to a varying extent with brown or blacki streaks, which also extend over the should on to the back. Usually, the throat, belly a undertail coverts are pale brown. Final many of the wing feathers have pale edges a at times these result in two narrow wing ba

Flight and call Apart from its gene appearance, the other main identificati features of the meadow pipit are its way flying and its flight call. These are well wo memorising, since it often flies off witho allowing an observer to approach close Notice how jerky and hesitant the bird's flig is, with very short bursts of flapping. Th listen to the call: a single, very high-pitch and distinctive 'sweep'. Only rarely will t meadow pipit take flight without calling; mo

CHECKLIST

*This checklist is a guide to some of the mammals you will find on mountains and moorlands. Although you will not see them all in the same place, you should be able to spot many of them throughout the changing seasons. The species listed in **bold type** are described in detail.*

Bank vole
Brown hare
Common shrew
Dale pony
Dartmoor pony
Exmoor pony
Fell pony
Feral goat
Field vole
Fox
Hedgehog
Mole
Mountain hare
Otter
Pine marten
Polecat
Pygmy shrew
Rabbit
Red deer
Reindeer
Roe deer
Scottish Highland pony
Shetland pony
Soay sheep
Stoat
Water shrew
Weasel
Welsh mountain pony
Wildcat
Wood mouse

Left: A fine red deer stag in winter coat. In spring and summer red deer can find enough to eat on the hills and mountains of Scotland, but in winter they must move down to lower ground if they are to survive.

153

MOUNTAIN AND MOORLAND MAMMALS

Many of our native land mammals are so highly adaptable that they can live almost anywhere in Britain. Some of them flourish on high moorlands despite the long cold winters, rather sunless damp summers, and unkind soils. Even so, none belongs exclusively to the uplands.

There is no mountain in the British Isles that is too high for at least a few of our mammal species. The tiny pygmy shrew, for instance, has been found at the top of our highest mountain, Ben Nevis; but most of our mammals thrive in a variety of habitats, and even the mountain hare, though so much at home on the Scottish moors, is found elsewhere on low-lying ground, notably in Ireland.

Mountain hare This hare is smaller than the much more widespread brown hare; its ears are shorter, and it tends to turn white in winter while the brown hare stays brown. The mountain hares of Ireland, however, seldom turn wholly white; some become patched

with white, others show no white at all. The white mountain hares of Scotland camouflage themselves in the snow to be less conspicuous to predators, but in Ireland, which lacks a steady winter snow cover, there is no need for this type of camouflage.

Although the brown hare is generally regarded as a lowland animal, a small proportion of its population lives on moorland up to about 500m (1500ft), where, in Scotland, its range overlaps with that of the mountain hare. It seems likely that when the two species meet they compete for food, and that the mountain hare keeps to the uplands because the brown hare is dominant at the lower levels. This could explain why in

Above: Red deer. There are thought to be about a quarter of a million in northern Scotland. They live in far-scattered herds, usually numbering two or three dozen, but occasional they assemble in larger numbers and up to 600 ha been seen together. They are red only in their thinner summer coats; in winter the pelage is longer and browner. They prefer life on the high moors in summer to avoid flies, but in winter they are driven by cold and hunger to seek food and shelter in valley bottoms and woodlands.

Originally the red deer wer forest dwellers, so those that live today up on the moorlands are really refugees. Subsisting for many generations on a die of heather and coarse grasses has reduced the body weight and antler siz of the Highland deer compared with that of those living in southern England.

Left: The mountain hare. Because mountain hares, like red grouse, prefer to feed on short, young, heather, they are commonest on the Scottish moors carefully preserved for grouse, for there the heather is systematically burned to keep it short. Elsewhere they graze on grasses and sedges and, in times of deep snow, can survive on gorse, juniper, and other tall plants. Their commonest natural predators are foxes, but some are seized by wild cats, eagles and other raptors. Leverets are taken by buzzards and hen harriers. By far their worst enemy is man. He has long persecuted them for sport and because they eat the heather shoots which are meant for grouse.

the other two shrews which are brown on the back, is, like the common shrew, distributed throughout mainland Britain. Far better known as a lowlander than as an uplander, the water shrew occurs only sparsely on moorlands and perhaps seldom moves above about 300m (1500ft), frequenting instead stream banks and the margins of lakes.

Hedgehog and mole Two other insectivores, the hedgehog and mole, also belong chiefly to the lowlands but both venture up the valleysides to the moorland rim in fair numbers. Occasionally you see the prickly skins of hedgehogs far above the tree line, but these may have been animals carried up by predators. Moles have a much better claim to be genuine dwellers on high moorland, for they have been found living at 1000m (3000ft). These occurrences are rare, however. The mole is dependent on an abundance of easily available earthworms and cannot tolerate soils that are either waterlogged, extremely stony or very sour, because they are all virtually wormless. As such soils prevail over

land, where the brown hare is largely absent, the mountain hare flourishes in lowland areas.

Upland rodents The hares' small cousins, the rodents, are also well represented on the uplands. Indeed one, the field vole, must at times outnumber all the other mammals put together. This little vole, grey-brown with small eyes and ears, short tail and blunt snout, occasionally multiplies in numbers so astonishingly that its multitudes eat the grass down to the bare earth. This plague of voles attracts predators from afar – hawks, owls and carnivorous mammals. Then quite suddenly a virulent disease runs through the famished vole population, reducing it to a low level, the predators quickly disperse and the episode is over. This vole is a hardy species on all levels of moorland, reaching 1300m (4000ft) on the Cairngorms. It feeds mainly on grasses and thrives especially in the deep grassland that develops when sheep are fenced out of moorland in preparation for tree planting.

The bank vole, distinguished by the redness of the adult pelage, though predominantly a woodlander of woods and hedgerows, is also really recorded on high moorland. Likewise the wood-mouse is by no means restricted to woods. Just as aptly described by its alternative name, long-tailed field-mouse it, too, is often a grassland dweller, occurring here and there on upland moors.

Our two smallest mammals also include the high ground in their range. Both pygmy and common shrews live well hidden in the grassland, feeding on worms, beetles and other invertebrates. They are voracious species that need to eat frequently to sustain their night and day activity that continues even in winter, when invertebrate life is often hard to find. The water shrew, which is a neat black colour above and white below, in contrast to

Above: The Scottish wild cat, once widespread in Britain (but never in Ireland), was exterminated nearly everywhere by the numerous gamekeepers of the last century. Its original habitat was forest and it still lives in high-level Scottish pinewoods wherever it can find them. Elsewhere it makes do with open country, especially heather moors. Its den is hidden among rocks, fallen tree trunks or deep heather.

wide areas of moorland the mole is inevitably scarce and local there.

Upland carnivores Six carnivores regularly frequent moorlands but they are seldom observed and are most often detected by their signs. Rather common throughout most British and Irish uplands, and quite likely to be seen by day is the fox, because in warm weather it likes to sleep out in the open where it is sometimes disturbed by hill walkers. Its droppings often contain hair, wool or feathers and tend to be blackish when fresh, bleaching to white eventually. Like those of many moorland carnivores, they are often purple with bilberry juice in summer.

The fox lives as readily among steep cliffs

and block scree as among level tracts of tall heather, or the cover of rushes and purple moor-grass. If you search around with binoculars from a high vantage point you can sometimes spot a fox lying curled up sun-bathing on a mountain ledge or on the sheltered slope of a peat-hag. Shepherds suspect the fox of preying heavily on lambs and they kill it whenever possible, although the mortality of upland lambs is often high through natural causes. The moor fox lives mainly on small mammals, birds, fruit and any sort of carrion.

The wild cat and four members of the family Mustelidae also regularly live on moorlands. Man's hand has long been against stoats and weasels but the polecat and the pine marten have been even more ruthlessly persecuted; however, the polecat can still be found throughout most of Wales, and the pine marten still thrives in northern Scotland and areas of Ireland, with smaller numbers in the Lake District and Snowdonia. Both are by preference woodlanders that have adapted to other habitats over the centuries as the tree cover has been destroyed. Both have doubt-less been helped by the great spreads of conifers which have invaded the moors this century and provide cover and food.

The red deer, the largest and most cele-brated of the moorland mammals, was originally a forest dweller, as was the much smaller roe deer which remains a shy wood-

land creature nearly everywhere. But in the Scottish Highlands the roe deer has to some extent followed the life-style of the red deer and taken to the treeless uplands in summer, especially where it can find the cover of tall heather. In at least one district roe deer live above the tree line all year. Scottish roe deer are indigenous, as distinct from those of low-land England which are the result of intro-ductions from the Continent. There are no wild roe in Ireland. It is interesting that although Wales has large areas of moorland it has no deer of any sort. There used to be plenty of red deer, but they were exterminated centuries ago and have never been re-introduced.

Above: One member of a herd of reindeer which has been on the Cairngorms since 1952 but which, sinc they are managed like cattl cannot be thought of as ev semi wild.

Opposite page: A rare mammal of the moorlands, found now mainly in Wale the polecat, recognisable from its 'bandit' mask.

Below: The stoat, usually a lowland species, can sometimes be found in upland areas.

THE FRENZIED RUT OF THE RED DEER

For three weeks every autumn, the graceful red deer stag changes almost beyond recognition. One day he will be grazing peacefully with his fellow stags, the next he has become a roaring, restless beast, antlers at the ready to defend his harem of hinds.

RED DEER
(*Cervus elaphus*)
Size Max height at shoulder: male 122cm (48in), female 114cm (45in). Av weight: male 85kg (187lb), female 58kg (128lb), variable.
Breeding season Young born mainly late May and June.
No of young (calf) 1.
Lifespan Max 20 years.
Food Mainly grasses, sedges, rushes. Also heather, tree leaves, bark, herbs, lichens, ferns, mushrooms.
Predators Man; foxes and eagles take the young.

Red deer, indigenous to Britain, are our largest land mammal. They were at one time much more widespread, inhabiting the woodland that covered much of the country. Today, British red deer can be divided into two groups: those that still exist in scattered herds in English woodland, and those that now live on mountains and moorland, notably in the Scottish Highlands, but also in Martindale in northern England.

Antlers Only the stags have antlers, which are generally lighter and shorter on Highland deer than those of southern, woodland deer, and with fewer points (tines). This is due to their poorer, harsher habitat. Average Highland stags have six to eight points on each

antler. Some may have 10 or 12 points an exceptionally, up to 16—or none at a Woodland stags average 10 to 12 points, a may have as many as 20.

The number of points is no guide to t age of a stag. But a mature stag has thicke longer, and often darker, antlers than young stag with a similar number of points

Changing coats Red deer grow new coa twice a year. The winter coat consists of tw layers: an undercoat of soft, blue-grey, clos knit fur and an overcoat of long, crinkly ha which varies from very dark, blackish-brow through red-brown to sandy yellow. Th warm double coat is replaced in June by thin single coat of glossy red hair.

Peaceful prelude The long days of summ are spent peacefully grazing on the high mountain slopes, the sexes segregated in groups. Stags of three years and above mo about quite separately from the hinds, wł also keep in single-sex groups. The fe antlered animals still with the hinds are you males (staggies).

Autumn aggression Towards the end September the stag groups begin to gro restless. Their antlers are now hardened ai darker in colour, from off-white to near black in some cases. The mature stags ha grown tremendously shaggy, leonine man which make them look front-heavy in contra to their heavily muscled but slim haunches.

After a day or two of voicing their unrest

Left: If a stag slips and falls during combat, his opponent will do his best to gore him. The brow points of the antlers (those points that jut out just above the forehead) are used for this purpose. Fights to the death are rare, however. Usually one stag senses defeat and retreats.

Below: Except during the rut, red deer live mainly in single-sex societies. Young males (staggies) stay with the female group until the age of three years, when they break away to join a stag group.

liminary roaring, some of the stags break ay to roam through the hills in search of ds. Once a stag has found a hind group, he els every male in the group except the male ves of that year, and endeavours to hold hinds for the three weeks' duration of the in rut – or until his strength fails.

He becomes an animal possessed, and his neanour alters dramatically. His gait nges from a graceful stride to a stiff-legged, ted, menacing strut. His expression alters m one of almost bovine placidity to one of en aggression. His mane, already shaggy l thick at the onset of the rut, appears even cker as a result of his wallowing in peat or d – the individual hairs standing out stiff l spiky. His beautiful coat of summer red imilarly daubed and darkened. The hairs ling along the middle of his belly become , black and smelly with continual urinat- . This, together with his habit of rolling vegetation liberally sprayed with urine, e him the pungent, rank odour that is racteristic of the rutting stag.

Roaring incessantly, always on the alert the incursion of any male, he is kept at er pitch by the roaring of other stags rby. Stags still searching for hinds, evicted gies hanging around the group and hinds mpting to sneak away, all contribute to continual state of unrest. He can neither p soundly nor eat properly, and it is dly surprising that he loses weight and

strength. It is an exceptional stag who can last the three weeks of the rut without being deposed by a fresher stag.

Furious combat Some fighting takes place each rutting season, as aspiring stags venture to dispute ownership of hinds. Challenger and challenged first size each other up by pacing, stiff-legged, around the group of hinds. The defending stag always keeps a head in front of the challenger, and on the inner side of the paced circle. If the intruder decides he is overmatched, he will break off from this pacing and strut away to find an easier opponent. He may give vent to his anger and disappointment by viciously demolishing a patch of heather with scything antlers, then roaring loudly over this 'victory'.

If the preliminaries end in combat, however, the two pacing stags suddenly wheel towards each other, apparently simultaneously, bringing their antlers together with a reverberating clash. With heads and necks bowed and straining, there ensues a titanic struggle of balance and strength. Each stag tries to gain uphill ground advantage, in order to push his opponent backwards in one tremendous rush. There is an uncanny silence during all this violent action, broken only by the occasional clicking and clashing of antlers.

Quite as suddenly as the combat started, the stag sensing defeat breaks off and literally runs for his life. The victor, if incensed enough, may follow for a few metres, scything at the

Left: The stag roars incessantly during the rut and is continually incensed by the roaring of other stags within hearing distance. He mates with his hinds as they come into season; no more than one or two hinds in his group will be in season on any one day. The hind stays in season for about 24 hours

Red deer distribution

defeated stag's haunches with his antlers. He roars in breathless triumph, then returns to his hinds—if he is lucky enough to find them still there.

Fights which last long or end in fatalities are exceptional. Most last only a few minutes. Superficial wounds, like torn ears or forehead skin are fairly common, with occasionally more serious wounds such as punctured eyeballs which, of course, mean permanent blindness in the affected eye. There can be few red deer haunts which do not have a one-eyed stag from time to time.

After the rut By the end of October most of the rutting is over, and stags and hinds go their separate ways for the winter and spring months. Stags tend to spend these hospitable months on lower ground, close to human habitation, where the grazing better but the risk of discovery greater. T is mainly a consequence of their reduc vitality and physical condition after the rut mature stag may have lost 13kg (2st) dur this time.

In really severe weather, the hinds a come further down the hillsides to find fc and better shelter. There is generally suffici grazing to see the deer through the wint but by spring there is little left, and a per of scarcity follows until the growth of n vegetation. This is the most difficult time deer, particularly in the Highlands, and o the strongest and fittest survive. Mortalit mainly among weaker calves and age adults whose teeth or constitution are longer adequate.

By mid-March the stags begin to cast th antlers, looking donkey-like and bereft of dignity without them. Their winter coats now bleached and shaggy. April is perh the hardest month of all, the deer still hav to subsist on the scant remains of last yea vegetation.

The new growth of vegetation begins May. Then the deer can gradually desert lower ground for the higher, safer slopes. June their new year is fully under way, w new grazing, renewed strength, new co fast-growing antlers and young calves.

Calving The hind gives birth relativ easily. Once she has dropped her calf, licks it assiduously, eating the opaque me brane that covers it. At first the wet, bla new-born calf lies still beneath these minis tions, but after about ten minutes it begin struggle weakly. Within about 30 minute is standing on its feet, swaying precariou sometimes falling, but always struggling again.

On wavering and apparently unco-or ated legs, it pursues a weaving, lurch course to find the hind's udder and take first, vital drink. It suckles for about minutes, then collapses again and lies beneath the mother's renewed licking grooming.

Peat and mud wallows

Red deer take peat or mud baths (wallows) throughout the year. They wallow most frequently during the rut and on hot, summer days, but also in cold, frosty weather, sometimes breaking ice to bathe.
The animal first urinates into the wallow and stirs it up with its antlers (or, in the case of the hind, with a foreleg). It rolls over on one side in the smelly liquid, then makes another half-roll to coat the other side. Finally, the deer rubs its neck and head on the side of the wallow and emerges glistening but stinking.
Wallowing helps deer keep cool, soothes itching caused by warble fly grubs or moulting, and provides a protective armour of insect repellent.
The dried-on coat may be black or varying shades of brown or red, depending on whether the wallow is of peat or mud.

Daytime concealment For the first ten days of the calf's life, it is left alone from dawn to dusk, usually under some kind of cover. This may be long heather, the shadow of a rock or thick clumps of rushes. Very occasionally calves are left in conspicuous places, such as bare green slopes or equally bare expanses of black peat.

The mother returns to her calf in the evening to let it suckle. She remains with it all night, then leaves it once again to continue her own grazing. If the calf is discovered alone on the hill in the first two days of life, it remains absolutely motionless. Later on, it may rise and run.

During its first weeks, the calf may use a penetrating, high-pitched emergency call, to appeal to the hind for help when danger threatens. This call carries over long distances and can bring as many as seven hinds stampeding to the rescue, all with calves hidden in the same area.

The hind has fiercely maternal instincts, and is utterly selfless in protecting her calf against predators. She will kill both foxes and eagles, trampling them into the ground with her flailing front hooves.

The stag, on the other hand, is an utterly selfish individualist who would not even recognise his own offspring. When in his prime, he mates with perhaps 20 hinds in each season. The romantic concept of the family proud father stag is pure myth. In a mating system based on polygamy, this could not occur.

Equally mythical is the romantic idea of the stag as proud leader of the herd. Even during the rut, it is the hind who takes the lead in times of danger. Although the stag may appear outwardly dominant over the hinds, it is one of the senior hinds who leads off in flight, the stag invariably bringing up the rear.

Revenue from red deer It is estimated by researchers that over 255,000 red deer live in the Scottish Highlands today. In their virtually sterile mountainous habitat they do provide an important factor in the economy of the Highlands. Deer-stalking and the venison trade to hotels provide much-needed jobs for a number of people, and a revenue of over two million pounds is collected annually from these concerns. Deer conservation is therefore an important issue.

Above: Calves are generally born in early summer. They keep their cream-dappled coat until they are about three months old.

Below: Red deer can subsist in all but the severest weather conditions. They scrape through soft snow to vegetation beneath, using a flailing foreleg.

RETURN OF THE REINDEER

Usually thought of as a semi-domesticated nomadic animal of the Arctic Circle landscape, the reindeer was returned in 1952 to the glens and hillsides of the Cairngorms in the Scottish Highlands.

To see reindeer in the wild in the Briti[sh] Isles you have to go to the heart of t[he] Cairngorms in Scotland and climb the hi[lls] of Glenmore outside the popular resort [of] Aviemore. The fact that this is the only wi[ld] herd of reindeer living in this country m[ay] seem strange. Discoveries of reindeer bon[es] and antlers show that reindeer could be fou[nd] over a wide ranging area in prehistoric time[s] although it is accepted that they had all di[ed] out by 7000 BC. In fact, the Scottish reinde[er] alive today are an example of a species th[at] has been reintroduced successfully into t[he] British Isles by the efforts and determinati[on] of the late Mikel Utsi and his wife Dr Eth[el] Lindgren.

Sweden to Scotland Reindeer breeder Utsi transplanted a few beasts from his own Swedish mountain reindeer herd to the Cairngorms in 1952. This cool mountainous region has conditions broadly similar to parts of northern Scandinavia. Later fresh stock from both Sweden and Norway reinforced the herd, and a Russian strain was added when a bull joined the herd from Whipsnade Zoo in Bedfordshire. Carefully managed, the reindeer flourished. By the late 1970s there were 80 beasts, and by the late 1980s about 300 calves had been born since the herd was first established.

Reindeer and red deer look similar from a distance, but there are several features that clearly distinguish the reindeer from red deer and indeed from all other types of deer. One important difference is that both sexes carry antlers (in other deer only the male grows antlers), although the bull's antlers are larger than the cow's. Another difference is that the first forward branch of one side of the antlers is often itself branched, and juts out above the face rather like a hand with outspread fingers. Reindeer are also able to survive nearer to the North Pole than any other deer.

Reindeer and caribou are thought by most authorities to be different races of the same species. Reindeer flourish in Europe and Asia where over one and a half million roam inhospitable areas of mountain and tundra. The caribou, which lives in a truly wild state unlike its semi-domesticated Eurasian counterpart, is found in North America.

In Scotland the reindeer roam thousands of acres of the mountain slopes of Glenmore Forest 400–900 metres (1400–3000ft) above sea level. Their range is not entirely unrestricted because the Reindeer Company that owns them sometimes corrals the beasts to check

for ailments and to cull individuals for the venison meat market. Also each year the herd keeper (or volunteer guides) takes thousands of interested visitors on walks to see the reindeer. But apart from the time spent in enclosures when they are checked by the deer warder, they feed and breed much like their semi-domesticated counterparts in northern Europe and Asia.

Herd behaviour Like other reindeer, those found in Scotland form a herd containing animals of both sexes and all ages. Sex and age help to determine rank or 'pecking order'. During the autumn mating (or rut) the strongest bulls – often those with the largest antlers – tend to dominate all other bulls and the cows. However, mature cows outrank yearling bulls, which are smaller and weigh less than the cows. Calves come bottom of the pecking order unless a calf is close to its mother, when it shares its mother's status.

Cows become boss in winter. This is because the bulls shed their antlers soon after the autumn rut, but the cows retain theirs until the following spring. Thus cows move up the

Above: Reindeer cows in the Cairngorm snow, with Loch Morlich and Glenmore Forest visible behind. The herd of some 80 deer has been established since 1952 when the reindeer were first brought over from their Swedish mountain home by Mike Utsi. After quarantine they were released on 300 acres near Aviemore. Two years later they were released in the Highlands. More reindeer followed, some of the forest type and also a young Russian bull from Whipsnade Zoo.

Below: Full speed ahead. A reindeer can run as fast as a horse over uneven or frozen ground. The antlers of this cow are developing and show their velvet covering.

Splayed hoofs for slippery slopes

Each half of a reindeer's splayed hoof roughly resembles a half moon. The whole hoof print is almost round with a clear-cut rim and two small marks to the rear are made by the large, low-positioned dew claws. Cows leave smaller, more pointed tracks than bulls.

The splayed, broad, flat and deeply cleft hoofs aid walking on soft ground and snow, as well as being well-designed to paw away deep snow to reach lichens underneath. Indeed this habit has earned the North American native reindeer their Red Indian name 'caribou' which means shoveller.

The hoofs also help to spread out the weight of the reindeer so that each hoof exerts a much smaller pressure than most hoofed mammals on the surface supporting the deer's weight. This helps to prevent the reindeer from sinking too much when travelling over deep snow or boggy ground. Hairs at the base of each leg grow quite long over and between the hoofs and help the deer to grip ice.

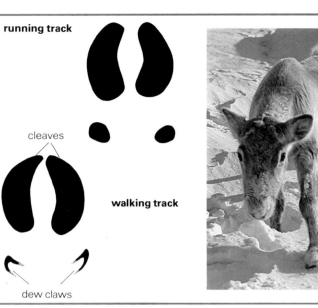

running track

cleaves

walking track

dew claws

Right: Reindeer moss—the basic diet for reindeer in winter. It is not a moss, but a many branched lichen that grows to a height of about 15cm (6in).

Below: Creating a 'crater'— this is a hole pawed out by the deer in the snow to expose the lichen. It is thought the reindeer is able to smell the plant growing under the snow.

social rank, often driving the bulls away fro the females in the herd.

The herd remains grazing in a relative small area when not disturbed or lured aw by the discovery of richer pastures. The re deer keeper rounds up any strays that occur, but a strong homing instinct mea that these are just as likely to find their o way back in time.

The Scottish herd does not migrate up a down the mountains as do Scandinavi herds, because the winters are not as harsh those of northern European mountains. Ho ever, when deep snow cloaks the lower slop in winter, the deer tend to climb to dr ground.

Food for all seasons The reindeer is oft thought to eat only reindeer moss. Althou it does eat this plant, which is really a lich the deer has a varied diet including vario other kinds of lichen—ground, rock and tr species. The reindeer in Scotland will sear out lichens all the year round and in t Cairngorms the reindeer lichen is quite co mon.

In winter, when snow covers much of t ground, the reindeer knows exactly where paw away the snow to expose the lichen car beneath. No one knows how the deer loca the plant but it may smell it.

In spring, signs of the winter foraging visible as 'paths' grazed bare on lich covered ground. At this time, the reindeer a eats fresh green leaves of birch, willo blaeberry and grasses that grow low down the mountains. Some tender heather sho are also cropped. In late summer and ea autumn the deer search out fungi, ev munching decaying specimens.

Like other deer, the reindeer also ch any shed antlers, as well as deer and b bones they find—these are rich in phospho and calcium and help to maintain the mine content of their bodies. The reindeer kee puts out mineral licks and rock salt which a help to keep the animals healthy.

Autumn breeding Reindeer mate from late September to the end of October. With their antlers fully grown and hardened, bulls compete with one another for the cows during this period. When rutting, adults repeat a throaty roar and wield their hooves or antlers against any rival that comes too near. During the rut, each male mates with as many cows as his strength and opportunities permit.

The calves—usually one per cow—are born the following May or June. A newborn reindeer is on its feet within an hour, and soon makes its first attempts at running. The calves stay with their mothers in the herd, and within a month they are taking lichens and other plant food. But each calf is suckled with its mother's milk until the onset of winter.

Antlers for defending The cow's antlers become extremely important in the winter, especially if she is with her calf. The cow exposes lichens in the snow which she and her offspring can eat. She uses her antlers to defend her feeding patches; this keeps other cows at bay as well as driving some bulls from exposed lichen feeding sites. (The bulls have by now shed their antlers, and are thus ill-equipped for fighting with protective females.)

Pests and enemies When reindeer were introduced to Scotland in 1952 they needed treatment for reindeer warble flies that had travelled with the deer in the form of eggs in the skin. The eggs hatch into maggots that eat the deer's flesh. Although this was cleared up by treatment with insecticides, native insects—including horseflies, black flies, mosquitoes and warble flies—are still troublesome at times. The reindeer normally escape these summer pests by climbing a mountain top, where the winds keep the insects at bay. However, in the few periods of warm weather, from June to the end of August, groups of animals are brought down to a corral for treatment. The insect repellent suited to the reindeer was selected in consultation with a chemical firm.

Above: A reindeer cow with her calf. The single calf is born in May or June and can keep up with a running herd within four hours. The calf's legs are quite long at birth compared to the rest of its body, the front ones being straight when it stands, and the back ones splayed out at the hocks to provide good support for the body.

Coping with the cold

The reindeer is remarkably well adapted to cope with the cold. It is virtually unaffected by low temperatures due to the extraordinarily effective insulation given by a coat of long, hollow hairs underlaid by short, dense, soft woolly fur. It is also able to avoid losing heat through bare extremities, such as its nose, hoofs and legs, by maintaining two different internal temperatures—normal body temperature of around 38°C (100°F) in the bulk of its body, and a temperature near to its external surroundings in extremities such as its nose, its legs and its hoofs.

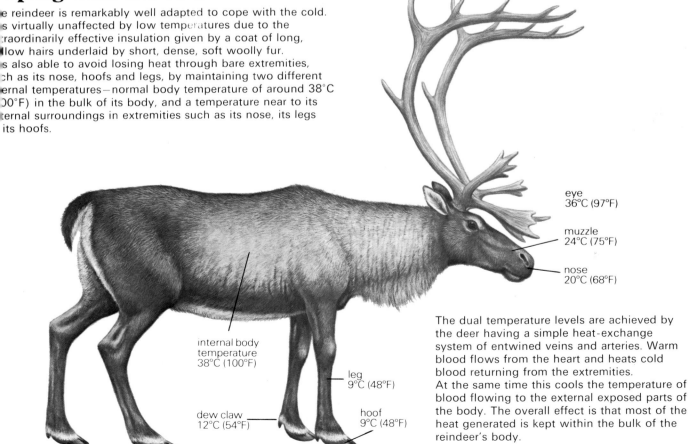

eye
36°C (97°F)

muzzle
24°C (75°F)

nose
20°C (68°F)

internal body
temperature
38°C (100°F)

leg
9°C (48°F)

dew claw
12°C (54°F)

hoof
9°C (48°F)

The dual temperature levels are achieved by the deer having a simple heat-exchange system of entwined veins and arteries. Warm blood flows from the heart and heats cold blood returning from the extremities.
At the same time this cools the temperature of blood flowing to the external exposed parts of the body. The overall effect is that most of the heat generated is kept within the bulk of the reindeer's body.

THE WILDCAT: A FIERCE PREDATOR

Wildcats are to be found in the remote uplands and forest fastnesses of northern Scotland, where they hunt for small mammal prey such as rabbits. About one-third larger in size than a domestic cat, they have a distinctive thick black-ringed tail.

Above: Glen Affric, Inverness-shire in August, a traditional haunt of the Scottish wildcat. This species has expanded its range over the last 60 years, although the population is still far from its pre-20th century levels, and the picture over the last 10-15 years is unclear. A survey of the current population is now under way.

In historic times the European (or Scottish) wildcat was found throughout much of mainland Britain. However, centuries of persecution together with the clearance of forest for fuel, timber and agricultural purposes led to its eventual elimination from England by about 1850, and from Wales by the end of the century. At the same time it was steadily losing ground in Scotland. Although re-afforestation had begun during the 19th century, persecution continued and the wildcat was driven into the remoter areas of north-west Scotland; the population probably reached its lowest level at the beginning of World War I.

Professor James Ritchie, a wildlife expert

writing in 1920, was not optimistic about t[he] future of this species in the British Isles, b[ut] fortunately his fears were not realised. Ma[ny] gamekeepers went off to World War I, a[nd] since 1918 there have been far fewer e[m]ployed than at the turn of the century; th[eir] efforts have largely been devoted to trying [to] control the growing fox population. T[he] wildcat quickly responded to this change [in] the level of persecution, and it began [to] recolonize areas that it had originally [oc]cupied. It continued to expand its range, a[nd] surveys reported in 1946 and 1962 bo[th] indicated that new ground was being colo[n]ized.

The wildcat also suffered severely fr[om] persecution in mainland Europe, and it is n[ow] a completely protected species in a number [of] countries. Release programmes which [at]tempt to re-establish this species in su[it]able areas of its former range have a[lso] taken place in mainland Europe.

What is a wildcat? As a species, the wildc[at] has a wide geographical range, and it is fou[nd] in Scotland, central, southern and sout[h] eastern Europe, Africa, Israel and eastwar[d] to include north-west India and sou[th] Mongolia. The various populations spre[ad] over such a wide area have caused taxon[o]mists (taxonomy is the study of classificati[on] of animals or plants into groups) ma[ny] problems over the years. Many cats collect[ed] in Asia and Africa were thought to be separa[te] species and the classification of wildcats became confused.

However, after further study and deliberation the taxonomists realised that many of the cats were so similar to the European wildcat that they could not be considered as different species, and they were subsequently classified as sub-species.

There are now thought to be three major groups of wildcats: European–*Felis silvestris silvestris*; African–*Felis silvestris lybica*; and Asiatic–*Felis silvestris ornata*. The wildcats found in Scotland are obviously part of the European group, and have been renamed *Felis silvestris grampia*–so distinguishing them from the central European form–because of their more pronounced markings and darker general colour. However, within the British population there is variation in the colour and intensity of markings, and it is perhaps debatable if the taxonomic distinction is justifiable.

Wide-ranging habitat Wildcats live in a variety of habitats in Scotland, ranging from high moorlands and mountainous areas to pastures. However, they are usually to be found below 500m (1650ft) and their preferred habitats are deciduous and coniferous woodland and scrub, especially near areas of pasture and moorland where rabbits and small mammals are found.

Sometimes wildcats will also inhabit open moorland, but when bad weather and the cold of winter arrives they seek shelter in any available woodlands. Forest plantations provide valuable food and shelter, which has helped the spread of the species. They also live in the Highland Wildlife Park in Inverness-shire.

On occasion, a feral cat can be mistaken for genuine wildcat. Although feral cats –

domestic cats living wild and fending for themselves – tend to occupy areas around human habitation, exploiting whatever food is available, they can turn up in remote areas, miles from the nearest house or village. So, even in northern Scotland, the appearance of a tabby coloured cat on a moorland road at

Above: A portrait of a Scottish wildcat – note the stripes on the cheeks and on the forehead. Should the wildcat ever become established south of Glasgow and Edinburgh, there is an abundance of suitable habitat available. In time it may even colonize the north of England.

Left: A wildcat at the Highland Wildlife Park in Inverness-shire and (below) a map showing the population from 1960-76.

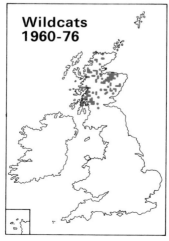

Wildcats 1960-76

night, in a car's headlights, is no guarantee that it is a wildcat.

Identification The genuine wildcat is considerably larger and more sturdily built than the average domestic cat. It has a more or less striped body, with a very well marked series of black rings or bands on the short, thick, blunt tail. There is a dark line of fur running down the spine to the tail, and there are touches of white around the chin and chest areas. The fur is a yellowish-grey or brown colour, with indistinct darker stripes or blotches. The wildcat can reach a weight of about 7kg (15lb); females tend to be smaller and lighter than the males.

Hunting by night The wildcat is active mainly at night, ranging far and wide in search of prey, but in autumn when the need to put on weight to face the coming of winter is paramount, it may forage by day as well. Most of the day is spent resting or sleeping – in a hollow under a rock, on a convenient ledge, up a tree or wherever the cat can bask in the sun. The home range consists of up to 70 hectares (170 acres) of territory, which is marked here and there along regularly used paths with secretions from a special gland.

Unlike domestic cats, the wildcat does not always bury its droppings; instead it just leaves them lying on the ground – possibly to inform other cats of its presence.

Wildcats are usually solitary hunters – it is uncommon to see a pair hunting together. At all times the wildcat avoids contact with man as much as possible. The prey consists mainly of mice and voles, but hares, rabbits and squirrels are also caught, as are birds, frogs, insects (such as grasshoppers) and sometimes fish. The techniques used for hunting are stealth, speed and surprise. The wildcat stalks its prey with great intensity, then pounces with all its strength. The initial blow, if it does not kill, throws the victim off balance; the wildcat then kills its prey by biting through the neck

Above: This is a wildcat in captivity – it has just been grooming, but something has attracted its attention. Notice the alert, 'interested' expression, and the intensity of its gaze – prime attributes of the hunter.

Below: Wildcat kittens in their den. They are usually born in deep forest but they are soon moved to various temporary dens, often in more exposed parts of the countryside.

and by raking slashes with its long claws.

Rearing kittens After mating in ear March the female wildcat gives birth in M to anything from two to five kittens. They a born in a securely hidden place – under fallen tree, among rocks or in a hollow in t ground. The kittens are born fully furred b blind; their eyes do not open for nearly fortnight and when they do they are blue colour – changing to yellow-green or go after several weeks. The kittens are fed on th mother's milk at first, but eventually she hur for prey to bring back to them.

At about ten to twelve weeks old the kitte accompany their mother on hunting trips. five months old they are able to leave th mother and fend for themselves, and they a fully grown at about ten months. Th disperse in the autumn, the males general ranging farther than the females.

Male and female wildcats do not mate f life, and therefore do not join the san partner year after year. Even during t breeding season each spring they do not li as a pair. The lifespan of a wildcat in t wild is often very short. Wildcats have natural predators, except that the kittens m occasionally be taken by a fox or eagle, accidents or an exceptionally severe winter which food becomes very scarce are the ma bars to the spread of the population.

Looking for wildcats A survey of the rar British carnivores, including the otter, pi marten, wildcat and polecat, has recently bee completed. In the case of the wildcat we kno that there has been an expansion of range ov the last 60 years, but the picture during t last 10-15 years is less clear. Although ne areas have apparently been colonized in rece years, wildcats have become scarce in oth areas. The overall spread seems to hav slowed down in recent years. Any informatic is welcome from gamekeepers, foresters, lan owners and naturalists (and anyone else) wł are likely to come across wildcats.

GREGARIOUS GOATS OF REMOTE HILLS

Country superstitions have linked goats with the devil for centuries because of their horns and cloven hoofs. No truly wild goat exists in Britain today, but there are over sixty feral herds, established from domestic flocks, living in wild, remote upland places.

Below: A herd of feral goats in the typically rocky, steep habitat they prefer. As they range over moorlands, hills and mountain slopes they feed on coarse grasses, the leaves and shoots of shrubs and heather and the bark of such trees as birch and rowan.

Owing to mixed origins from domestic breeds of goat, there is no fixed type of feral goat in Britain. In colour it can vary from pure white to jet black – although it is usually a mixture of brown, grey, black and white. The nanny (female) is more variable in colour than the billy (male) which tends to be grey or brown. The true feral goat normally develops a long, shaggy coat and fine, sweeping horns – present in both sexes.

Herding together Goats are strongly social animals, living together in family groups made up of several generations. Outside the breeding season males and females generally form quite distinct and separate herds, although males may be found at any time with female parties. In some cases the single-sexed herds occupy different geographical ranges.

'Female' herds, which in practice contain both females and their current offspring, are tightly knit units with a formal social structure. They are usually family groups, the females being related, as each female born tends to stay in her mother's group when she matures. The oldest female – the queen – leads the herd and each member knows its place and follows its leader in the clearly defined herd structure.

Billy herds are less rigidly organised than female herds, although a leader is usually present and a marked heirarchy is apparent. A number of old billies live solitary lives.

Horn-clashing fights Goats show a whole range of social behaviour. Aggressive displays are the most spectacular and resounding, as the contestants rear up on their hind legs and clash their horns together again and again. Although impressive, these combats are ritualised and the animals obey sets of rules imprinted in their behaviour. The animals meet only in head-to-head clashes or pushing matches, never attempting to jab a horn into the flank or underbelly. To take the shock of the clashing horns, goats have developed a specially reinforced forehead of thickened and spongy bone that strengthens the skull and absorbs the impact.

Horn-clashing displays are used not only in aggressive contests but also to strengthen the bonds within a herd and reinforce the position a goat holds in it. In such a contest, the 'fights' are still further ritualised, and the goats stop for short spells to lick each other's faces – a behavioural trait transferred from the more usual context of a mother licking her kids. Females do not fight, but nannies frequently whicker (a whinny-like noise) to each other when they meet and they may groom each other's neck and head.

Food at the top Like their truly wild counterparts, feral goats live mostly in rather rocky or mountainous areas on exposed cliffsides or hilltops. The nanny herds, with kids to support, tend to take over the more productive areas, while billies withdraw to the poorer parts of the range. This usually

results in the nanny herds feeding on the lower, more nutritious slopes of mountain areas with billies being found higher up on the poorer rocky tops.

The forage includes coarse grasses, herbs and dwarf shrubs such as heather or bilberry. Unlike sheep, goats feed extensively on shrubby materials when these are available, plucking leaves and shoots from trees such as birch and rowan. They also bite off quite thick, twiggy stems and chew them up with apparent relish. Many goats strip bark from trunks and stems with sharp jerks of the lower incisors. Bark is a highly nutritious foodstuff and may compensate in part for the poor quality of the rest of the diet.

Above: Family foraging. Although both sexes grow horns, those of a male (right) – the billy – can reach up to a metre in length.

Below: Feral goats on the Island of Skokholm, off the coast of Pembrokeshire, Wales. The goats share the island with colonies of breeding seabirds such as shearwaters, storm petrels and puffins.

Left: A 'queen' leads her nanny herd to new feeding grounds.

mazingly agile, goats frequently stand up on eir hind legs to reach further up into tall es.

Regular daily routines are followed by cks of goats. The herd leader – billy or een – knows all of its range in detail. cording to the season and weather, it lows a strict and rigid route. Leaving a safe sting place among the rocks where the herd s spent the night, the billy or queen leads herd each morning to favoured feeding aces. When the herd leader stops to feed, e flock feeds with it; and when the leader oves on, the whole flock moves too.

The herd makes about 12 stops in different eding areas during the morning, before settling down for the day on a suitable area of mixed forage. Here each animal feeds at its own pace and convenience, stopping for periods to chew the cud. The herd goes back to the safety of the rocks for the night.

Ardent smelly billies Males and females separated for most of the year, meet in early autumn to mate. The 'rut' is the time when males fight over individual females that are 'in season' (ready to mate). The rutting season begins in mid-August in the north of Scotland, but is delayed until mid-October in England and Wales. The billies – always somewhat smelly – develop an even more pungent odour at this time as special musk glands around the anus, at the base of the horns and

FERAL GOAT (*Capra hircus*)
Size Male 30–45kg (66–99lb) female 25–35kg (55–77lb).
Coat Shaggy; colour very variable – ranges from pure white or grey-brown to a mottled brown, grey, black and white.
Horns Grown by both sexes, large and backward-sweeping.
Length Up to 75cm (30in), sometimes more.
Breeding season Rut begins mid-Aug or mid-Oct depending on latitude.
Gestation 150 days. Usually 2 kids born.
Food Hill vegetation, browsing rather than grazing.
Predators None, other than man; shooting parties for horns organised by trophy hunters.

King of the castle

A baby goat – kid – is born from January to April, twins being more common than a single kid or triplets. The kid stands within a few minutes of birth and grows rapidly.
A favourite game of a kid with its mother is 'king of the castle', when the kid jumps on the mother's back, surveys the surrounds and hops off, only to repeat the action time and time again. No doubt this is practice for agile rock climbing.

below the eyes become highly active. The billy goats add little to the attractiveness of this effect by the curious habit of anointing themselves with urine.

Nanny goats become sexually mature from six months of age, but normally do not mate until they are about 18 months old. They come into season at 21-day intervals from the start of the rut and continue to come into season until January or February or when they conceive, (which ever occurs first).

Billies identify females in season by testing their urine. Each time a female urinates, the billy rushes to the spot and sniffs the ground, or goes to the female and sniffs her bottom. Some females respond by urinating all over the billy's nose. The billy stands rigid, with his neck outstretched, and his top lip curls right back in a pronounced 'leer'. This behaviour is called flehmen and a specialised sense organ is exposed at the base of the upper lip that is sensitive to the chemicals contained in the urine. Dominant females also display flehmen and sniff at the urine of other goats.

When a billy detects a nanny in season, he courts her carefully, runs around her sniffing and snorting, licks her head and flanks and strikes out at her from behind with a rigid forefoot. If the nanny accepts him, she allows him to mount and copulate. If she does not want him, she turns and butts him away. A determined nanny is more than a match for an ardent billy.

HARES OF HEATHER MOORLAND

The mountain hare, a mammal of moorlands rather than mountains (despite its name), is well adapted for detecting enemies such as foxes with its long ears and good vision.

Comparing hares

mountain hare in summer

white tail

brown hare

black top to tail

Mountain hares can be distinguished from brown hares by their appearance. A male weighs about 2.7kg (6lb), while a female is usually slightly larger at 2.9kg (6½lb); a male brown hare weighs 3.6kg (8lb), while a female slightly heavier. A mountain hare is also greyer (hence its alternative name of blue hare, which refers to the blue-grey flank colour), and it has shorter ears and the top of its tail is not black. In winter, however, a mountain hare is strikingly different because it is mostly white or in its transitional piebald coat.

Mountains and moorlands Mountain hares are indigenous only in the Scottish Highlands and Ireland (which has no brown hares except for an introduction into the north-west). The hares were introduced to the Scottish Lowlands between 1834 and 1862, and became numerous by the end of the century. Introductions to the Scottish islands came later and were less successful. The only really successful introductions south of the Scottish border took place in Yorkshire between 1870 and 1880.

Today, mountain hares are not uncommon in parts of the southern Pennines. In Wales mountain hares released near Bangor flourished briefly but then died out. Irish hares, which in summer are redder and in winter become piebald rather than white, were introduced into south Scotland in about 1920. Forty years later their descendants could be distinguished from the Scottish race, which occurred in the same locality, by coat colour and incomplete moults.

Forms, scrapes and burrows The home range of a mountain hare extends between 20 and [?] hectares (50 to 60 acres), and the hare sits within this area for most of the day in a form, scrape, or at the entrance of its burrow, only moving at dusk to begin feeding. The mountain hare makes its form in long heather by pushing through the stems until it has a space long enough to crouch in without being seen, as well as being sheltered from the wind. In summer, mountain hares mainly make their forms in long heather on the lower slopes. In autumn, winter and spring they are found on the higher, more open hillsides. A scrape may

be no more than a shallow depression scratched in the peat alongside a sheltering bank or boulder.

Most species of hares do not burrow, but the mountain hare digs short burrows a metre or two long, or takes over an isolated unused rabbit burrow. If disturbed by a man or a dog, the hare runs away from the burrow, usually to higher ground. The function of the burrow is uncertain. It is kept open during periods of snow, and probably the hare uses it as a shelter during storms. Leverets are not born in burrows but young leverets readily go to ground in burrows or cracks in peat.

Winter whitening In Roman times it was thought that mountain hares became white in winter by eating snow. In the wild, a mountain hare's coat begins to change colour in October. The colour changes gradually, with white appearing first on the flanks and then moving upwards, with the head not whitening until January or February, only a short time before a return to brown begins again. The winter coat is longer and denser than the autumn coat it replaces which is not moulted until the winter coat is almost fully grown, so that protection against the cold is not lost. It grows faster when the weather is colder, and is retained for longer on higher ground or in

Mountain hare distribution

Above: Mountain hares occur naturally only in the Scottish Highlands and Ireland, but they have been introduced elsewhere.

Opposite page: Mountain hare at the entrance to its snow-surrounded burrow.

Below: Late afternoon foray for three mountain hares on snowy grouse moorland.

Left: The heavily furred hind feet of a mountain hare leave unexpectedly large impressions in the snow. The track is rather larger than that made by this hare's lowland relative, the brown hare.

Below left: Conspicuous trails in heather are made and maintained by mountain hares biting off tender heather shoots as they move along. The uneaten pieces are discarded along the trail.

colder weather. The winter moult is in fact triggered off by decreasing daylength and can be brought about in captive hares at any time of year by shortening the periods of the hares' artificial daylight. Often, white or piebald mountain hares are conspicuous against dark heather not yet covered with snow. The spring moult lasts from mid-February to May, with the winter coat being shed freely as the new one grows. A third rather inconspicuous summer moult occurs between early June and mid-September.

Heather and cotton grass diet Mountain hares feed principally on heather, which in eastern Scotland makes up 90% of their winter diet and 50% of their summer diet. The hare prefers to feed among short heather, probably so that it can maintain a look-out for predators. With its long ears, good all-round vision and strong hind legs it is an animal adapted to identifying danger and well equipped to escape by running. Where hares are common, grazing on short heather may lead to a food shortage, and this forces some of them to move on to longer heather.

Another important plant of the mountain hare's diet is cotton grass. Its flower shoots appear early in April, about the time the first leverets are born, and provide nutritious food before the main growth of heather. In summer, mountain hares also eat moorland grasses. Bell heather or cross-leaved heath form only a very small part of their diet. When deep snow finally covers the heather, gorse, juniper, willow and rowan are important foods, with birch as a last choice. Juniper leaves, bark and twigs are all eaten on occasion. Twigs are bitten through to leave a characteristic clean sloping cut.

Winter feeding Mountain hares dig through soft snow to get at the vegetation, but if the snow becomes ice-crusted they are unable to do this and, if no protruding vegetation is available, many of them die.

When grazing, mountain hares feed with their backs to the wind, cropping an area within an arc of 90°. Then they move one front foot at a time slowly forward, ears raised to detect possible danger. The body is then eased forward, the hind feet are brought up and the ears lowered. During storms mountain hares congregate on the sheltered side of ridges in groups of up to 40, and make scrapes in the snow for shelter. They feed intensively in daylight during or immediately preceding storms.

As with rabbits and brown hares, food is passed twice through the gut. Soft faeces

MOUNTAIN HARE (*Lepus timidus*). Distinguished from brown hare by shorter ears, greyer coat, no black top to tail and smaller size. Turns white in winter. **Weight** of males about 2.7kg (6lb), females 2.9kg (6½lb). **Moults** three times annually: brown to white in autumn/early winter, white to brown in spring, brown to brown from June to September. **Food** principally heather in winter. In spring and summer about 50% heather, the rest cotton grass and other grasses. Usually feeds from dusk onwards, but occasionally grazes in the daytime. **Habitat** heather moorland but also mountain tops in W Scotland. Commonest on heather moorland (2 per hectare/2.4 per acre), rare in W and NW Scotland (1 to 80 hectares/190 acres). **Home range** on heather moorland 20-28 hectares (50-70 acres). Sits on higher ground by day in form or short burrow it digs for itself. **Breeds** April-August. **Gestation** 49 days. Probably three litters in each season. **Distribution** indigenous in Highlands and Ireland. Introduced Scottish Lowlands and Islands, Pennines in S Yorkshire and Derbyshire. Also North Wales.

Changing coats

In mountain hares the sex with the smaller body weight—the male—is the first to start to moult to a white winter coat. This is presumably because he is more susceptible to the cold—the autumn under coat is not shed until the long, dense winter coat is almost fully grown, so protection against cold is not lost. The heavier female is the first to shed her winter coat with the approach of spring. The moult takes several weeks to complete and so the change begins before there is snow cover. This means that for a while a mountain hare can be rather conspicuous, especially to such predators as foxes.

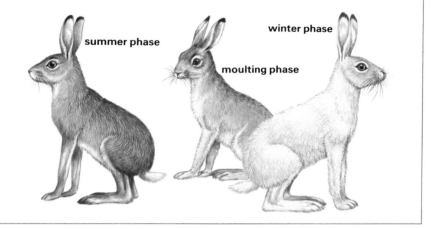

duced by day are ingested directly from anus. The hard pellets, the more familiar ppings, are excreted at night.

Courtship behaviour Mountain hares pear more subdued in their courtship than wn hares. At the beginning of the breeding son in February hares may be active during day. Occasionally groups of 20 or more es will gather in a small area from which y suddenly disperse in all directions, some hem in pairs.

Usually courtship consists of one or two les following a female at a slow lope. ntually she stops, one of the males roaches, there is a period of confrontation vhich the attitude of the ears may act as a al, and then the female strikes with her epaws and chases off the male.

After a gestation period of 49 days the crets are born in the heather. Early litters, n in April, normally consist of one or two crets, mid-season litters of two to three casionally four) leverets, with late season rs (August–September) down to one or again. This gives an average production ix to seven leverets per female. Mountain es mate as soon as their previous litter is

Above: Summer coat. The mountain hare sheds its spring coat between early June and mid-September. Decreasing daylight hours trigger off the winter moult, the hares' hind feet changing colour first, with the head whitening last (see below) in January or February.

born. When food becomes scarce the female absorbs all or some of her embryos–a useful device to ensure her survival and future opportunities to breed.

Population changes Mountain hares vary enormously in numbers, with peaks occurring about every ten years. Bad weather can bring about a population crash in the spring when numbers are high and food is becoming scarce. It takes several years before numbers build up again. When numbers are less, there is more food to go around; consequently, hares live longer (many of them for more than three years), and more of them survive to breed. Since females breed annually, those that live for three or more years produce a large number of young and hares become numerous again.

There are also big differences between different moorland habitats. Moorland with a rich, healthy flora may have one mountain hare per hectare but over poor rocky moorland with sparce vegetation they are much more widely spaced out.

Enemies on land and in the air Mountain hares form an important part of the diet of red foxes on heather moorland, and the fox is in fact the chief predator. Golden eagles and wild cats also take adult mountain hares. The fox breaks up the carcase, often biting it in two just forward of the pelvic girdle, and discards the stomach but eats part of the gut. The wild cat pulls off the skin as it feeds.

OTTERS IN A SCOTTISH WINTER

The hardiness of the otter is legendary; even in winter it sleeps in couches open to the elements, curled up in soggy piles of vegetation. Sometimes cubs are born in winter as well.

The Scottish Highlands are one of the last strongholds of the otter in the British Isles. But midwinter among the moors and mountains is a hazardous time for all wildlife. Snow blankets mountain and glen alike; ice sheaths the creepers and other vegetation hanging in the still-trickling rivers; the lochs are usually icebound; and the temperature remains almost constantly below freezing point. Many animals (such as frogs and toads) hibernate, and many birds migrate to warmer climates or move to more clement parts of the British Isles, but the hardy otter usually remains to confront the freezing, snowy conditions of winter, only moving to warmer coastal sites in times of extreme hardship.

Food shortages Diminished food supplies are a major hardship for the otter in winter. Favoured prey such as frogs, eels and freshwater crayfish retreat into deep mud or inaccessible crevices to overwinter in a state of inactivity, and shoaling fish commonly move into deep water where they are less vulnerable to cold; as a result the otter has difficulty reaching them. Mammals such as voles, and waterfowl, which the otter eats on occasion, die in the severe winter conditions, or are lessened in numbers by migration. In areas of Scotland that are remote from the sea the food sources are much reduced in quality and quantity. Then the otter must subsist on carrion, feeding on crows, rats and other animals that have been dead for some time. During the bad winter of 1979 red deer that had died of starvation in a remote area of Sutherland were eaten by many starving animals, including otters.

In some areas, salmon and trout move to shallow winter spawning grounds, becoming a fairly rich source of food for any otters in the area. Large fish, however, are not normally caught. Researchers have found that a large salmon or trout is a rare meal; the remains of prey present in the otter's spraint (droppings) consist mainly of small fish.

Coping with frozen waters When ice is widespread, otters break through it to enter the water beneath, producing holes about one metre long by half a metre wide (40in ×

20in). As many as 37 holes have been found in a 100 metre (110yd) stretch of ice. Like some seals, otters display remarkable precision in relocating these holes from underwater. Should the freeze last some time, making the ice too thick to break, otters may be forced to crowd temporarily into areas of naturally open water, such as that found at a lake outflow. There is one sad account from Wales of an otter being trapped by its tail—it had become ice-bound in a freezing river. Although rescued, the animal died within a few hours.

Coastal migration In some areas the otter avoids the worst effects of winter by migrating to the coast, where conditions are milder and food is more plentiful. The coastal habitat is the most beneficial to an otter, usually offering good sources of food and holt sites, but winter there still poses some problems.

The otter hunts most efficiently in calm or slow-moving water. In the marine environment, however, it often captures prey in or near the waters at low tide level, especially

Above: Winter foraging. At this time of the year, with many rivers frozen, the otters often make a fishing hole into which they can dive and hunt fish. Sometimes they are forced to scavenge rather than hu[nt]

Below: In the remote, little disturbed places where the[y] live, otters still find time t[o] engage in play, despite th[e] hardships of winter surviv[al]. They have been observed sliding down snowy bank[s] having family fun.

trail to top of the bank

otter hole

here great kelp beds are found. Winter orms and huge waves continuously break- g on the shores sometimes make hunting ry difficult, or even prevent it altogether. hen calmer weather returns, a hungry ter takes many risks to obtain food. After a olent, two-day storm, researchers observed e otter scavenging all morning (it is ually a nocturnal forager), clearing a stretch shore of shrimps, prawns and fish washed by the waves.

Inland storms are another common winter zard with which the otter has to contend. ese storms may increase the normal volume a river by three or four times, so that becomes a flood-river (called a spate), th enormously increased power. Over- nging trees that form favourable holt es for the otter are often uprooted. At this ne the rivers flow faster than an otter can im, making large stretches unsafe for nting.

Downriver, current speeds are slower, but ring spates the muddy and silty waters pede the otter's search for food (it hunts inly by sight). Even a little light enables the ter to glimpse a fish's shiny scales, but in al darkness the otter uses its long sensitive iskers to 'feel out' any prey, and so still nages to find some food.

Competition with feral mink is probably mething most otters face at some time ring their lives. The number of feral mink has increased dramatically in the last 25 years. How much the two carnivores compete is not known, but as they feed on the same animals – up to 70% of their prey is common to both species – it would seem likely that there is some competition. However, until further research is done in the field, the subject is still a matter of debate and most authorities believe that man alone is responsible for the otter's decline.

Winter cubs In Britain the otter has been found to produce young in every month of the year. In parts of Scandinavia and northern Europe, however, the same species of otter gives birth only in spring and summer. The reason why British otters can breed all the year round may well be linked to the fact that in this country winters are generally mild, a really hard, prolonged winter occur- ing only about every seven or so years. This means you may be lucky enough to see the delightful sight of playful otter cubs sliding down snowy banks in the coldest months. However, records of winter cubs succumbing to the weather are not uncommon.

Below: Gourmet dinner. It appears that the otter does not prey mainly on large fish, such as salmon and trout, but captures small, slow-moving fish such as roach and chub. For every large fish eaten, over 100 small specimens, including eels and coarse fish, will have been taken.
An otter avoids exhausting the food supply of a particular area by having a large home range that extends as far as 12 to 18 miles along a river. It also hunts inland within this district.

In times of severe weather conditions, otters have been recorded raiding chicken runs. They also help themselves by night to the easy pickings of trout hatcheries.

adult playing with cubs

otter slide

long heavy mane

short back

small neat head

long thick tail

deep body

silky feathering on legs

short cannon bone

LAKELAND FELL PONIES

Above: The Fell pony's thick winter coat begins to appear in about September. It consists of a very thick, short undercoat and a longer, coarser top layer.

A tough, hardy breed, the Fell pony is well adapted to the rigours of its natural habitat – the Fells of northern England where its ancestors have lived since prehistoric times.

Opposite: The most common coat colours among Fell ponies are black and dark brown, but there are a few bays and greys. Chestnuts are not permitted by the Breed Society.

Fell ponies take their name from the Fells or hills of northern England, west of the Pennines. Until the end of the last century Fell ponies were virtually indistinguishable from the Dales ponies of north-east England, but now they have developed into two separate breeds, the Fells on the west of the Pennines and the Dales on the east.

Small but strong The modern Fell is a sturdy pony, standing not more than 14 hands (140cm/56in) at the withers (top of the shoulder). Ponies that live wild in their native habitat tend to be smaller than their stud-bred relatives and average between 13 hands and 13 hands 1in. There are two principal reasons for this. First, the available food is scarce and of relatively poor quality, and so does not encourage growth. Second, the smaller the pony, the less the surface area from which it loses body heat during the winter. Thus natural selection has, over the centuries, operated in favour of the smaller animal.

The head is small and neat and the body deep and short backed, giving the impression of great strength and compactness. The breed is noted for its long, thick mane and tail and for the straight, silky leg feathering

FELL PONY
Size Maximum height, 14 hands (140cm/56in) at the withers (top of the shoulder).
Colour Black, brown, a few bays, occasionally grey.
Breeding season Late April until August.
Gestation Approximately 11 months.
No of young Normally one.
Life span 20-25 years.
Food Coarse grasses, rushes, moss, gorse, heather, ling.
Distribution Originally the Fells of north-west England, now restricted to the Ullswater area of the Lake District.
Breed society Fell Pony Society.
Where to see Fell ponies The main shows are: Fell Pony Society Show, Penrith; Fell Pony Stallion Show, Dalemain, Penrith; The Royal Windsor Show; National Pony Society Show, Malvern.

horse hoof   Fell pony hoof

Above: The hoofs of the Fell pony are round and broad compared with those of a horse. The large surface area enables the pony to cross soft, boggy ground into which a narrower hoof would sink.

which, in winter, extends up to the knee, although in summer all but a little feathering at the point of the heel may be lost.

The most common colours are black and dark brown, but there are a few bays and even fewer greys. Chestnuts are not permitted by the Breed Society, nor are white markings other than a small star on the forehead or a few white marks on the heels—piebalds and skewbalds are also debarred by the Society.

Upland habitat Until about a hundred years ago large numbers of Fell ponies ranged freely over the higher parts of northern Lancashire, Cumbria, Northumberland and the Scottish borders, but there are now probably only about a hundred ponies living

Left: This stallion has the small, neat head which is characteristic of the breed. The broad forehead tapers to a narrow nose, the ears are small and well formed, the nostrils are large and the eyes are prominent.

Below: The breeding season lasts from when the first foals arrive in late April or May, until August. The foal begins grazing when it is about a week old.

on the fells, and these are mainly confined t the Ullswater area. Today most ponies ar bred on private stud farms situated in variou parts of Britain, although these tend to b concentrated in the north of the country Those that still live on the Fells are als privately owned. They lead a semi-wil existence in the true Fell country between 30 and 610m (1000-2000ft) where it is sti possible to see the ways in which they hav adapted to their native habitat.

Adaptations to environment Retention body heat is vitally important during th cold, bleak winters of the northern hill The Fell pony's long, thick mane, tail an thick winter coat protect the animal again the cold. The winter coat begins to appear September and is not shed until May, or eve June. It consists of a thick, short undercoa and a longer, coarser top layer, and is a extremely effective form of insulation. Th insulation is improved by natural oils whic help to waterproof the coat. The ponies a much more susceptible to wet than they a to cold.

The feathering on the legs protects again cold and also stops rain and melting sno running down the legs and irritating the ski

The insulating quality of the coat strikingly illustrated by the fact that pur bred Fell ponies can frequently be seen wi thick blankets of snow on their backs after heavy snowfall whereas part-breds, which not have such thick coats, stand out stark black because the heat escaping from them sufficient to melt the snow.

Fell ponies avoid becoming buried snow drifts by stamping their feet. Th causes the snow under and around them become hard-packed, until the ponies a left standing on a little mound instead being completely covered with snow, as often happens to sheep.

The feet of the Fell pony are sufficient round and broad to allow it to cross so boggy ground where an animal with narrower foot would tend to sink in. T hoofs are of typical 'blue' horn. This is dar almost black, horn renowned for its toug ness and its ability to withstand hard use rough, stony ground.

The cannon bone (the long bone below t knee) is short and thick and about 20cm (8 in circumference. This gives considerab strength and sturdiness, vital for an anim which is constantly travelling over rou or hard ground. A thoroughbred race hor of say, 16 hands, which does not have cope with such hard, rough ground, wou have a cannon bone much longer than that the Fell pony, but of about the same c cumference and therefore weaker.

The Fell pony moves with a very high kn action, picking its feet up much higher th an average thoroughbred horse. This mea that the pony can move over rough grou without stumbling, or falling and hurti

self.

Herd life The ponies that live wild on the ells form small family groups, usually con-sisting of six or seven animals, each group occupying a territory which varies with the time of year. In the days when there were many more ponies living in the wild, the groups were much larger, and each was led by a stallion. Now, however, there are very few stallions out on the hills. The few that do exist move from group to group during the breeding season.

As in all pony breeds, the breeding season lasts from when the first foals arrive in late April or May, until August. The gestation period is approximately 11 months and when a mare is ready to foal, she leaves the group, and does not return until her foal is a few days old and steady on its legs.

The foals are brought down from the Fells in autumn. They are registered with the Breed Society and each is marked on its ear for identification.

Seasonal choice of food On the Fells a considerable proportion of the ponies' time, both day and night, is spent foraging for food. In the summer the groups move up to the higher ground, where they feed on a variety of coarse grasses, rushes, ling and heather. They also eat gorse, when it is available, for it is very nutritious. The ponies paw the gorse with their front feet in order to break down the prickles. They eat the gorse with great care, rolling back their upper lips so as to avoid the prickles.

In winter the groups of Fell ponies come down to the better grazing available in the valleys, where their owners put out hay for them. They eat bog moss, when it is available, and also bog grass. In spring, when the new season's bog grass is coming through, they

are sometimes tempted to venture too far into the bog to eat it, and occasionally become trapped and have to be rescued.

Hard working ponies From earliest times, the ponies of the Fells have been used by man–the uses changing as the life of the countryside changed. Before the Industrial Revolution they were used on farms for ploughing, shepherding and transport. They were also used as pack animals carrying contraband for smugglers, and wool from farms, often travelling as far as London. Later the ponies were used in the mines for transporting lead ore, iron and coal. Today they are used by sportsmen for carrying deer and grouse panniers, and for children to ride.

Above: The ponies on the Fells live in small family groups, usually consisting of six or seven animals. In the days when there were many more ponies living in the wild, the groups were much larger.

Below: In the wild, the foal may not be weaned by its mother until just before the next foal is due. Nowadays, the owners usually take the young foals off the hills in the autumn before the worst of the winter weather.

THE WELSH MOUNTAIN PONY

The Welsh mountain pony is widely regarded as the most beautiful pony in the world. It has enormous presence, and a stallion, whether silhouetted against the skyline of his native hills, or in a showring, is an especially memorable sight.

Above: A Welsh pony making the most of a patch of grass in the middle of winter.
Native ponies are instinctive weather forecasters, and Welsh hill farmers usually get up to 24 hours warning of bad weather, as the ponies come down to the valley bottoms or into the small dingles where streams are running. During winter they spend much of their time sheltering away from the exposed high ground.

Wales is fortunate in having four breeds of native ponies, each with its own characteristics but which, in some respects, may appear rather confusing to the uninitiated.

The smallest–and the breed from which the other three have developed over the centuries–is the Welsh mountain pony. This lovely little pony stands up to 12 hands in height. It is registered in Section A of the Welsh Stud Book, and is frequently referred to simply as 'Section A'.

Next in size is the Welsh pony, described as being a larger version of the Welsh mountain pony and standing up to 13.2 hands. It is registered in Section B of the Stud Book. Section C is devoted to the Welsh pony of the Cob Type, also standing to 13.2 hands.

The largest of the Welsh breeds is the Wels cob, or Section D, which stands over 13. hands, and is a larger edition of the Section C The Welsh cob is of special interest, as it is th only breed of British mountain and moorlan pony that may stand over the maximum pon size of 14.2 hands–there are even cobs c nearly 16 hands.

The Welsh mountain pony At best this pon possesses an attractive, small, typically pony shaped head, tapering to wide, flaring nostril and with a distinctively 'dished' (slightl concave) profile. The ears are small, and th eyes large, set well apart, bold and expressiv Blue eyes are still found in some ponies, an are indicative of descent from some of th oldest breeding lines. The mane, whic crowns an elegantly arched neck, is profu and flowing, and the well-set tail is long, fu and carried gaily. The action of the ponies distinctive (see box). It is interesting to no that when the ponies are bred away from the native environment, they tend to have flatter foreleg action, which is not considere correct.

The Welsh pony This pony, or Section is very similar to the Section A, but is large and more suitable as a riding pony. Th means that it shows possibly slightly less kn action and a little more refinement than smaller relative, but it should still possess t good bone (the circumference of the forel below the knee) and the sturdiness of the tr native pony.

There are still a small number of Section ponies on the Welsh hills, but in commo with the other Welsh breeds, far more a now bred on private studs all over Britain ar in many countries of the world.

Section C and **Section D** Both of these cob although developed from the Welsh mou tain ponies, have hardly changed sin medieval times. It is unlikely that the Sectic Ds ever lived wild on the hills. Any pony th is in excess of about 13.2 hands at the mo is too large to be able to eke out a living und the rigorous conditions prevailing.

The cobs have been developed as ridi and harness animals, especially for far work, and in comparatively recent times th have been subjected to infusions of Hackn blood, from which it is believed that much their spectacular high knee action come This action is generally regarded as bei typical of harness animals, but as well going well in harness the cobs of both Sectio have been renowed as riding ponies for mal centuries. Their best pace is the trot, and t 'trotting out' of Welsh cobs by their handle who hold them on a single long rein, is oft the highlight of show classes. In the pa animals were assessed for breeding almo entirely on the results of trotting races.

The cobs are of much heavier build th the Section A or B, and the Section D cob also taller. In spite of this, both cobs shou

[...]ght: Mutual grooming
[...]tween a mare and her foal.
[...]hey are parted the foal
[...]stinctively returns to
[...]here it last saw its mother
[...]d waits for her to return.

WELSH PONIES AND COBS
Size Welsh mountain pony
(Section A) Maximum height
12 hands (122cm/48in);
Welsh pony (Section B) and
Welsh pony of cob type
(Section C), both maximum
height of 13 hands 2 inches
(137cm/54in); Welsh cob
(Section D) over 13 hands 2
inches.
Colour Bay, brown, black,
palomino (gold), grey. Never
piebald and skewbald.
Breeding season May until
August.
Gestation Approximately 11
months.
No of young Normally one.
If twins born, one often dies.
Life span 20-30 years.
Food Coarse grasses, rushes,
reeds, gorse, heather, ling,
some bog mosses.
Distribution Black
Mountains, Brecon Beacons,
Prescelly Mountains, the
Long Mynd and some of the
hills of North Wales.
Breed Society Welsh Pony
and Cob Society.
**Where to see Welsh
ponies and cobs** The Royal
Welsh Show, Lampeter
Stallion show, Ponies of
Britain shows, Northleach
Show.

[...]ght: The head of a
[...]ction A pony, showing the
[...]shed' profile, small ears
[...]d large eyes. Welsh ponies
[...]e famed for their
[...]telligence, good
[...]mperament and superb
[...]mping ability.

retain their native pony characteristics of
small heads with neat, small ears, and with
proportions such that the depth of the body,
measured just behind the front legs, is the
same as the length of the legs.

Ponies of the mountains The ponies that
remain on the Welsh mountains (many fewer
now), be they Section A or Section B, live the
hard, rugged life that has been the lot of their
breeds since prehistoric times. Their food
varies according to the time of the year.
During spring and summer the ponies are
more often found near the tops of the hills
where they eat the grasses that are then at
their best. In early spring, a few ponies that
have fared badly during winter, may venture

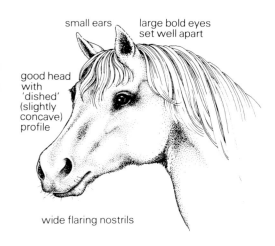

small ears   large bold eyes
set well apart

good head
with
'dished'
(slightly
concave)
profile

wide flaring nostrils

into the mountain bogs in search of the new
season's grass. Unfortunately, some are too
weak to struggle out again, and each year a
few are lost in this way.

During the foaling season (from about May
to late July) mares and foals may come down
from the highest ground to where the bracken
grows, perhaps to gain some respite from
biting flies or from the heat, or to eat some
of the grasses that grow in and near the
bracken. Bracken itself, if eaten in anything
but small quantities, can cause illness and
some foals die from bracken poisoning.

Today's ponies It cannot be said that the
majority of ponies on the Welsh mountains
live an entirely natural life these days, as their
breeding is to a large extent controlled by
human intervention. So as to eliminate the
possibility of mares foaling early in the year
when the weather is still likely to be bad, few,
if any, stallions are left out on the mountains
all year round. The great majority are not
turned out until May 1st, so that, with a
gestation period of 11 months, no full-term
foal should be born before April at the
earliest. Nowadays, many owners also take
their mares off the hills during the worst of
the winter.

When the stallions are turned out, they
gather their own herd of mares around them—
usually the same ones as in previous years.
Sometimes, a stallion will 'poach' a mare that
belongs to another; the robbed stallion will

Welsh ponies on the move

The action of the Welsh
mountain pony, as in
most native breeds,
shows a certain amount
of bending of the knees of
the forelegs, matched by
picking up of the feet of
the hind legs. This results
in a slightly shorter stride
so they can move freely
and easily over rough
ground. Cobs have a
spectacular high knee
action; their best pace is
the trot.

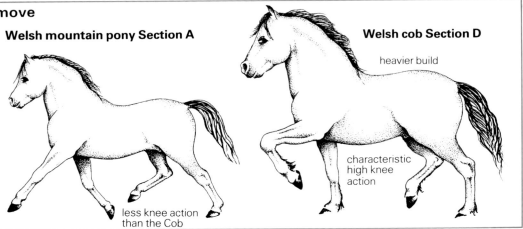

Welsh mountain pony Section A

Welsh cob Section D

heavier build

characteristic
high knee
action

less knee action
than the Cob

Above: A cob mare and her foal. Cobs are stronger and of much heavier build than either Section A or B ponies, and in the past they have been used for riding and harness animals, especially for farm work.

Opposite page: A mare with her filly. Welsh ponies can be bay, black, brown, grey or palomino (gold) — but never piebald or skewbald.

Below: Welsh ponies in the Brecon Beacons. The ponies used to be extremely shy and ran from humans. However, today, many parts of the Welsh mountains have become National Parks and the ponies are more used to people and have become less suspicious.

then go into the poacher's herd and retrieve his property, usually without any marked aggression. In general, only stallions aged five years or over have any success in collecting a herd of mares.

When a mare is ready to give birth, she goes off on her own, and stays away until her foal is strong enough to join the herd. Sometimes, however, the herd stallion will notice that a mare is missing and retrieve her, even if she has only foaled a few hours previously. With ears flat (a threat posture in horses), and mouth wide open, he will gallop her back into the herd, leaving the unfortunate foal to follow if it can. On occasions the pony owner will find such a foal, and carry it back to its mother.

As winter approaches, the hill ponies begin to grow their long, thick winter coats – much earlier than those living in lowland areas. It has been observed that the poorer, thinner animals seem to grow thicker coats than their better-conditioned relatives. Most have their coats through by mid to late September, and do not shed them until the following May.

A striking illustration of the difference i protective qualities of coats grown by the hi ponies and those that have not been expose to such rigorous conditions was seen in 195 when a bout of extreme weather came in mic May. The ponies that had wintered on th hills and still had their coats survived, whil the others, which had already shed most c their protection died in the exceptionall harsh conditions.

The ponies are rounded up two or thre times a year, by their owners mounted o other ponies, and the foals are taken for sal or are ear-tagged and allowed to rejoin th herd. In times past, the ponies were so wil and unused to humans that the only way t approach them was to 'stalk' them fro behind.

Although fossil remains and ancient re ords show that the ponies have lived on th hills since pre-historic times, they have bee subjected to the influence of other breed since at least medieval days. Arab stallior have been turned out, and have undoubtedl instilled more quality into the breeds, b whether the typical dished profile (the hal mark of the Arab horse) actually came fro them is a matter for discussion. Som authorities consider it a characteristic c various mountain species, and instance breed of mountain sheep which have the sam feature. Small thoroughbreds were also use which again would have imparted refinemen but, less favourably, would have detracte from the native hardiness.

The two cob breeds have also been i fluenced by others. The Hackney influenc has already been mentioned, and it is assume that there must have been an infusion c heavy or carthorse blood, giving the grea strength and substance for which the cob are rightly famed.

Above: A herd of Highland ponies living on the remote and unspoilt Hebridean island of Rhum.

HIGHLAND PONIES
Size 13-14.2 hands (132-147cm/52-58in).
Colour Grey, brown, and various different shades of dun.
Breeding season Spring and early summer.
Gestation Approximately 11 months.
No of young Normally one. If twins are born, one very often dies.
Life span 20-30 years.
Food Grasses, gorse, some seaweed if available for essential minerals.
Distribution Scottish Highlands and Western Islands.
Breed Society Highland Pony Society.

ADAPTABLE HIGHLAND PONIES

The Highland pony is the largest and heaviest of our nine British breeds and, with its range of colours and markings, one of the most interesting.

Although there are variations in height and size, the typical Highland pony presents a solid, powerful and compact appearance, with noticeably sturdy legs. In the wild, or when it is turned out for the winter, the most prominent features are the long, thick fore-lock which reaches from the top of the head sometimes right down to the muzzle, the pro-fuse, almost curtain-like mane of slight wavy hair, and the thick, bushy tail.

Many colours In addition to the commo greys and browns, the Highland's colou include a remarkable variety of duns, de cribed as mouse, yellow, grey, golden, crea and fox.

Perhaps even more interesting than th colours is the existence in most ponies of dark dorsal eel stripe; many also have zebr like dark stripes on the inside of their foreleg These suggest the Highland's links with th primitive ponies of northern Europe, ar similar marks are found in some moder northern European breeds.

Ancient origins The Highland's norther European origins are generally accepted, b ponies, albeit of smaller stature than th present ones, have been in Scotland for mar thousands of years, as fossil remains son 60,000 years old indicate. With the coming man and when sea communications were suf ciently advanced, the indigenous ponies we subjected to infusions of outside blood, i cluding that of Arab, Percheron, Clydesda

Adaptations to the cold The Highland is well adapted to a generally harsh environment. The generous forelock gives the eyes protection from wind and rain when the pony is grazing, and the mane acts as a shield for the throat and neck, channelling much of the rain and also helping with heat conservation, particularly for the lengthy and superficially sited jugular vein, through which body heat can also be lost.

In common with other breeds, Highland ponies normally stand with their backs towards bad weather and the abundant tail hairs blow between the legs, giving protection to the hairless inguinal region and the thinly covered inside surface of the thighs.

The extreme density of the winter coat, especially over the hind-quarters and back, acts as insulation and prevents snow, rain, and ice from penetrating to the skin. The

Above: A Highland pony mare on Rhum. Older mares act as leaders of the herd.

Below: On Rhum the Nature Conservancy Council protects the ponies. They live something approaching a 'natural' life, competing for food with other fauna on the island, and roaming over large areas according to the weather and the season. The breeding and foaling is not completely natural as the mares are brought to a stallion in the field and then kept close to the house for winter.

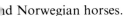

d Norwegian horses.

Because the ponies were widely scattered rough the Highlands and Western Islands, e same influences did not necessarily affect e breed as a whole. For instance, the ponies Barra were probably influenced more than me others by Arab blood, due to the pres-ce of Arab stallions within that com-ratively small area. The result was lighter, ther more refined ponies. On South Uist a lydesdale stallion was used which produced heavier type.

In general, too, the environment on the naller islands has influenced the ponies. here are few, if any, trees, and little other elter. A constant on-shore wind makes heat nservation even more of a problem, and nies survive better if they have smaller dies with less surface area from which to se heat. Consequently, by natural selection, e ponies on such islands tend to be smaller, hile those on islands such as Skye, where ere is more shelter, tend to be larger. This s also been encouraged to some extent by lective breeding.

comparatively small amount of featherin around the fetlocks channels the rain an stops excessive wetting of the heels whic could lead to irritating skin conditions. I summer the mane, tail and forelock give son protection from insects.

Front view The Highland pony, togethe with some of the other British and Europea breeds, has certain characteristics of eye an orbital positioning that differ from some oth breeds and appear to be a direct adaptation their environment.

In many breeds the eyes are set very muc to the side of the head, giving considerab all-round vision, the only blind-spot bein the width of the animal's own body. Th means that they do not normally have bino ular vision. This feature, combined with t structure of the eye, gives the horse rathe poor forward vision, and it finds it difficult

Above: A Highland mare and her foal. Like most mountain and moorland ponies, the Highland easily becomes overweight if it spends too much time in lush pastures without enough exercise.

Left: The head of a two-year old Highland filly. The eyes of Highland ponies are set rather more to the front and on either side of a slightly narrower nose than those of ponies which do not have to graze on rough terrain and herbage.

Below: Highland ponies are used as pack ponies to carry the carcases of red deer in the annual cull.

focus well on objects more than about 1.3 (4ft) ahead. When a horse manages to focu its eye on a close object in front, it cann see clearly and it also loses its ability to see t the side and rear. The animal can compensa to some extent by moving its head and nec to one side or another.

Some breeds also have more promine eyes which allow them more scope for visu accommodation, but for the Highlands an similar breeds which habitually graze amor rough herbage, eyes of this type could easi be damaged by sharp twigs, thorns and th branches of trees.

It appears, however, that over the centuri the Highlands have undergone a structur adaptation of the position of the eyes and th proportions of the face to improve their fo ward vision. Although the eyes are sti placed laterally, they are set rather more the front on either side of a slightly narrow nose than those of breeds which do not ha to graze in such rough areas. This gives degree of binocular vision and better overa

ght: Highland ponies and
ttle grazing together. On
um they also have to
mpete with red deer for
od. To be sure of food the
nies are now returning to
e 'inbye' fields near the
use around February, and
ey are kept there until the
st bite comes through at
e end of April or the
ginning of May.

low: Highland ponies are
ll adapted to a wet and
d environment. They are
e, friendly and reliable
ride, and are often used
pony-trekking.

forward vision so the pony can focus more
accurately on the ground in front and, therefore feed more advantageously. The eyes are
also set further down the head than in many
other breeds, thus further improving the
close-to-ground vision.

Working ponies There are not many Highland ponies still living under completely
natural conditions; as in most other British
pony breeds, the emphasis has moved to the
private studs, but there is still a small herd of
ponies on the Isle of Rhum.

Here they are primarily used as working
animals, being used as pack ponies to carry
the carcases of the red deer that have been
shot in the annual cull. This is one of the
traditional tasks of Highland ponies, many

of which are strong enough to carry a 111kg
(16 stone) stag across the rough, steep terrain
of the Highlands and Islands.

On Rhum three-year old ponies are introduced to deer-carrying by first being given
a trial run with weighted sacks smeared with
blood, so they will not be upset when the real
thing is slung across their backs. They are
then used to carry hinds, which are lighter
than stags. The following year they are expected to work for the whole hind season,
after which they carry stags. There are two
short culling seasons: late July until mid-
September, and late October until Christmas.
Six ponies are shod and used for each period
and then turned out on the hill.

In general the breeding life of Highland
ponies differs little from other native breeds
in their natural habitat. On Rhum the herd
(apart from the breeding mares) is turned out
for most of the year. The animals roam
between Harris on the south-west coast and
Kilmory on the north–about five miles. At
Kilmory on the machair (grassland behind the
sand dunes) there is good grass on land that
was formerly cultivated by crofters, and the
ponies go there in spring for the 'early bite'.
At other times they eat grass, chiefly *Agrostis*,
a little *Molinia*, and seaweed for important
minerals including iodine.

As the stallion is never turned out with the
mares, the herd structure remains much the
same all year, instead of the male being the
leader during the breeding season. The older
mares act as leaders; when a few of them were
removed several years ago, the pattern of
seasonal movement was disrupted and has not
yet been fully re-established.

For centuries Highland ponies were used
by crofters as all-purpose animals. Today
they are popular riding ponies, notably for
pony-trekking.

daptations for survival

profuse mane protects throat
and neck, channelling away rain
and reducing heat loss

extremely dense winter coat,
especially over hind quarters,
insulates and prevents rain,
snow and ice from reaching skin

pony stands with back to bad weather

thick bushy tail

set more to
and lower
than in most
breeds,
ving forward
round vision

ably sturdy legs

aratively small
nt of feathering
d fetlocks
els the rain and
excessive
ng of heels

tail hairs protect
inside surface of thighs

INDEX

The entries listed in **bold** type refer to main subjects. The page numbers in *italics* indicate illustrations. Medium type entries refer to the text.

A

adder *29*, 32
Ajuga pyramidalis 69
Alchemilla alpina 70
alevins
    salmon *94*
    trout *97*
alpine . . .
    bearberry 54, *55*
    cinquefoil *68*, 69
    clubmoss *82, 83*
    fleabane *64*
    forget-me-not *64*
    lady fern *81*
    lady's mantle *70*
    meadow-rue *68*, *69*
    mouse-ear *68*, *69*
    saxifrage *74*
    willowherb *22*
    woodsia *80, 81*
Alpine plants 62-9
    arctic- 62-6, 70-1
alternate-leaved golden saxifrage *74*
Andromeda polifolia 59
Androniscus dentiger 16
Anthus **148**
antlers *154, 158, 159, 160, 162, 163, 165*
Aquila chrysaetos **107**
Arbutus unedo 54, *55*
arctic-alpines *see* **Alpine plants**
Arctostaphylos 54, *55*
Aulacomnium palustre 88, 89

B

Baetis 102, 103
bank vole *155*
bats *16, 17*
Bayberry 50-1
bearberry *38*, *52*, *53*, 54, *55*
bell-heather *19*, 56, *57, 59*
Ben Lawers (Perthshire) 62-6
Ben Lomond scree slope (Scotland) *19, 21*
Ben Nevis (Scotland) 11
Berwyn Mountains (Wales) 11
Betula nana 45, 46
bilberry *10*, *26*, *53*, 54, *55*
birch sawfly *42-3*
birch shieldbug *41*
Birches 40-3
    dwarf *45, 46*
Birds 104-51 *see also* eggs, nests
    camouflage *132*
    crow family *141*
    falconry *113*
    gamebird habitats *134*
    lek behaviour *135*
    mountain regions 9-10, 11
    radio tracking *124*
Black grouse 133-5
Black Mountains 11
blackbird 142, *143*
Blackstairs Mountains (Ireland) 11
bladderwort *30*, 32, *76, 77*
Blanket bogs 28-33, 36
bloody cranesbill *14*
blue heath 54
bog . . .
    asphodel *36*, *65*
    bilberry 54, *55*
    myrtle 50-1
    rosemary *35*, 57, *59*
    violet (common butterwort) *83*
bogbean *28*
bogs
    blanket 28-33, *36*

formation *33, 35*
insectivorous plants 75-7
mosses/liverworts 84-9
peat (Ireland) 34-7
boletus fungi *41*
Bracken 78-9
Brecon Beacons 11, *151, 184*
bristle fern 80, *81*
brook saxifrage *74*
brown birch bolete *41*
brown hare *154-5, 173*
Brown trout 95-7
bryophytes, bogs *89*
Buteo 119, **120**
Butterflies *43*, **100-101**
butterworts *32*, 76, *77*
Buzzards 11, *107*, **118-21**

C

Caenis 103
Cairngorms *8*, 11
Calluna vulgaris **56,** 59
Cambrian Mountains 11
campions *63, 66*
Campylopus paradoxus 89
capercaillie, habitat *134*
Capra hircus **170**
Carex bigelowii 65, 71
carnivorous plants *see* **Insectivorous**
Carrauntoohil (Ireland) 11
carrion crow *141*
catkins *44, 46, 51*
Caves, limestone 15-18
Cerastium alpinum 68, 69
Cervus elaphus **158**
Charr 98-9
chequered skipper *43*
Cheviot Hills 11
Chough 139-41
Chrysoplenium **74**
cinquefoils
    alpine *68, 69*
clints *13*
Cloëon 103
Clubmosses 82-3
Cobs, Welsh 182-5
Coenonympha tullia 101
Comeragh Mountains (Ireland) 11
common . . .
    bladderwort *76, 77*
    butterwort *76, 77*
    buzzard 11, *107*, **118-21**
    lady fern *81*
    shrew *155*
Cornish heath *59*
Corvus corax **141**
cotton grass *26, 32*
cowberry 54, *55*
cranberry 54, *55*
cranesbill, bloody *14*
creeping willow *44, 46*
Croagh Patrick (Ireland) 11
cross-leaved heath *31*, 57, *58, 59*
crow family *141*
crowberry *10*
Cryptogramma crispa 81
Cuillins (Skye) 11
Cumbrian Mountains 11

D

Daboecia cantabrica 59
Daphnia 77
damselfly *90*
Dartmoor (Devon) *24, 25*
deer
    aggressive behaviour *158-9*, 160
    antlers *154, 158, 159, 160, 162, 163, 165*
    peat and mud wallows *160*
    red *152*, *154*, 156, **158-61**
    reindeer *8*, 156, **162-5**

roe 156
Deschampsia flexuosa 71
Diapensia lapponica 70, 71
Dinocras cephalotes 103
Diphasiastrum alpinum 82, 83
Dolomedes fimbriatus 86, 87
Dorset heath *59*
Dotterel 11, **136-8**
Dovedale moss *72, 73*
dragonfly, golden-ringed *90-1*
Drepanocladus exannulatus 89
drooping saxifrage *64*, *65, 74*
Drosera 30, 76
Dryas octopetala 69
dwarf birch *45, 46*
dwarf juniper *46*
Dwarf trees 44-6

E

Eagle, golden *32*, **106-9**
eggs
    black grouse *134*
    dotterel *138*
    golden eagle *109*
    golden plover *138*
    mayfly *102*
    meadow pipit *149*
    merlin *125*
    peregrine falcon *113*
    ptarmigan *132*
    raven *139*
    red grouse *132*
    ring ouzel *142*, 144
    trout *96*
    wheatear *147*
Ephemera 102-3
Equisetum palustre 44
Erebia 100, 101
Erica 57, *59*
Eudromias morinellus 138
evolution, plants *83*

F

Falco **111,** *125*
Fell pony 178-81
Felis silvestris grampia 167
fen (raft) spider *86, 87*
ferns
    bracken 78-9
    mountain 80-81
    parsley *23*, 80
    rusty back *14*
field vole 11, *155*
field (wood) mouse *155*
filmy ferns 80, *81*
fir clubmoss *82, 83*
Fishes 92-9
    salmon growth stages *94*
    trout life cycle *96-7*
fleabane, alpine *64*
Flowering plants 60-77
fly agaric fungus *42-3*
forget-me-not, alpine *64*
fox 11, *22*, 155, *156*
frost action on rock *23*
fungus, cave *18*
fungus gnat *16*

G

Galty Mountains (Ireland) 11
Gamebirds 130-2, 133-5
    habitats *134*
Gaultheria shallon 55
Geranium sanguineum 14
Glen Affric (Scotland) *166*
Glenmore Forest Park *8*
globeflower *67, 68, 69*
Gnaphalium supinum 71
Goats, feral 169-71

olden eagle 11, *32*, **106-9**
olden plover 11, *104-5*, **136-8**
olden saxifrages *73*, *74*
rampian Mountains (Scotland) 11
reat sundew *30*, *75*, *76*
reater horseshoe bat *16*
rey partridge, habitat *134*
rey plover 136-8
rikes (pavement cracks) *12*, *13*, *14*
ouse
  black 133-5
  habitats *134*
  lek behaviour *135*
  red 130-2

ares *10*, *154*, *155*, **172-5**
eather family **52-5**
eathers and heaths **56-9**
edgehog 155
erald moth *16*
ighland ponies 186-9
oney buzzard *119*, *121*
ooded crow *141*
uperzia selago 82
ylocomium splendens 43
ymenophyllum tunbrigense *81*

sectivorous plants **75-7**
sects **100-103**
mountain regions 11
errupted clubmoss 83
sh butterwort **76-7**
sh heath *59*
sh mountain hare *10*
sh saxifrage *73*

kdaw *141*
141
ncus trifidus 64
iper, dwarf *46*
niperus communis nana *46*

mia angustifolia *54*, *55*
arney fern 80, *81*
ockmealdown Mountains (Ireland) 11
enigia islandica *71*
zia pauciflora 89

y fern, alpine *81*
y's mantle, alpine *71*
gopus **131**, *132*
ge emerald moth *42-3*
ge heath butterfly *100-101*
st cudweed 70, *71*
st willow *44*, *46*, *71*
dum palustre 55
behaviour *135*
us timidus **174**
ser clubmoss 83
ser twayblade *42-3*
ens
en Lawyers (Perthshire) 63, *64*
ountain *10*
eindeer moss 164
nestone pavements 12-14
(heather) 56, 58, 59
erworts **88-9**
nberis Pass (Snowdonia) *23*
eleuria procumbens *54*, *55*
don Pride (saxifrage) 73
g-leaved sundew *30*, *60-1*
g-tailed tit *42-3*

Lycopodium clavatum 83
Lyrurus tetrix **135**

M
Macgillycuddy's Reeks (Ireland) 11
Mackay's heath *59*
magpie *141*
Malham Cove limestone pavement *12*
Mammals 152-89
marsh horsetail *44*
Mayflies 90, **102-3**
Meadow pipit 11, **148-51**
meadow-rue, alpine 68, *69*
Merlin *104*, **122-5**
Meta 16, 17
Minuarta verna 69
mole 11, 155
Monadhliath Mountains (Scotland) 11
Moorlands 24-7
  blanket bogs 28-33
  gamebirds 130-35
  heather's central role *25*
  mammals 154-7
  map *27*
  merlin 122-5
  mountain hare 172-5
  red deer *156*, **158-61**
mosquitoes *16*
moss campion 63, 66
mosses
  birchwoods *42-3*
  mountain 10, 63, *64*, 70
  peat bogs 88-9
  sphagnum 84-7
mossy cyphel 63, 66
mossy saxifrage *72*
moths 11, *16*
mountain ash *see* **Rowan**
mountain avens 67-8, *69*
Mountain hare *10*, *154*, *155*, **172-5**
Mountains 8-11
  butterflies 100-101
  ferns 80-1
  fishes 92-9
  golden eagle 106-9
  mammals 154-7
  osprey 114-17
  peregrine falcon 110-13
  red deer 158-61
  reindeer 162-5
  ring ouzel 142-4
  saxifrages 72-4
mountain ringlet butterfly *100-101*
Mourne Mountains (N. Ireland) 11
mouse, wood 155
mouse-ear, alpine 68, *69*
Mweelrea Mountains (Ireland) 11
Mylia anomala 89
Myrica **50**

N
natterer's bat *17*
nests
  black grouse *134*
  buzzard *119*, *121*
  chough *141*
  dotterel *138*
  golden eagle *32*, *109*
  golden plover *136*, 138
  meadow pipit *149*, *150*
  merlin *124*, *125*
  osprey *114*, 115, *116*, *117*
  peregrine falcon *112*, *113*
  ptarmigan 130, *132*
  raven *139*, *140*
  red grouse *130*, *132*
  ring ouzel *142*
  snowy owl *127*
  wheatear *145*, *147*
Niphargus fontanus 16, 17

Norber Boulders (Ingleborough) *13*
North-West Highlands (Scotland) 11
Nyctea scandiaca **127**

O
oblong woodsia 80, *81*
Odontoschisma sphagni 89
Oenanthe oenanthe **147**
opposite-leaved golden saxifrage *73*, *74*
Osprey 114-17
Otter 176-7
Otter Hole Cave *15*
Owl, snowy 126-7

P
pale butterwort *76*
Pandion haliaetus **115**
parr
  salmon *94*
  trout *97*
parsley fern *23*, 80, *81*
partridges, habitats *134*
Pavements, rock 12-14
peat
  blanket bogs 28-33
  Irish bogs 34-7
  mosses and liverworts 84-9
Pennines (England) 11
Peregrine falcon 110-13
Perla 103
Perlodes microcephala 103
Pernettya mucronata 55
Pernis apivorus 119
Perthshire moorland *24*
petty whin *40*
pheasant, habitat *134*
Phyllodoce caerulea 54
pill millipede *16*
pine marten 156
Pinguicula **76**
Pipits 148-51
pitcher plants *77*
Plagiothecium undulatum 43
Plectrophenax nivalis **129**
Pleurozia purpurea 89
Pleurozium schreberi 43
Plovers *104-5*, **136-8**
Pluvialis
  apricaria **138**
  squatarola **137**
polecat 156, *157*
Polytrichum 70, 88, 89
ponies
  Fell 178-81
  Highland 186-9
  Welsh 182-5
Porrhomma 17, 18
Potentilla 68, *69*
Proasellus cavaticus 16, 17
Ptarmigan 9, 11, **130-2**
  habitat *134*
Pteridium aquilinum **79**
purple pitcher plant *77*
purple saxifrage 60, *71*, 73, *74*
pygmy shrew 11, 155
pyramidal bugle 68, *69*
Pyrrhocorax pyrrhocorax **141**

R
radio tracking, merlin *124*
raft spider *87*
rainbow trout *97*
Raven 11, *127*, **139-41**
red campion *66*
Red deer *152-3*, *154*, 156, **158-61**
Red grouse 130-2
  habitat *134*
  moorlands *25*, *26*
red-legged partridge, habitat *134*

redpoll *42-3*
Reindeer 8, 11, *156*, **162-5**
   coping with cold *165*
reindeer moss *164*
reticulate willow 44, *46*
rhododendron *55*
Rhododendron 55
Rhacomitrium 63
Rhum (Hebrides) 11
Rhytidiadelphus loreus 43
Ring ouzel 11, **142-4**
Rock pipit 148-50
rock structures 9
   frost action *23*
rodents, upland 155
roe deer 156
rook *141*
roseroot 68, 69
rough-legged buzzard *119*, 121
round-leaved sundew *30, 76*
Rowan *38-9*, **47-9**
rusty back fern 14

S
St Dabeoc's heath *59*
Salix 44, *46, 71*
Salmo
   gairdneri 97
   salar **93**
   trutta **97**
Salmon 92-4
Salvelinus alpinus **99**
Sarracenia purpurea 77
Saxifraga **72-4**
Saxifrages 65, 71, **72-4**
Scafell (Cumbria) 11
Scoliopteryx libatrix 16
Scotch argus butterfly *100-1*
Scotland, mountains (map) *11*
Scottish wildcat *155*, 156, **166-8**
Scree slopes 19-23
Sea trout 93-4
sedges 63, 70, *71*
Sedum rosea 68
Selaginella selaginoides 83

Shetlands, snowy owl discovery 127
shrews 155
Sibbaldia procumbens 70, *73*
silver birch *40, 42*
silverweed *13*
Skokholm Island goats *169*
skylark *149*
Slieve Mish Mountains (Ireland) 11
small mountain ringlet butterfly *101*
smolt (adult salmon) *94*
Snow bunting 128-9
snow gentian *66*
Snowdon (Wales) 11
Snowy owl 126-7
Sorbus aucuparia **49**
Sphagnum 30, 35, 37, **86**, *88*
Sphagnum moss 84-7
   Ben Lawers 63
   blanket bogs **28-33**
   peat (Ireland) *35, 37*
spiders 11, *16, 17, 18, 87*
spring sandwort *69*
stag's horn clubmoss *83*
stalactites/stalagmites *15, 16-17*
starry saxifrage 70, *72*
stiff sedge 63, 70, *71*
stoat 11, *41*, 156
Stoneflies 102-3
strawberry tree 54, *55*
sundews 36, *60-1, 75-7*
   blanket bogs *30, 32*
Sweet gale (bog-myrtle) **50-1**

T
Thalictrum alpinum 68, *69*
tormentil *69*
trailing azalea 54, *55*
Trechus micros 17, 18
tree pipit *149*
Trees 40-9
   birchwoods 40-3
   dwarf 44-6
   mountain tree line *10*
Trichomanes speciosum 81
Triphosa dubitata 16

Trollius europaeus 68
Trout 95-7
tufted saxifrage 73, *74*
Tunbridge filmy fern 80, *81*
Turdus torquatus **143**
twayblade, lesser *42-3*
Tweedsmuir Hills (Scotland) 11
Twelve Bens of Connemara *34*

U
Utricularia 30, *76*

V
Vaccinium 53, *54, 55*
voles 155

W
Wales, mountains (map) *11*
water pipit 150
water shrew 155
wavy hair grass 70, *71*
weasel 156
Welsh ponies and cobs 182-5
Wheatear 11, *21, 23*, **145-7**
Wicklow Mountains (Ireland) 11
wildcat *152, 155*, 156, **166-8**
willow warbler *42-3*
willowherb, alpine *22*
willows, dwarf species 44, *46*
Wilson's filmy fern 80, *81*
Wistman's Wood (Dartmoor) *25*
witch's broom *42-3*
wood sorrel *42-3*
wood (field) mouse 155
woodlands, **birch 40-3**
Woodsia 81, 82
woolly willow 44, *46*
wren 11

Y
yellow marsh saxifrage *74*
yellow mountain saxifrage *22, 71, 73*

ACKNOWLEDGEMENTS
Photographers' credits Heather Angel 8, 10 (centre left, right), 12, 13, 14, 21 (top), 23 (middle), 24, 26 (middle), 28, 31, 32 (bottom), 34, 35 (right), 38-9, 44 (top), 48 (bottom), 49, 50, 59, 62, 63 (top left, bottom), 64, 65, 66 (right), 68, 70 (bottom), 72 (top), 76, 78, 79, 81, 82, 83 (bottom), 84, 86 (bottom right), 87, 88 (bottom), 92, 94, 102 (bottom), 103 (bottom), 142 (bottom), 160, 162, 163 (top), 164 (top, bottom), 184 (bottom): Aquila Photographics/GG Bates 109 (middle), 113 (middle), 132 (bottom); GG & IM Bates 135; SC Brown 146 (bottom); PT Castell 139, 147 (middle), 148 (bottom); J Lawton Roberts 136 (top); T Leach 63 (top right), 73 (top, middle); C Linford 144 (top); DI McEwan 57 (middle); RT Mills 147 (bottom); AT Moffett 143; N Rodney Foster 145; R Siegal 133; EK Thompson 127 (bottom): Ardea/J-P Ferrero 176; A Lindall 174 (top); W Moller 177; Ian Beames 16, 18 (middle), 118, 152-3, 157, 159, 165: Biofotos/G Kinns 155 (middle), 168 (top): Bob Gibbons Photography/R Fletcher 51 (top), 101 (top), 166; Bob Gibbons 36 (right), 40 (bottom), 44 (bottom), 55, 73 (bottom); P Wilson 35 (left): Britain on View front cover: Bruce Coleman Ltd/Jane Burton 167, 183, 184 (top); R Burton 99; E Crichton 185, 187 (top); LR Dawson 128 (top); F Erize 112 (bottom); D Green 138 (top left); P Helo 114, 116 (bottom); G Langsbury 161 (bottom); L Lee Rue III 115 (bottom); C Ott 129; A Purcell 111; Hans Reinhard 110, 158, 182; Jos van Wormer 115 (top); P Chapman 17 (middle), 18 (top): Michael Chinery 103 (top): David Corke 102 (top): Anne Cumbers 178-9, 180, 181, 188 (top): Dennis Green 120, 121 (top), 122, 124, 125, 138 (bottom), 140 (top), 149

(middle): Harry Smith Photographic Collection 57 (top), 72 (bottom): RT Hewson 172, 174 (bottom): George Hyde 48 (top), 83 (top), 101 (bottom): Leslie Lane 186, 188 (bottom): Richard Lindsay 29 (top): M King & M Read/G Dore 19 (left); M Read 41 (bottom left), 175 (top): John Mason 25, 46 (middle), 51 (bottom), 54, 60-1, 69, 77, 83 (middle): Richard Mills 37 (top), 141: Colin Molyneux 20, 151: Pat Morris 17 (top), 40 (top), 88 (top), 126, 127 (top), 168 (top): Natural History Photographic Agency/HR Allen 188 (middle): J & M Bain 138 (top right); R Balharry 10 (top), 106 (top), 108; GJ Cambridge 36 (left), 85; L Campbell 53 (middle), 54 (top), 89; RJ Erwin 156 (bottom); J Good 109 (top); J Goodman 95, 97; B Hawkes 112 (top), 154, 163 (bottom); E Martomäki 121 (bottom): Natural Science Photos/Don MacCaskill 173, 175 (bottom): Nature Conservancy Council/ME Ball 187 (bottom); Rhum 188-9: Nature Photographers Ltd/T Andrewartha 130 (top); AS Beamish 170 (bottom), 171; SC Bisserot 169; FV Blackburn 47, 56; D Bonsall 6-7, 21 (bottom), 146 (top), 150 (bottom); B Burbidge 19 (right), 22 (middle), 23 (top), 67, 70 (top), 71; R Bush 53 (top); AA Butcher 75; NA Callow 22 (top); K Carlson 41 (bottom right), 45, 104-5, 119, 150 (top); RJ Chandler 137 (left); A Cleave 80 (bottom), 98; AK Davies 130 (bottom); AK Downes 18 (bottom); MR Hill 137 (right); J Hyett 54 (middle); Lea McNally 155 (top); C Mylne 116 (top), 132 (top), 144 (bottom), 164 (middle), 170 (top); O Newman 22 (bottom); C Palmer 46 (top), 52; WS Paton 109 (bottom); D Sewell 30; D Smith 26 (top), 32 (top), 113 (top), 134 (top), 149 (bottom); P Sterry 57 (bottom), 90-1, 128 (top); R Tidman 136 (bottom):

A Wharton 66 (left): Arthur Oglesby 96: Premaphotos Wildlife/KG Preston-Mafham 37 • (bottom), 41 (top), 74, 86 (middle, bottom right): John Robinson 161 (top): Richard Revels 43, 10█ Bryan Sage 127 (middle): Paul Sterry 9: Sally An█ Thompson 189 (top): Roger Tidman 29 (bottom) 148 (top): BE Watts 80 (top): Clive Westlake 15 Wildlife Services/M Leach 140, 142 (top), 156 (top): Woodfall Wildlife Pictures/I Nicol 123.

Artists' credits Stephen Adams 100, 101: Gra█ Allen/Linden Artists 152, 160, 165, 173, 175, 17█ Russell Barnett 93, 94, 183 (top): Robert Burns/ Drawing Attention 83: Sarah De Ath/Linden Arti█ 71, 74, 89: Elizabeth Dowle 38, 55, 59: Eugene Fleury 31 (airbrush): Wayne Ford 104, 107, 111, 115, 119, 120, 125 (colour), 127, 129, 131, 132█ 135, 137, 141, 143, 147, 149: Will Giles 108: Sa█ Hartley-Edwards 183 (bottom): Hayward Art Gr█ 10, 25, 60, 68-9, 95, 96-7: Elaine Keenan 179, 1█ 189: Richard Lewington/The Garden Studio 16-█ 103: Josephine Martin/The Garden Studio 81: D█ More/Linden Artists 46, 49, 51, 79: Paul Nesbitt█ Denys Ovenden 99: Liz Pepperell/The Garden S█ 30: Sandra Pond title page, 31 (line), 76, 77, 85█ 125 (line), 134, 171: Gordon Riley 90: Colin Sa█ (maps), 27, 36, 66, 101, 125, 129, 133, 137, 13█ 142, 145, 149, 164 (tracks artwork), 167, 173: Ed Stewart 11: Debra Sumpter 35: Phil Weare/ Linden Artists 43.

Index compiled by Richard Raper, Indexing Specialists, Hove, East Sussex.